IMAGES OF ****

MW00789089

HITLER'S DEATH TRAINS

THE ROLE OF THE *REICHSBAHN* IN THE FINAL SOLUTION

RARE PHOTOGRAPHS FROM WARTIME ARCHIVES

Ian Baxter

Pen & Sword
MILITARY

First published in Great Britain in 2023 by
PEN & SWORD MILITARY
an imprint of Pen & Sword Books Ltd
Yorkshire – Philadelphia

ISBN 978-1-39904-008-2

A CIP catalogue record for this book is available from the British Library.

Typeset by Concept, Huddersfield HD4 5JL.
Printed and bound in England by CPI Group (UK) Ltd, Croydon CR0 4YY.

Pen & Sword Books Limited incorporates the imprints of After the Battle, Atlas, Archaeology, Aviation, Discovery, Family History, Fiction, History, Maritime, Military, Military Classics, Politics, Select, Transport, True Crime, Air World, Frontline Publishing, Leo Cooper, Remember When, Seaforth Publishing, The Praetorian Press, Wharncliffe Local History, Wharncliffe Transport, Wharncliffe True Crime and White Owl.

For a complete list of Pen & Sword titles please contact
PEN & SWORD BOOKS LTD
47 Church Street, Barnsley, South Yorkshire, S70 2AS, England
E-mail: enquiries@pen-and-sword.co.uk
Website: www.pen-and-sword.co.uk
or
PEN & SWORD BOOKS
1950 Lawrence Rd, Havertown, PA 19083, USA
E-mail: uspen-and-sword@casematepublishers.com
Website: www.penandswordbooks.com

Contents

About the Author

Ian Baxter is a military historian who specializes in German twentieth-century military history. He has written more than fifty books including *Poland – The Eighteen Day Victory March*, *Panzers In North Africa*, *The Ardennes Offensive*, *The Western Campaign*, *The 12th SS Panzer-Division Hitlerjugend*, *The Waffen-SS on the Western Front*, *The Waffen-SS on the Eastern Front*, *The Red Army at Stalingrad*, *Elite German Forces of World War II*, *Armoured Warfare*, *German Tanks of War*, *Blitzkrieg*, *Panzer-Divisions at War 1939–1945*, *Hitler's Panzers*, *German Armoured Vehicles of World War Two*, *Last Two Years of the Waffen-SS at War*, *German Soldier Uniforms and Insignia*, *German Guns of the Third Reich*, *Defeat to Retreat: The Last Years of the German Army At War 1943–45*, *Operation Bagration – the Destruction of Army Group Centre*, *German Guns of the Third Reich*, *Rommel and the Afrika Korps*, *U-Boat War*, and most recently *The Sixth Army and the Road to Stalingrad*. He has written over a hundred articles including 'Last days of Hitler', 'Wolf's Lair', 'The Story of the V1 and V2 Rocket Programme', 'Secret Aircraft of World War Two', 'Rommel at Tobruk', 'Hitler's War With his Generals', 'Secret British Plans to Assassinate Hitler', 'The SS at Arnhem', 'Hitlerjugend', 'Battle of Caen1944', 'Gebirgsjäger at War', 'Panzer Crews', 'Hitlerjugend Guerrillas', 'Last Battles in the East', 'The Battle of Berlin', and many more. He has also reviewed numerous military studies for publication, supplied thousands of photographs and important documents to various publishers and film production companies worldwide, and lectures to various schools, colleges and universities throughout the United Kingdom and Southern Ireland.

Introduction

The Holocaust trains were a railway transportation run exclusively by the *Deutsche Reichsbahn* (the national railway) and controlled by the Nazi government and its allies. Due to the immense rail network across Europe and the Eastern countries, the Germans utilized the railway system for transporting the Jewish community and those regarded as hostile to the Reich to the ever-growing concentration camps being erected across Europe and Poland. The Nazis' 'Final Solution' was totally dependent on the railway system. This book describes in graphic detail how their hapless victims were transported from the ghettos to the vast concentration camp network to either work or die. Although these trains reduced valuable track space for the German war effort, their use allowed the Nazis to perfect the process of the Holocaust swiftly and efficiently. Under the command of Adolf Eichmann who facilitated and managed the logistics involved in the mass deportation of millions of Jews from the ghettos to the concentration camps by railway, it was ensured that the transports were disguised as mass resettlement to the east. However, most of these transports meant only death at places such as Belzec, Chełmno, Sobibor, Treblinka or Auschwitz-Birkenau.

The Nazi government knew that without the *Reichsbahn* the industrial murder of millions of people would not have been possible. In fact, some 3 million Jews and Roma (gypsies) – including around 1.5 million children – were gathered from across the Reich and Nazi-occupied Europe and transported by train in cattle wagons, destined for the extermination camps.

Chapter One

Plans for Genocide

Even before the defeat of Poland in September 1939, plans were already being drawn up to facilitate the movement of vast numbers of people destined for what would be initially known as the General Government of the Polish-occupied areas. It comprised the Polish province of Lublin and parts of the provinces of Warsaw and Kraków. Thousands of people would be more or less dumped in this region and were regarded by the Nazi government as enemies of the state.

Many of those who were resettled in the General Government were often moved on foot, which was time-consuming and a logistical nightmare for the planners. The scale of the relocation was enormous and soon became chaotic. By February 1940 the immense difficulty of simultaneously attempting to relocate Poles, Jews and other ethnicities had become such an administrative problem that it was agreed the Jews should be forced to live in ghettos. This would not only relieve the burden of the resettlement programme, it was a way of temporarily getting rid of the growing Jewish problem. After all, the Nazis hated and feared the Jews and to isolate them in ghettos was deemed immediately practicable.

It was agreed that in order to move large numbers of Jews to the ghettos, especially if they were some distance from their dwellings, the *Deutsche Reichsbahn* would be used along with the Polish National Railways (PKP), which had been handed over to the Germans to operate. Together they established what was called *Generaldirektion der Ostbahn* (DRB) with its headquarters in Kraków. The Polish railway was governed totally by the *Deutsche Reichsbahn*, with all managerial jobs given to German officials. The rail line was operated totally independently from the German railway and encompassed some of the largest locomotive factories in Europe. It comprised some 2,372 miles of railway with an additional 350 miles of narrow-gauge lines.

In order to operate this vast railway network, all Polish railwaymen were ordered to return to their place of work or face death. Their main employment was to transport large numbers of people across Poland to the individual holding areas or ghettos, and then to the camps that were being hastily constructed. The whole operation evolved in stages. Initially the trains were used only to concentrate the Jewish populations in the ghettos. German government ministries and state organizations, including the Reich Security Main Office (RSHA), the Transport Ministry and the Foreign Office planned, coordinated and directed the deportations. It was the Transport Ministry that organized the train schedules and later the following year it would be the Foreign Office that would plan with its German-allied states the handing over of their Jews. Adolf Eichmann, who had been assigned to head the RSHA (RSHA Sub-Department IV-D4), was tasked to oversee the transportation of all Jews into occupied Poland. His job included arranging with police agencies the removal of the Jews, dealing with their confiscated property and arranging financing and transport. Initially some 600,000 Jews were moved into the General Government area. By the end of 1941, approximately 3.5 million Polish Jews had been moved in a massive deportation action using the vast railway network. In fact, some of the large, more permanent ghettos had their own stations or railway sidings built to accommodate the vast influx of Jews being shunted in on cattle cars.

While the Jewish community was being transported to the ghettos, other people regarded as hostile to the Nazi regime such as Polish nationalists and other political enemies were being rounded up and transported by railway to the growing detention centres and concentration camps. Those who were incarcerated there were often set to work as stonebreakers and construction workers for buildings and streets.

One of the most famous concentration camps built in Poland was in the town of Oświęcim, which was situated in a remote corner of south-western Poland in a marshy valley where the Sola River flows into the Vistula about 35 miles west of the ancient city of Kraków. The town was virtually unknown outside Poland, and following the occupation of the country Oświęcim was incorporated into the Reich together with Upper Silesia and renamed as Auschwitz by the German authorities.

Auschwitz was a perfect location with a main railway hub. In 1940 it was deemed technically a quarantine camp for labour exchange. However, the camp would soon evolve and become one of the largest concentration camps in Europe.

When the Germans unleashed their invasion of the Soviet Union on 22 June 1941 (Operation BARBAROSSA), the Jewish problem escalated further. For the Nazi empire the prospect of a war against Russia entailed a transition from one policy of murder to another. This in effect brought about the most radical ideas imaginable in the eyes of the SS. A bloodbath ensued, and preparations for murder on an industrial scale entailed utilizing the railway network as the pivotal way of accelerating the operation.

Chapter Two

Special Trains
(*Sonderzüge*)

In order to plan for the destruction of the Jews, Nazi leaders got together to discuss the 'Final Solution'. This meeting was known as the Wannsee Conference, and was held in Berlin in January 1942. The conference was to legalize the discrimination and removal of the Jewish race from existence in the occupied territories and present were representatives from several government ministries, including state secretaries from the Foreign Office, the Justice, Interior and State Ministries and representatives from the SS. Also present was none other than Adolf Eichmann who was charged with collating information and preparing the minutes.

During the conference it was agreed that it would be the Jews in the General Government who would be dealt with first. Already a pool of experts had been drafted in to undertake this mammoth task. Eichmann was fully aware that the problems of transporting large numbers of Jews to Russia by rail and liquidating them would pose huge logistical problems, especially when the war in Russia had not been won. It was agreed that it was more practical to transport German and other Jews to Poland and kill them immediately rather than sending them further east. It was therefore suggested that a series of extermination camps, unlike that of Auschwitz, was to be constructed in Poland and used primarily to transport by cattle wagons those who were deemed unfit for work and would be killed.

The first phase of the process using the *Reichsbahn* was Operation REINHARD (German *REINHARDT*), the code name given to the systemic annihilation of the Polish Jews in the General Government. This operation would mark the beginning of the most deadly phase of the programme: the use of extermination camps. Nazi authorities outlined that although it was imperative for the movement of Jews by rail for the operation, the logistics of the *Reichsbahn* were also crucial to the conduct of Germany's military offensives on the Eastern Front. As a result, officials planning rolling stock for transportation to the concentration camps were to take into consideration that military supply was top priority. Providing army supply lines with food, armaments, ammunition, vehicles, spare parts and the transportation of the troops themselves were of the utmost importance. Meanwhile, civil logistics were also taken into consideration which dealt with the movement and storage of raw materials, semi-finished and finished goods. For organizations that provided services such as mail deliveries and public utilities including daily passenger train services, these were all taken into serious consideration and the planning. Daily timetables and schedules were drawn up including the increase in operatives that would service and maintain the trains and the wagons. Up to now the trains transporting Jews, called *Sonderzüge* or 'special trains', had low priority for movement and would generally operate on the main line only after all other transports had completed their services for the day. When Jews were transported to the ghettos, especially those who paid for their journey, they were often moved in third-class passenger carriages. However, the majority would now be moved from the ghettos using freight cars or cattle cars. These cattle cars were known as *Güterwagen* boxcars. SS regulations proposed that no more than fifty persons would be transported in these boxcars, but this number varied considerably in order to lessen main line usage and maximize capacity. Although these trains took away valuable track space, planners knew that it allowed mass-scale transportation and would shorten the time required for the extermination of the Jewish people. The vast numbers of people who were to be transported to the concentration camps meant that the service operator had to take military supply trains into consideration and allow these to pass first. This meant that the boxcars would be filled first at the departure hubs which were often train yards. Frequently these trains would have to wait many hours before departure and would sometimes leave overnight.

In order to perfect and run the railway system effectively, the special trains had to be scheduled around and fitted in between trains in the regular local timetables. The *Reichsbahn* had kept available appropriate coaches and began amassing boxcars from various rail yards across Europe including Poland, the Baltic States and Russia. Secrecy of advance arrangements of these trains was part of the plan and considerable efforts were made to ensure this was adhered to. Transport Ministry officials were informed to let their railway people know of the transportation of what was termed 'human livestock'. Listed names of those destined to be transported to the concentration camps were catalogued where possible. Many hours were often required just to work out the numbers of people who would be travelling by train, the route of the locomotive and its desired destination. Special code-words were given out along a number of the main routes for the railway police for provision of additional railway personnel and guards along the way. Special instructions were given to the locomotive drivers and preparations were made for scheduled and unforeseen stops. Regular scheduled trains were not to meet or run parallel with the *Sonderzüge*. Freight trains, maintenance trains and military trains had to be given right of way. Because of the nature of what was being transported, reserve locomotives were often kept on hand, particularly if there were mechanical problems or where delays had to be made up. Trains following could not be allowed to proceed close behind or stop at a station or yard where a *Sonderzüg* had halted. Uninvolved *Reichsbahn* officials and family members of those involved in the whole operation were not to be told anything about the train runs, especially their destination. It was imperative that the minimum number of people were told, and the information given to individuals was not to go beyond their various functions. If anyone asked questions, all information relating to schedules and other aspects of the train runs was labelled as a resettlement transportation programme. It was strictly forbidden to give any information relating to the trains' destination. If a train had to stop for any reason in a station, then regulations outlined that the platform had to be cordoned off and guarded by the railway police. When the trains were in motion, communications were carried out by radio to other rail officials. However, for more secret and classified information which was often sent to the train's destination or the offices at the RSHA, the Transport Ministry and the Foreign Office, a *Reichsbahn* Enigma machine was frequently used.

Once a communiqué had been sent through the appropriate channels, SS, Ukrainian guards and local auxiliaries including members of the *Ordnungspolizei* (*Orpo* or Order Police) were ordered to assist in receiving the transports. The guards were told to receive the arrival of Jews with an element of calm in order to ensure that there was no initial panic. Deception and disguise were vital to the whole operation. Yet the plan to transport thousands of people into the General Government area would be overwhelming for the first three killing centres, which were known as the Reinhard camps.

A famous photograph of *SS-Obersturmbannführer* Adolf Eichmann. It was Eichmann that was tasked with facilitating and managing the logistics involved in the mass deportation of Jews to the ghettos and extermination camps in Nazi-occupied Europe. Eichmann had been assigned to head the RSHA (RSHA Sub-Department IV-D4) which was tasked with overseeing the transportation of all Jews into occupied Poland. His job included arranging with police agencies for the removal of the Jews, dealing with their confiscated property and arranging financing and transport. Initially some 600,000 Jews were planned to be moved into the General Government. By the end of 1941, some 3.5 million Polish Jews had been moved in a massive deportation action using the vast railway network.

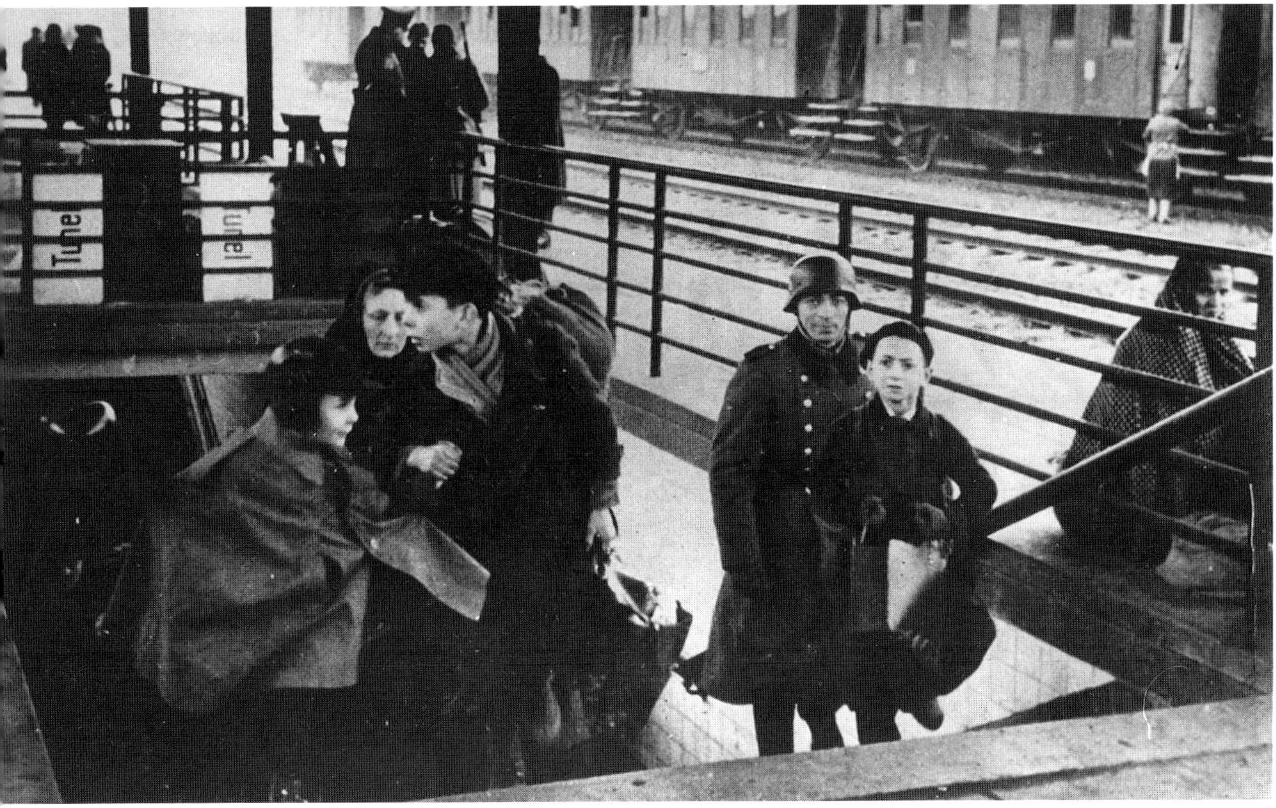

A Jewish family climbs the stairs to the train platform at the railway station during a deportation action from the Kraków Ghetto. *(USHMM)*

A still from period film footage depicting the deportation of Jews from an unidentified ghetto. *(USHMM)*

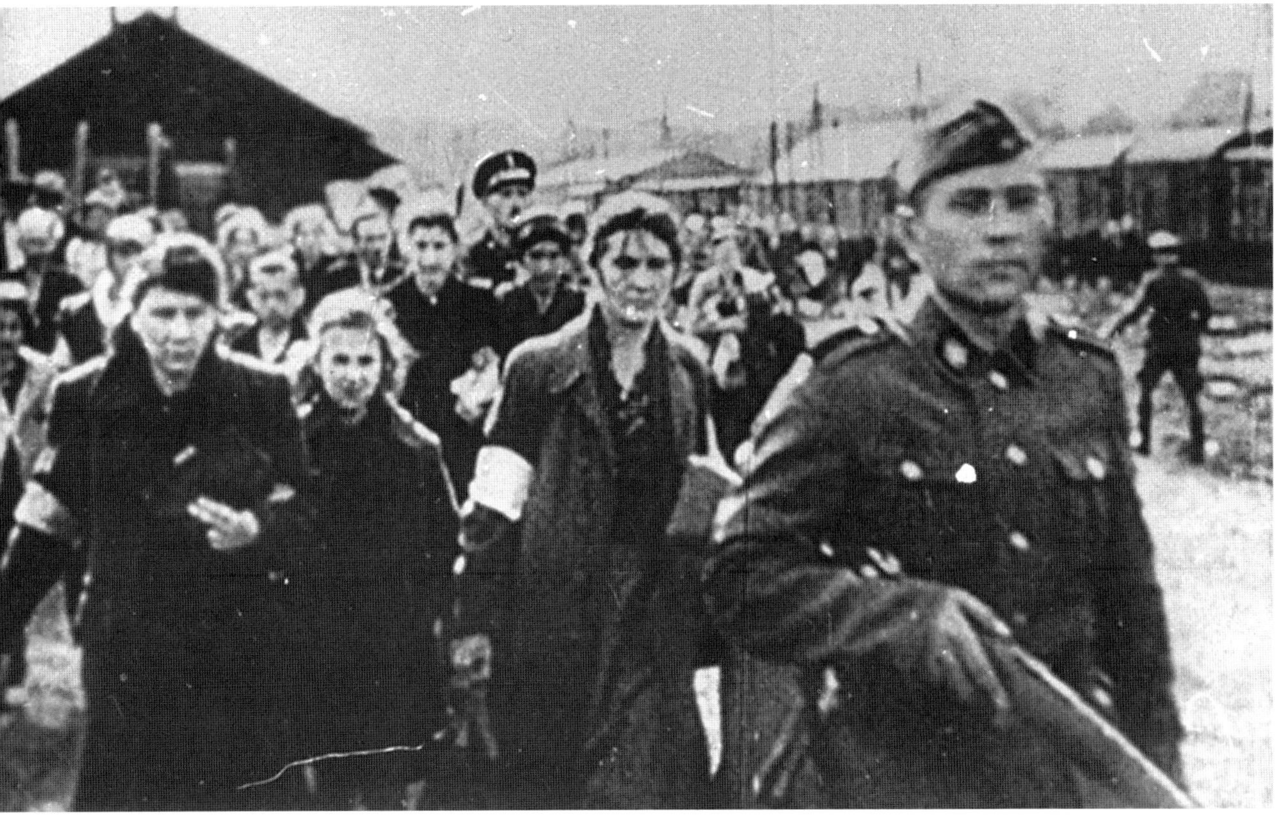

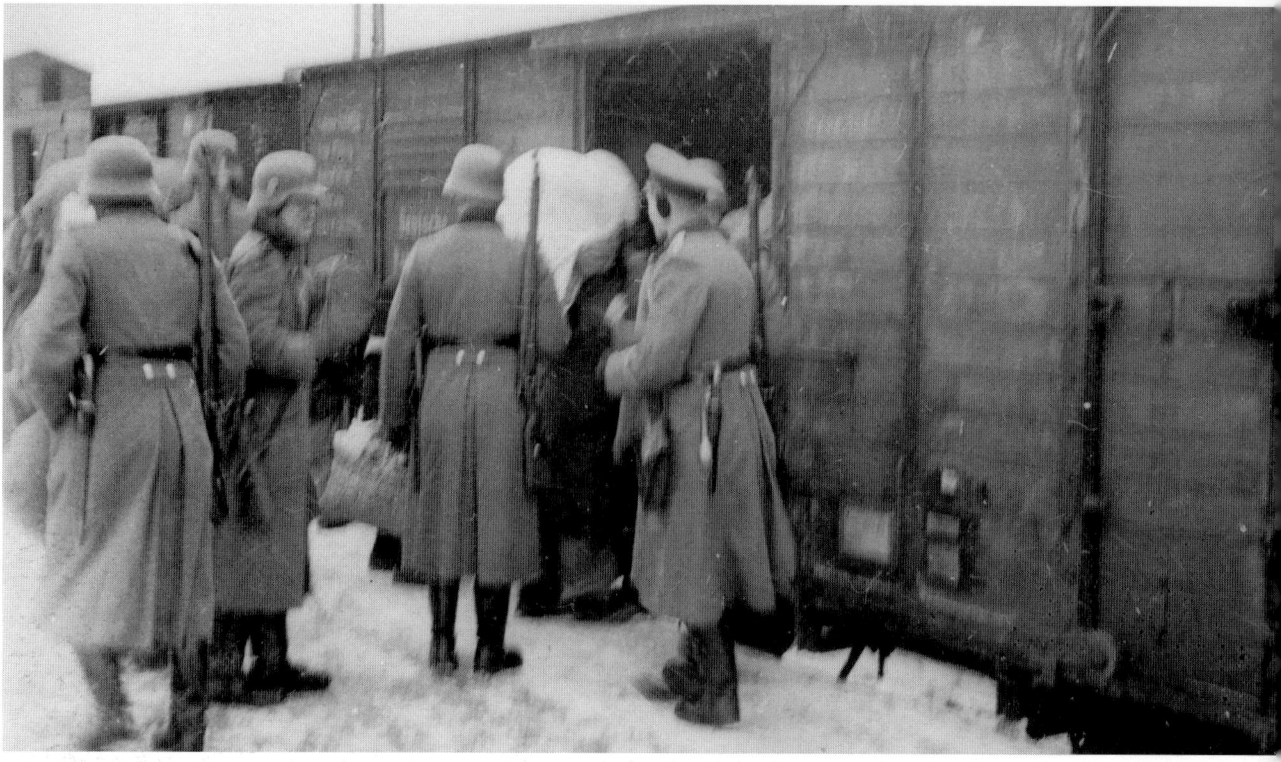

German soldiers oversee the boarding of Jews from the Zyrardow ghetto onto a deportation train. The standard means of transportation of the Jewish community was by boxcar or freight car. The size of the boxcar was 10 metres long. However, third-class passenger carriages were also used for the same purpose. A published SS manual covered a section relating to transportation of 'human cargo' and suggested a carrying capacity per 'train set' of 2,500 people in fifty cars, each boxcar loaded with fifty prisoners, but they often exceeded this capacity. *(USHMM)*

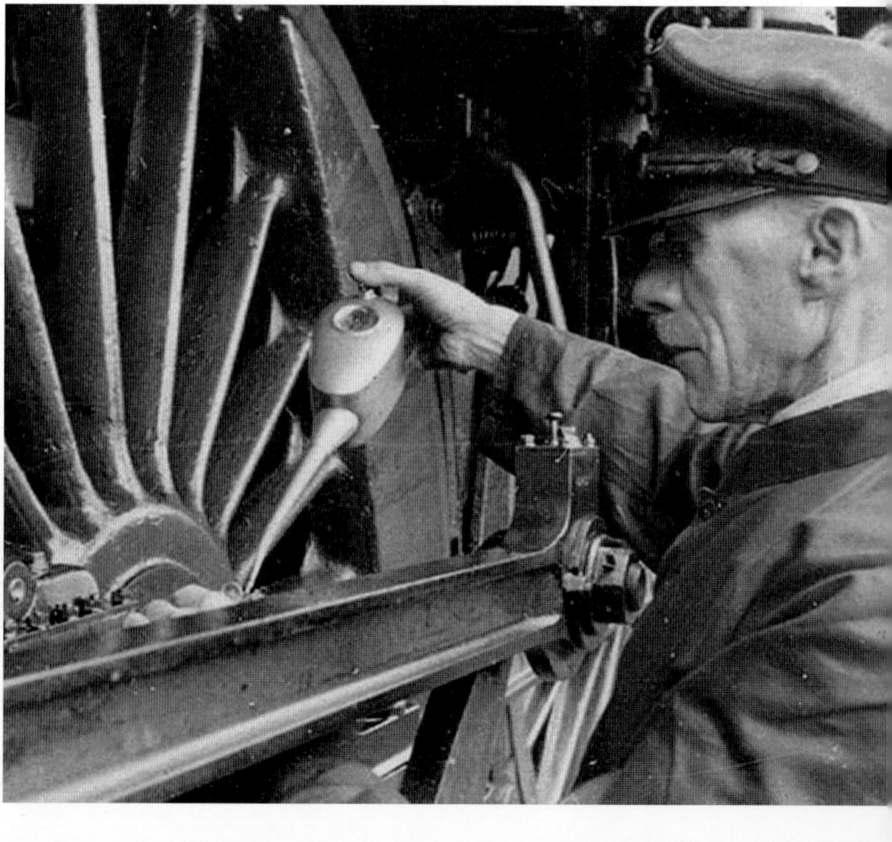

Two photographs of a German locomotive driver belonging to the *Deutsche Reichsbahn*. Throughout the war these locomotives were primarily responsible for the forcible transportation of the Jews, as well as other victims of the Holocaust, to various ghettos, forced labour camps, concentration camps and eventually the death camps. *(NARA)*

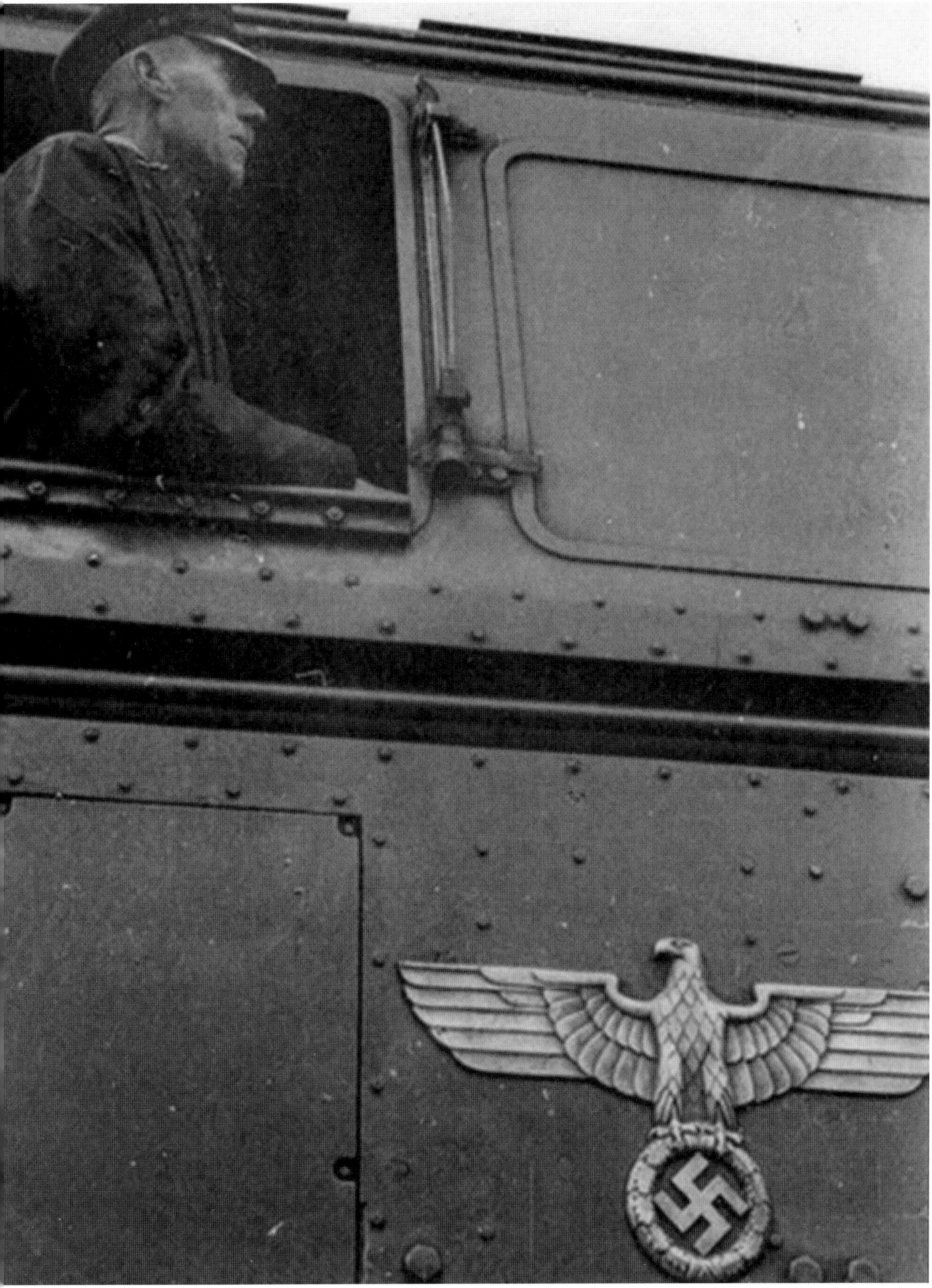

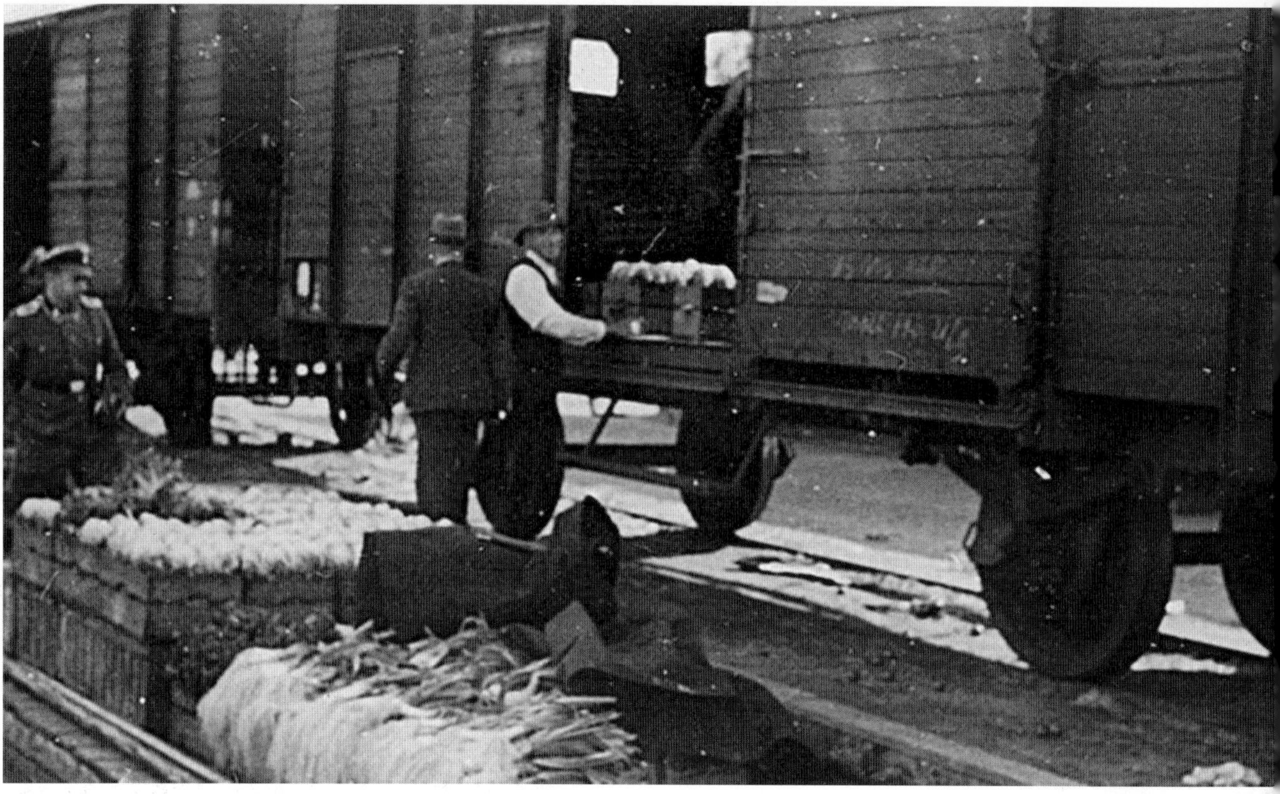

Five photographs taken in sequence showing *Deutsche Reichsbahn* rolling stock being used to transport materials from a dockside. It was this rolling stock that would be utilized in great volumes by the German railway to transport Jews across Europe. The logistics of transportation were immense. The vast numbers of people who were to be transported to the concentration camps meant that the service operator had to also allow for not only the transportation of military supply trains but general cargo materials for the basic requirements of the public as well. *(NARA)*

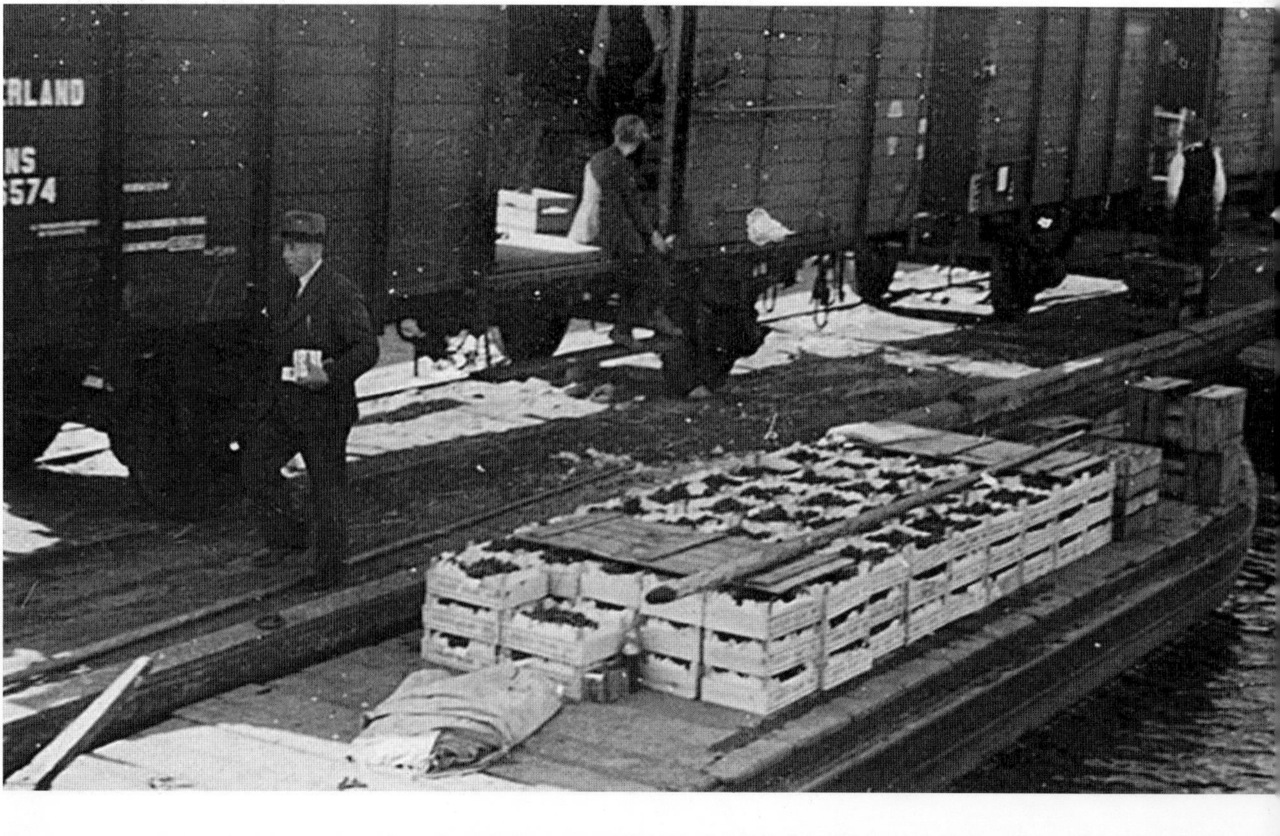

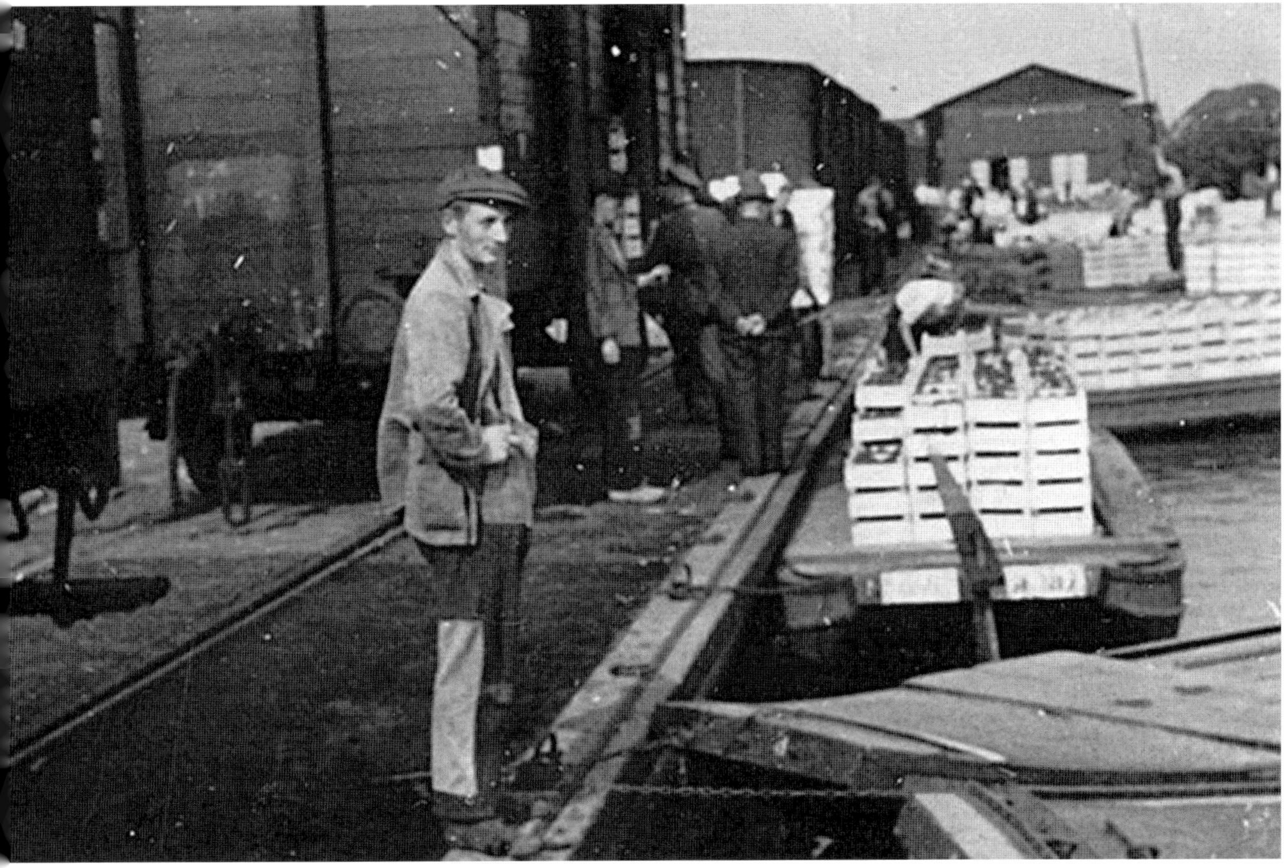

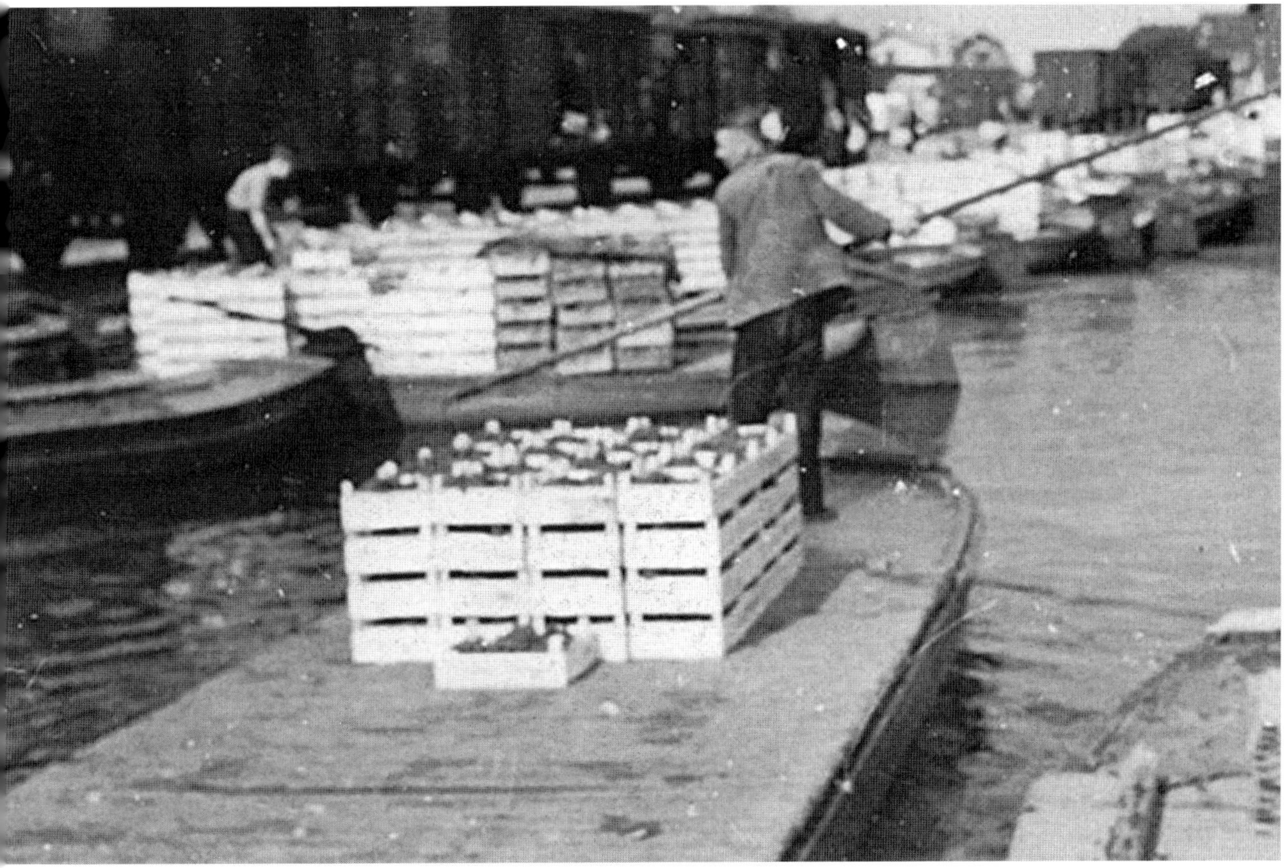

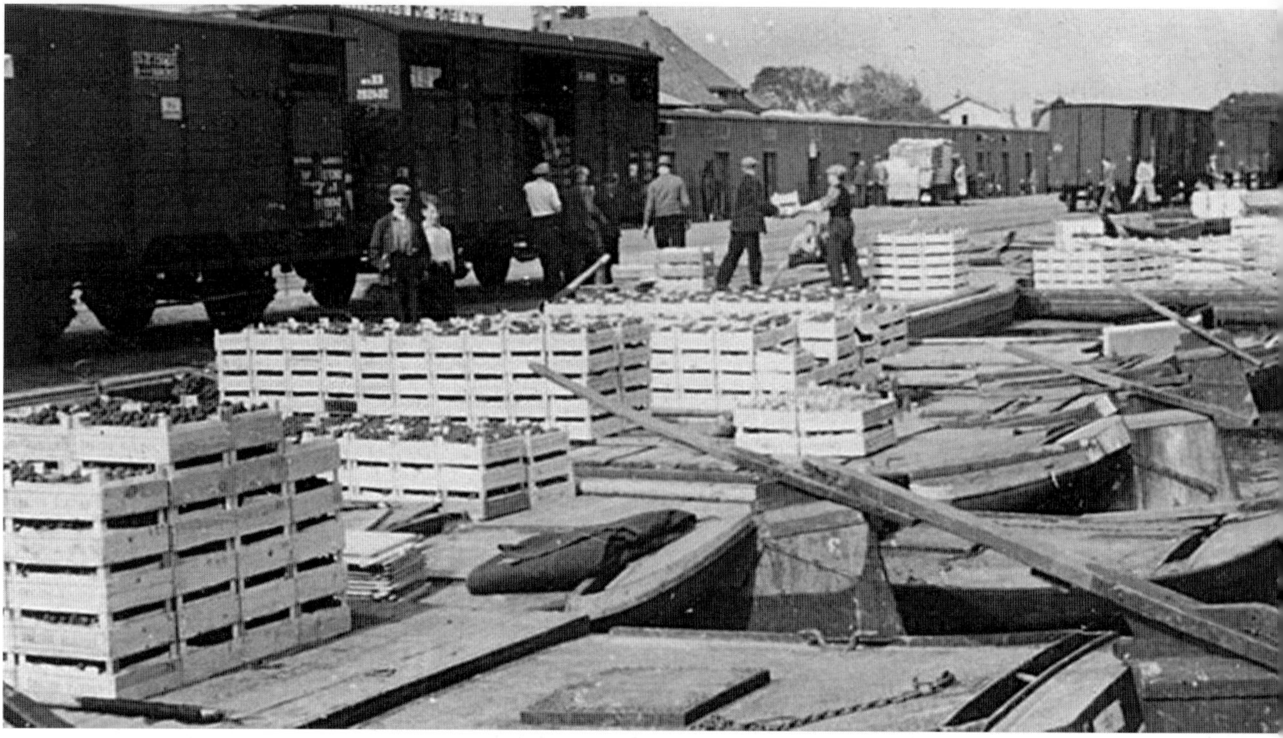

(**Below**) German troops loading sacks of supplies on board a train destined for the front. During the war military supplies took precedence over the transportation of the Jews to the concentration camps. However, the planning and timetables were often a logistical nightmare for the *Reichsbahn*.

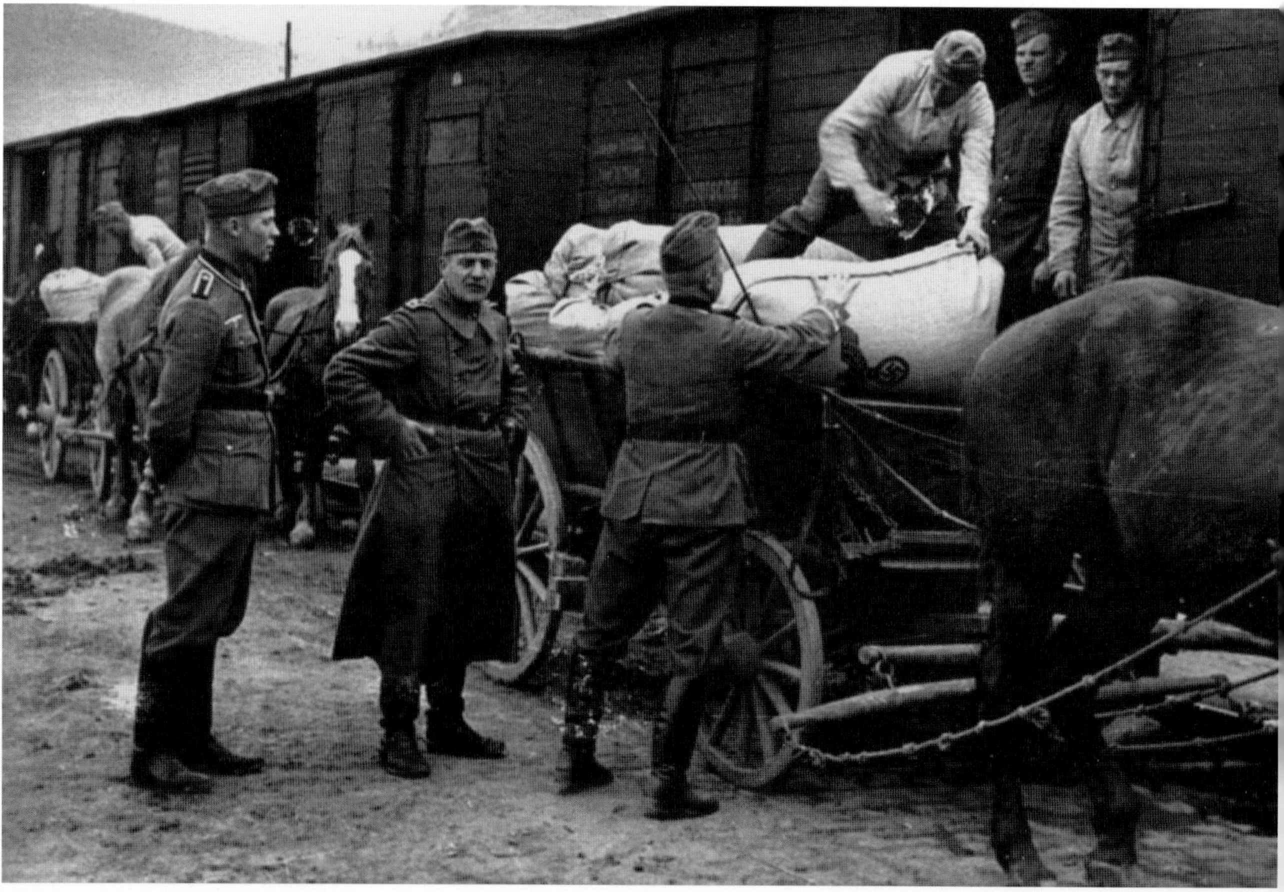

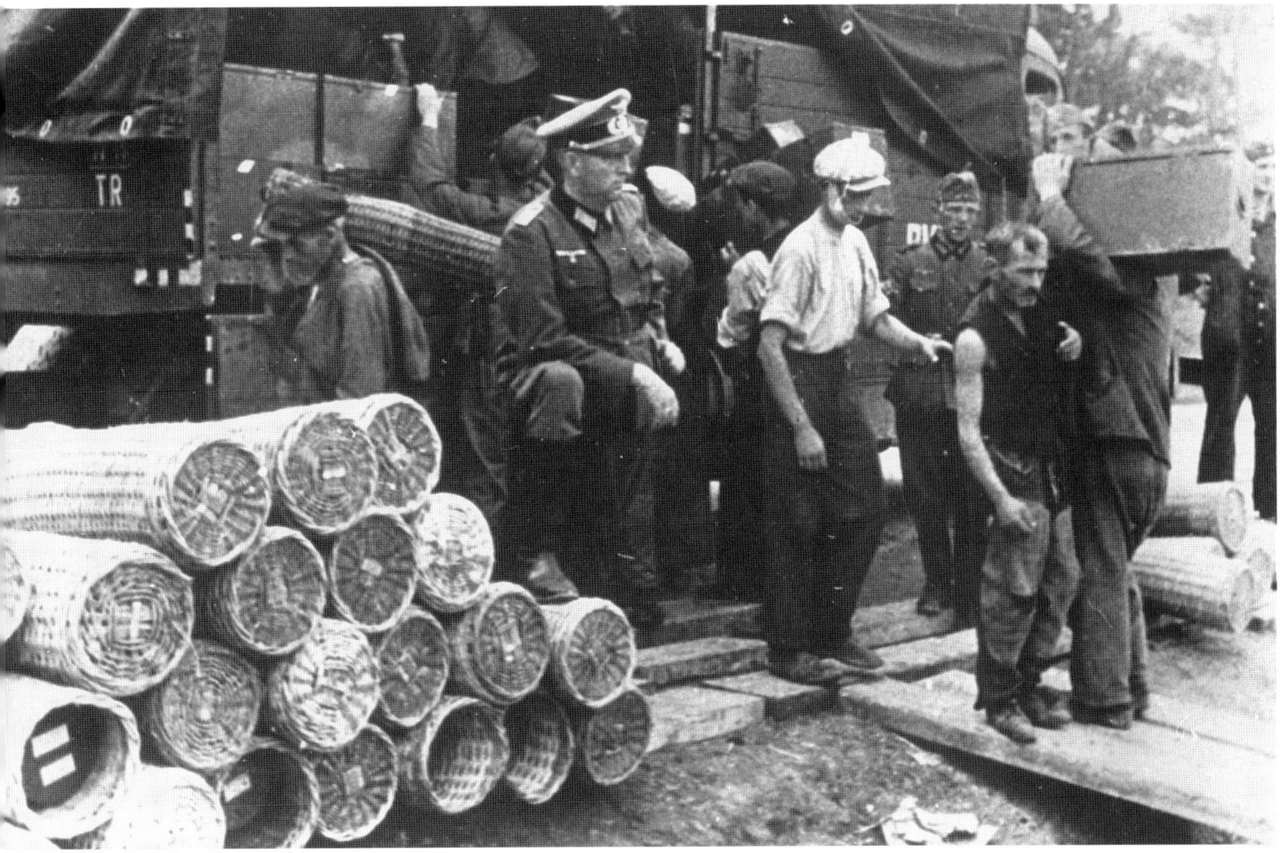

Two photographs showing Jewish men forced to load a munitions train under German supervision. *(USHMM)*

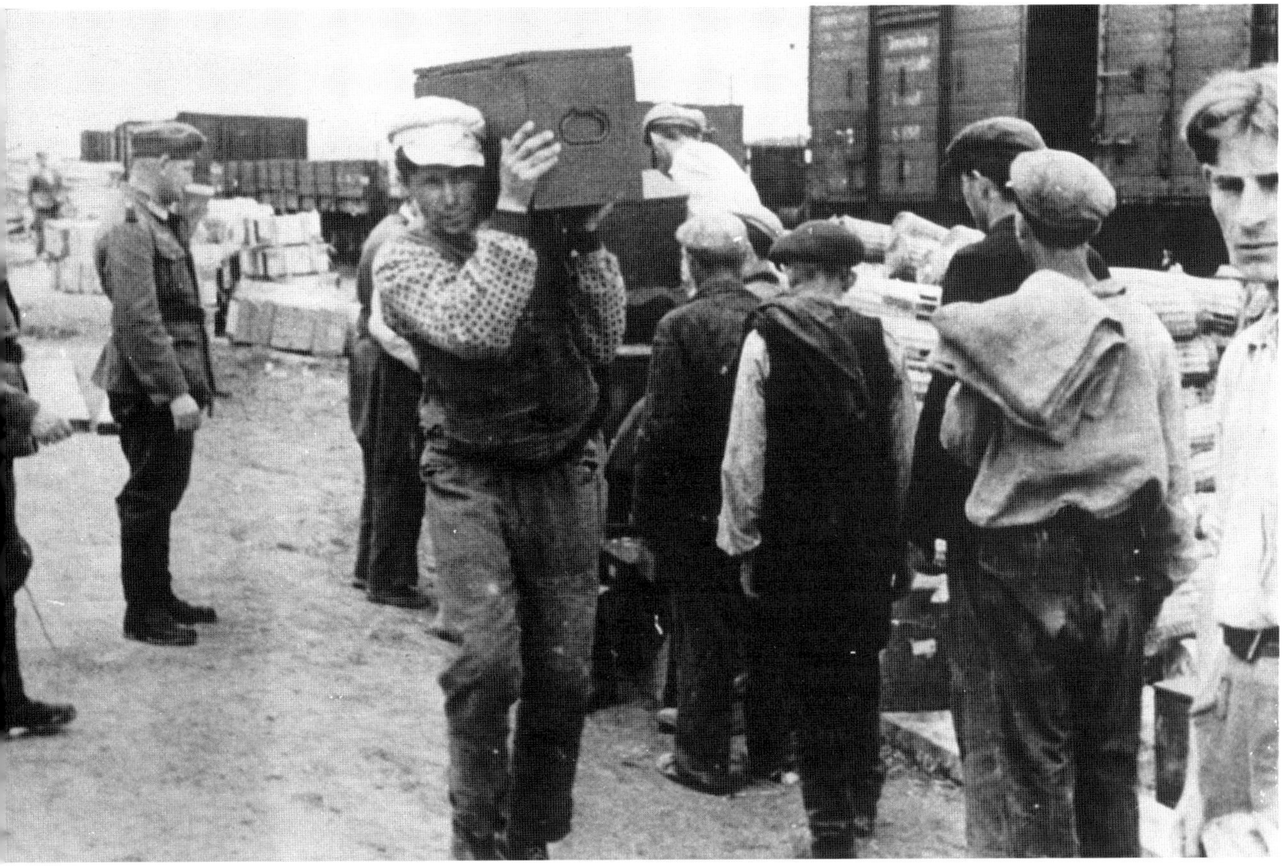

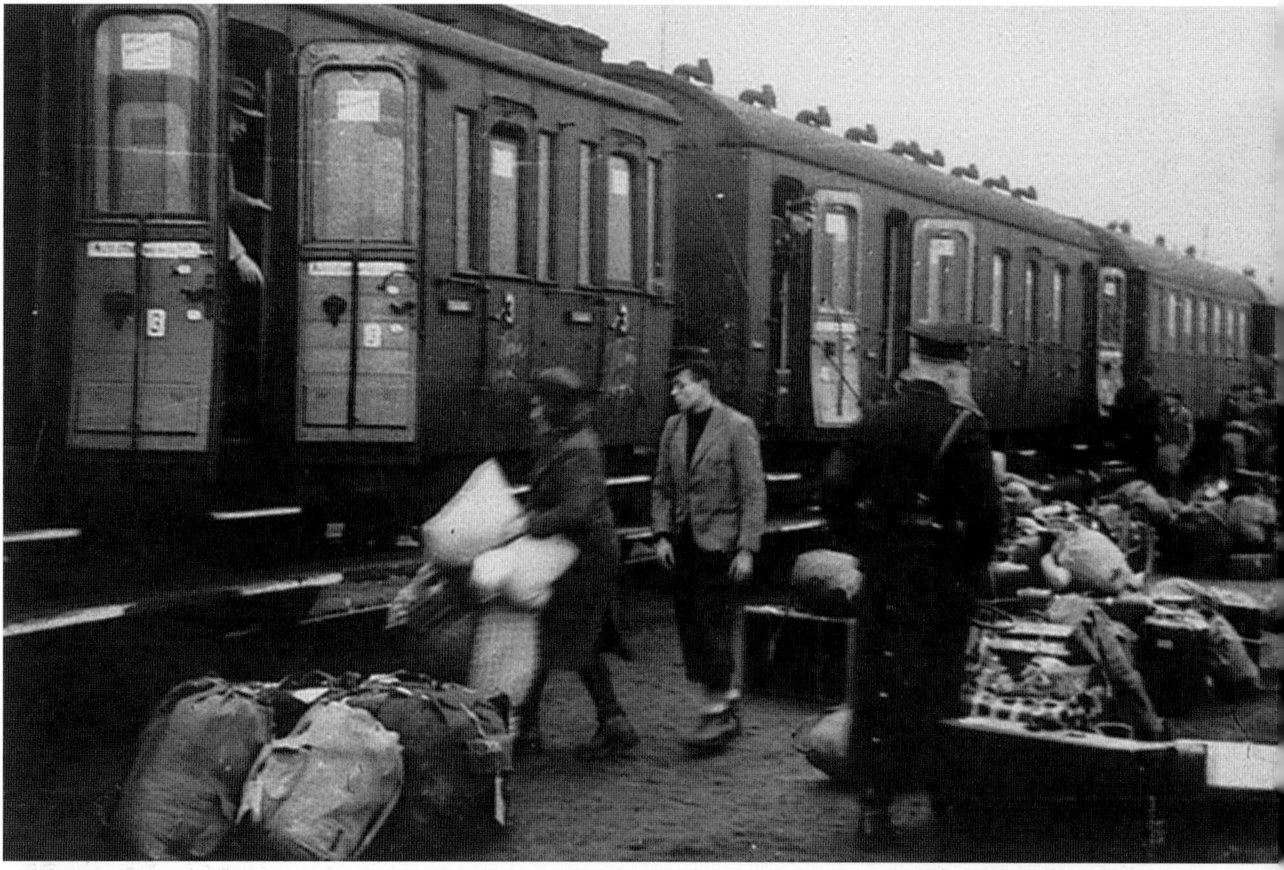

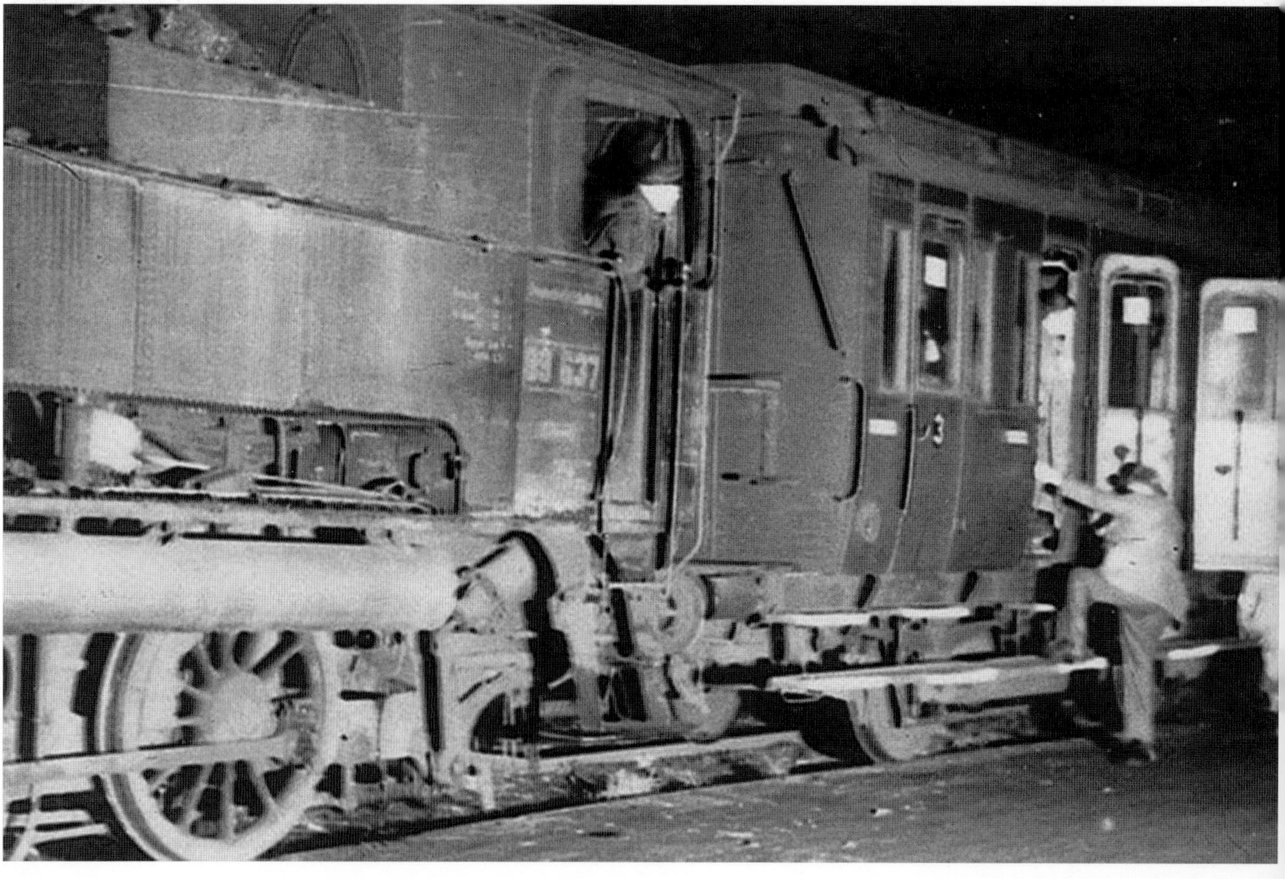
89 637

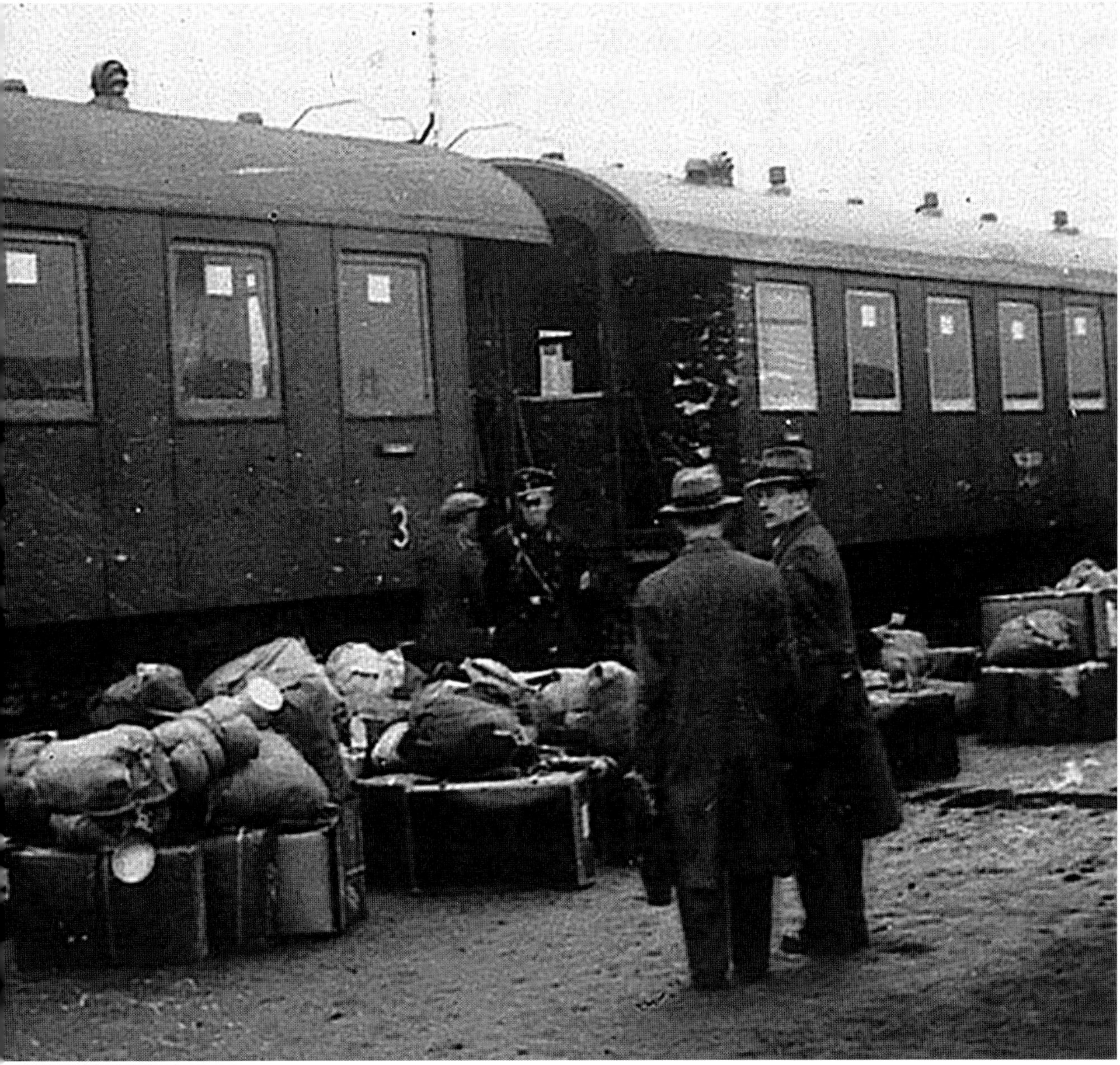

Three photographs taken in November 1941 showing Jews from Würzburg boarding a deportation train bound for Riga. The Jews were taken by third-class passenger train to Langwasser concentration camp on the outskirts of Nuremberg, from where they were transferred two days later to Riga. This was the first deportation of Jews from Germany to Riga. The transports arrived at the Jungfernhof concentration camp. A total of 1,008 Jews were deported on this transport. The transport list noted that 516 were from Nuremberg, 202 from Würzburg, 118 from Bamberg, 89 from Fürth, 46 from Bayreuth, 25 from Coburg, 8 from Forchheim and 4 from Erlangen. Only 52 people survived from this transport, 15 of them from Würzburg. *(Yad Vashem/USHMM)*

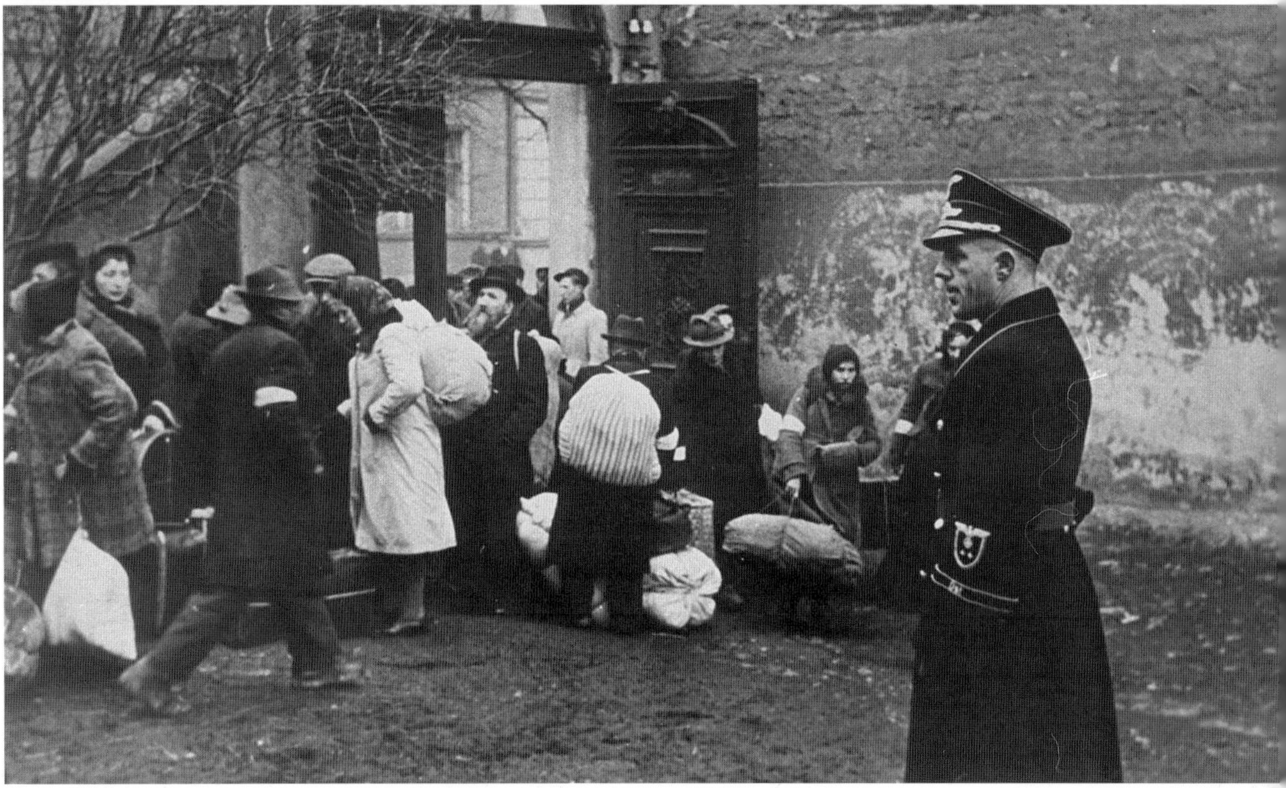

A German official supervises a deportation action in the Kraków Ghetto. Jews are assembled in a courtyard with their belongings awaiting further instructions. From 30 May 1942 onward, the Germans began deportation actions from the Kraków Ghetto to surrounding concentration camps. Headed by *SS-Oberführer* Julian Scherner, the Jews were first assembled on Zgody Square and then escorted to the railway station in Prokocim. The first transport of 7,000 people and the second of an additional 4,000 Jews were deported to Belzec death camp on 5 June 1942. *(USHMM)*

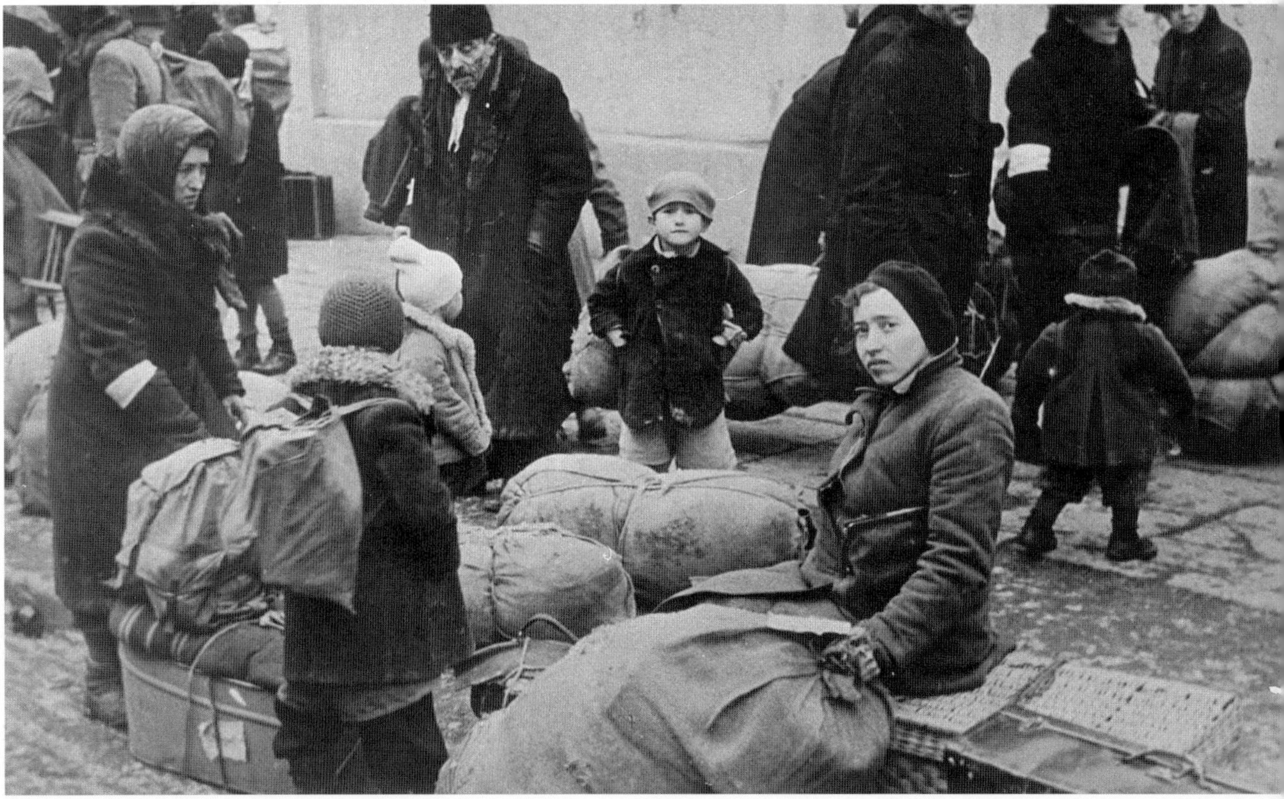

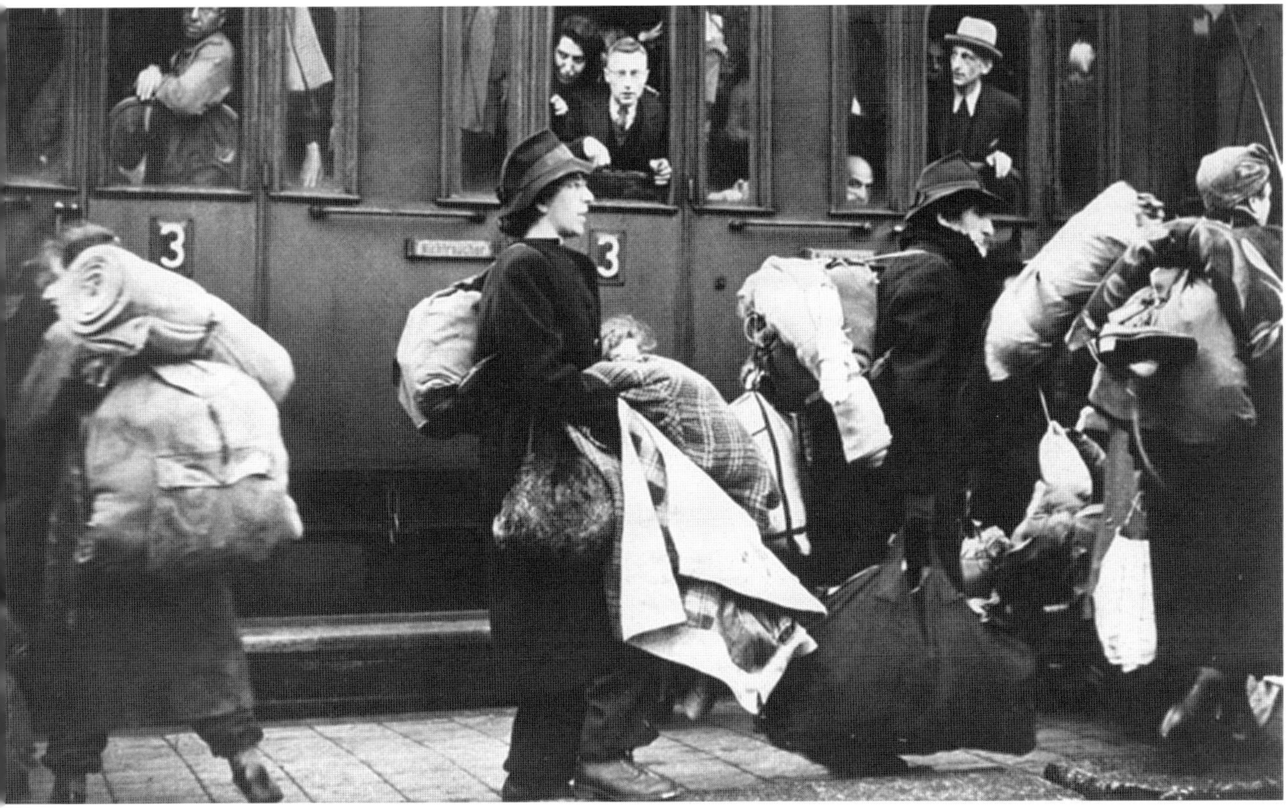

Two photographs showing a deportation action of Jews from Germany to Latvia by passenger train. In December 1941, the Jewish community of Bielefeld in Germany was gathered together prior to their deportation to Eastern Europe. On 13 December some 1,000 Jews from Bielefeld were deported to Riga and almost all were shot on arrival. A few were selected and transported to the Riga Ghetto. However, hardly anyone survived this action. *(USHMM)*

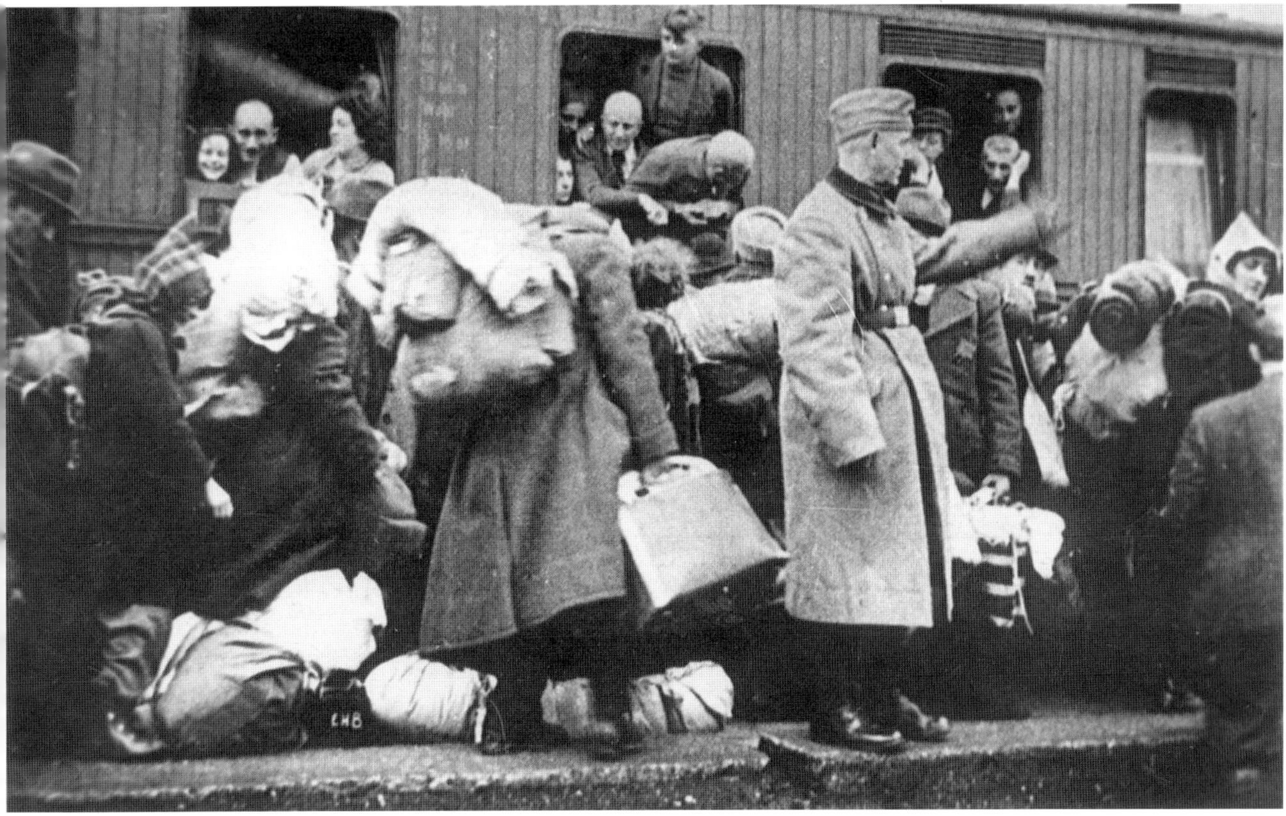

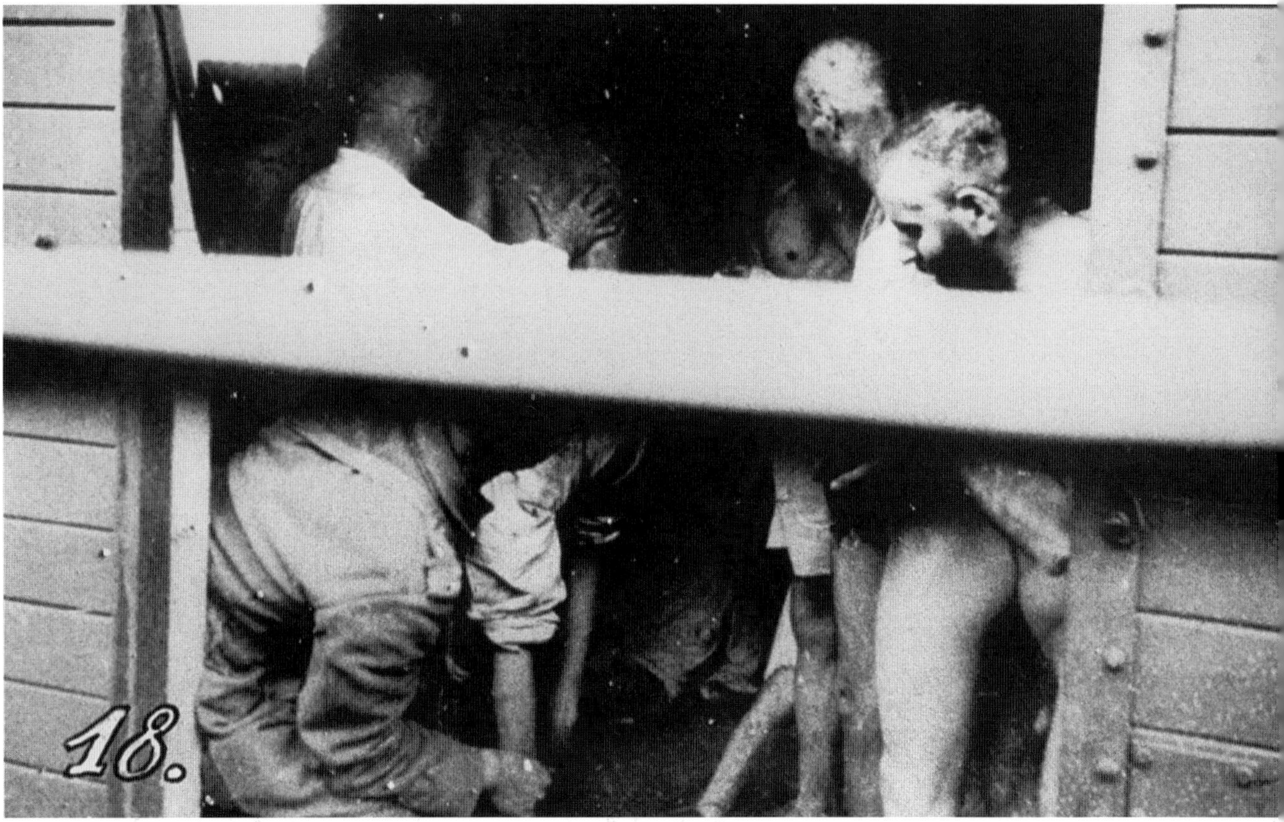
18.

Two photographs showing Romanian military physicians examining Jews during a stop on the Iași-Călărași death train in Săbăoani. During the journey more than 1,400 Jews died in the overcrowded boxcars. The survivors of the death trains were set free after two months of camp detention in Călărași and Podu Iloaiei. *(USHMM)*

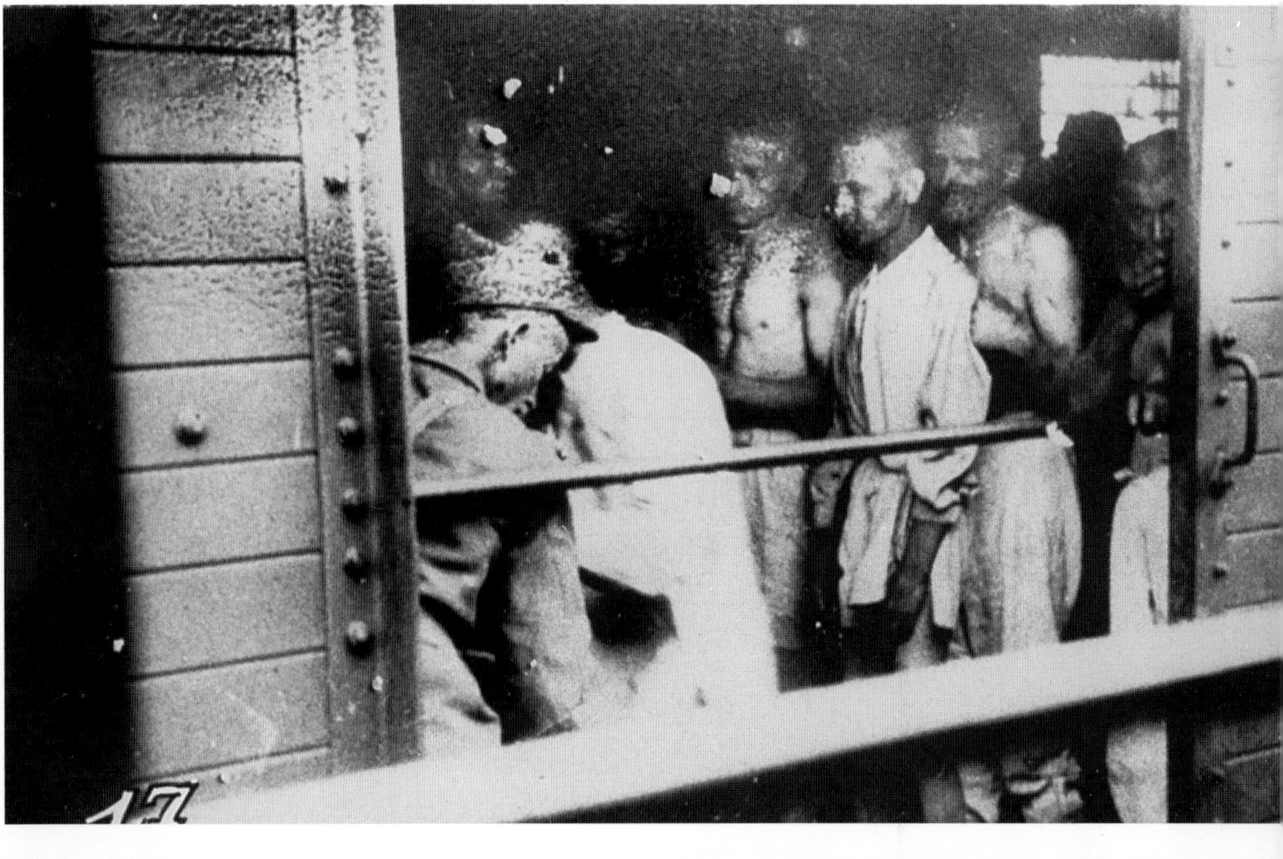
17

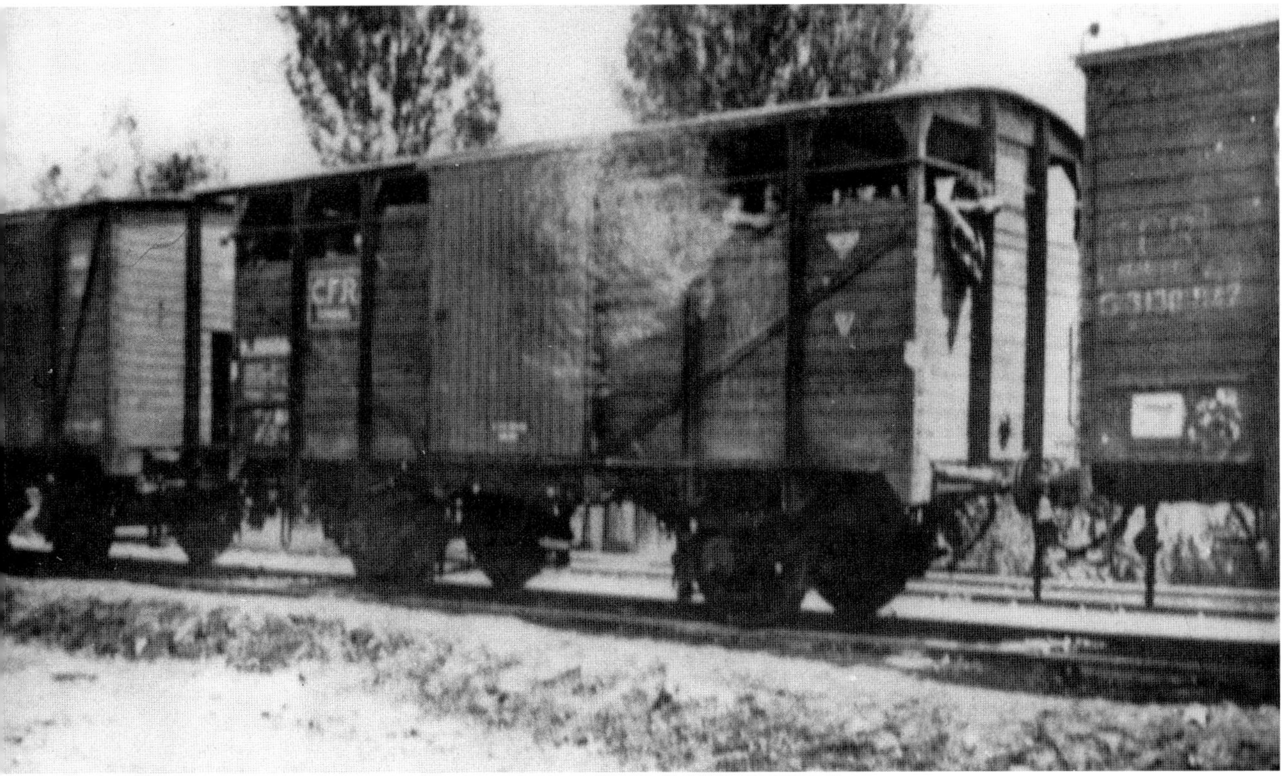

Boxcars containing Jews at a railway station in Târgu-Frumos. During the first days of the German invasion of Russia 13,000 Jews were murdered by Romanian army and police units in the town of Iași and on two train transports. A total of 2,500 Jews were deported to Călărași and was known as the Iași to Călărași death train. *(USHMM)*

Under the supervision of Romanian guards, Romani men load the corpses of victims of the Iași-Călărași death train onto trucks in Târgu-Frumos. *(USHMM)*

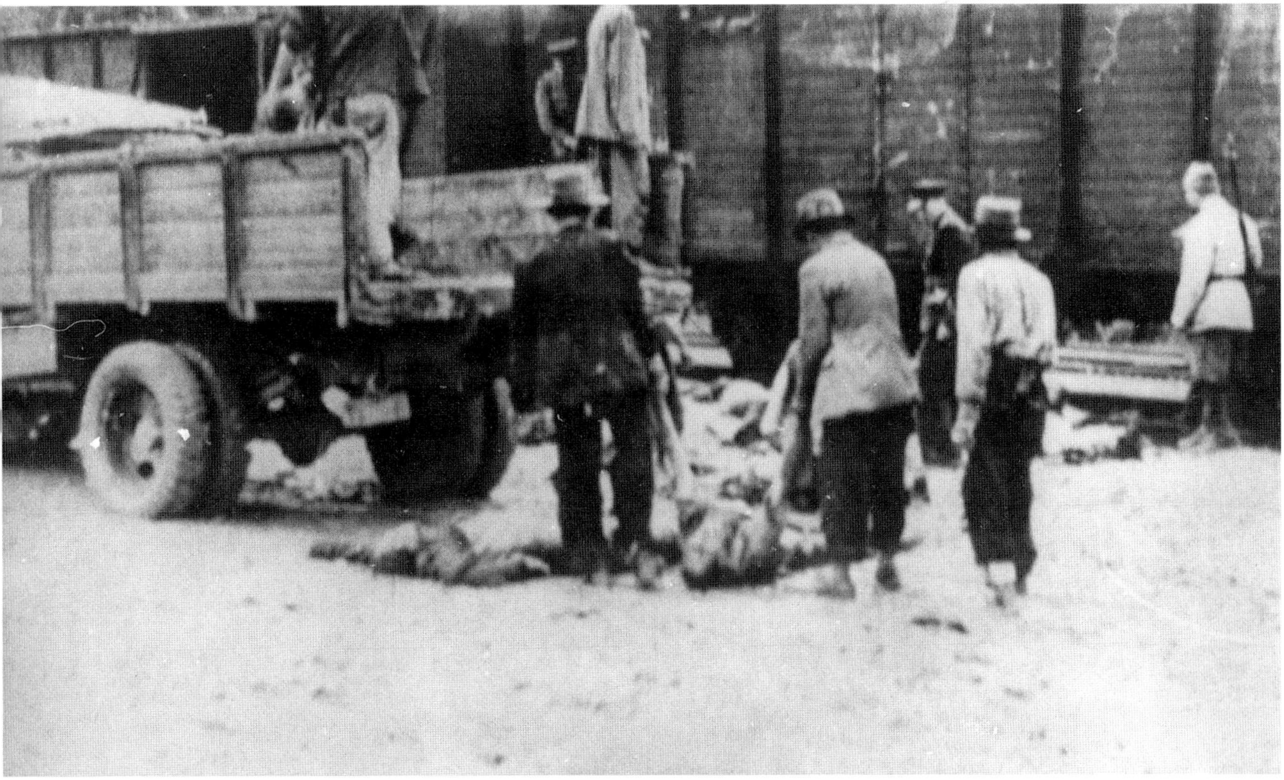

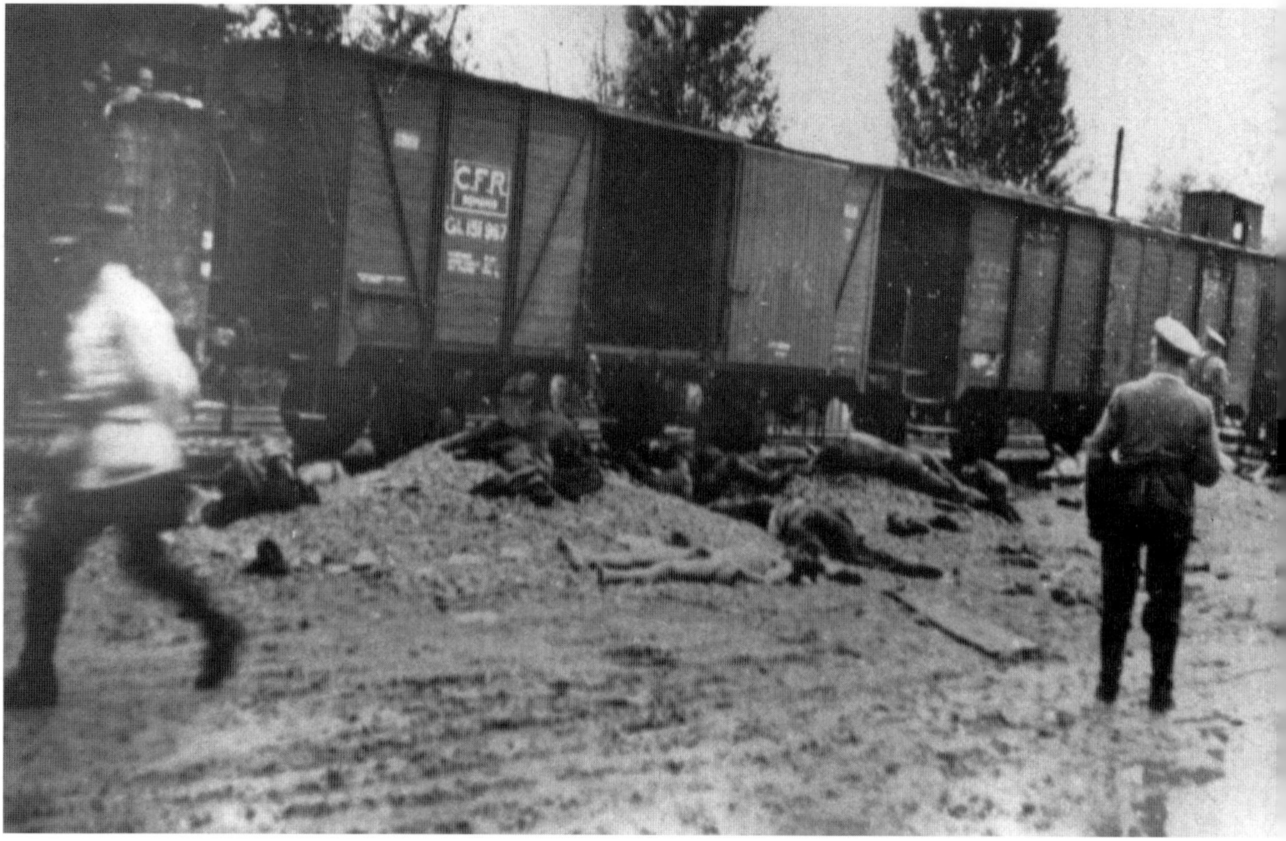
C.F.R.

Two photographs showing Romanian police walking past the bodies of Jews removed from the Iași-Călărași death train in Târgu-Frumos. *(USHMM)*

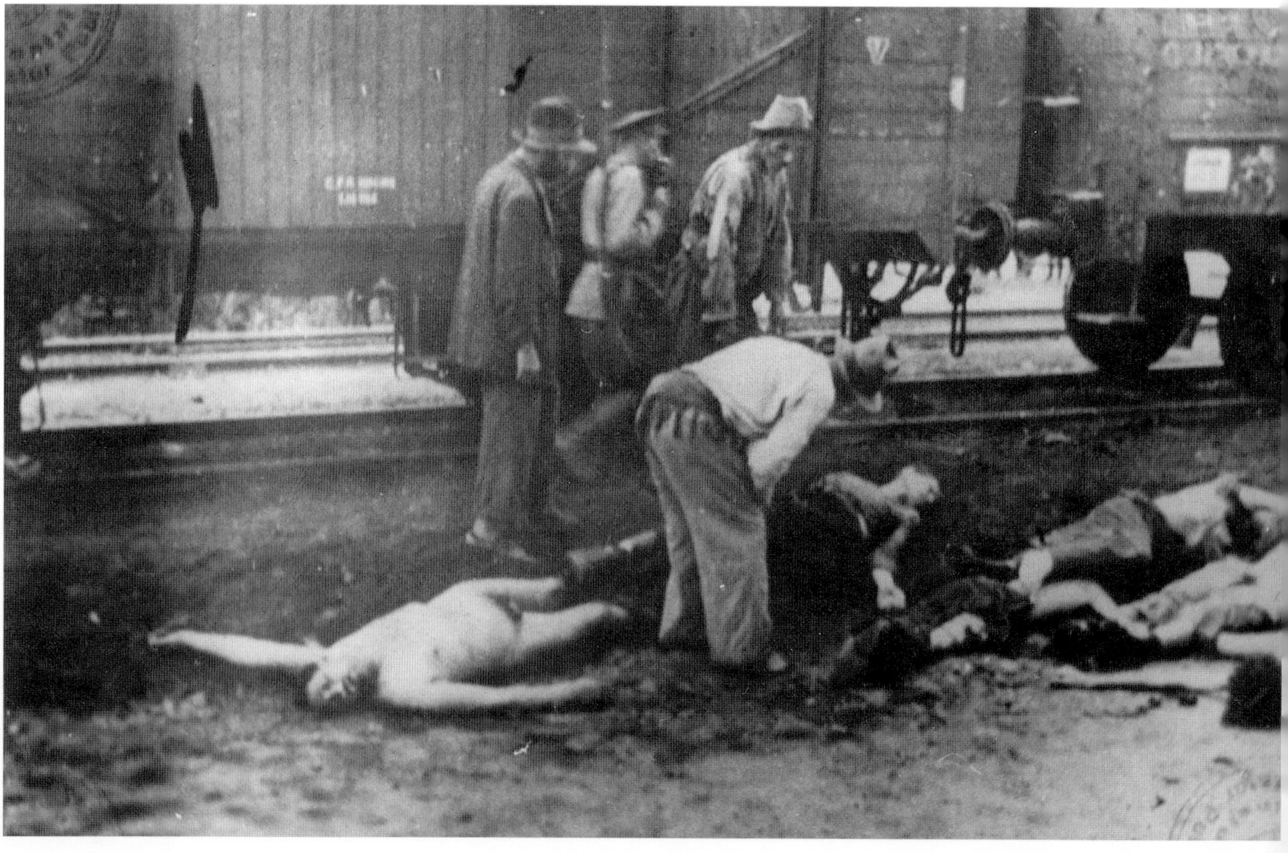

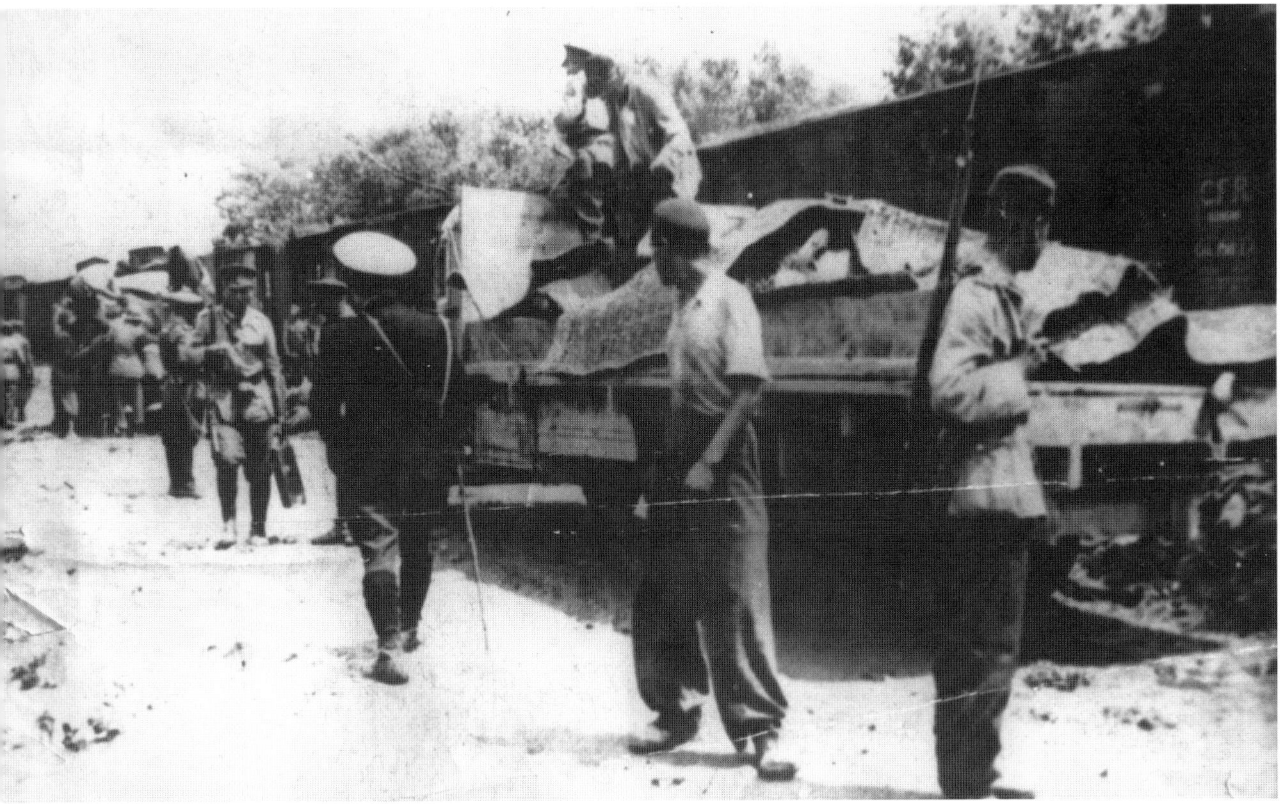

Romanian guards supervise the removal of bodies from the Iași-Călărași death train in Târgu-Frumos. *(USHMM)*

Romanian police supervise the removal of hundreds of bodies from the Iași-Călărași death train during its stop in Târgu-Frumos. *(USHMM)*

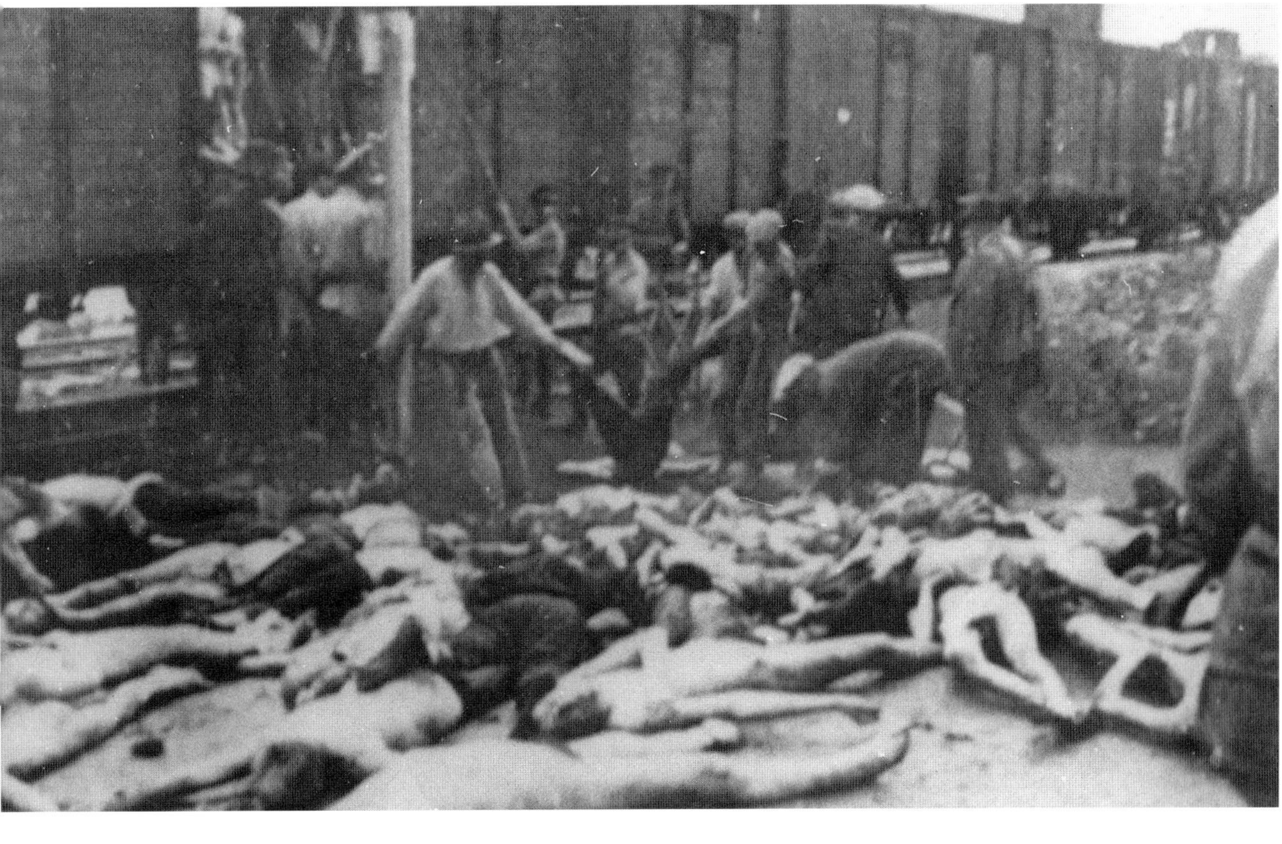

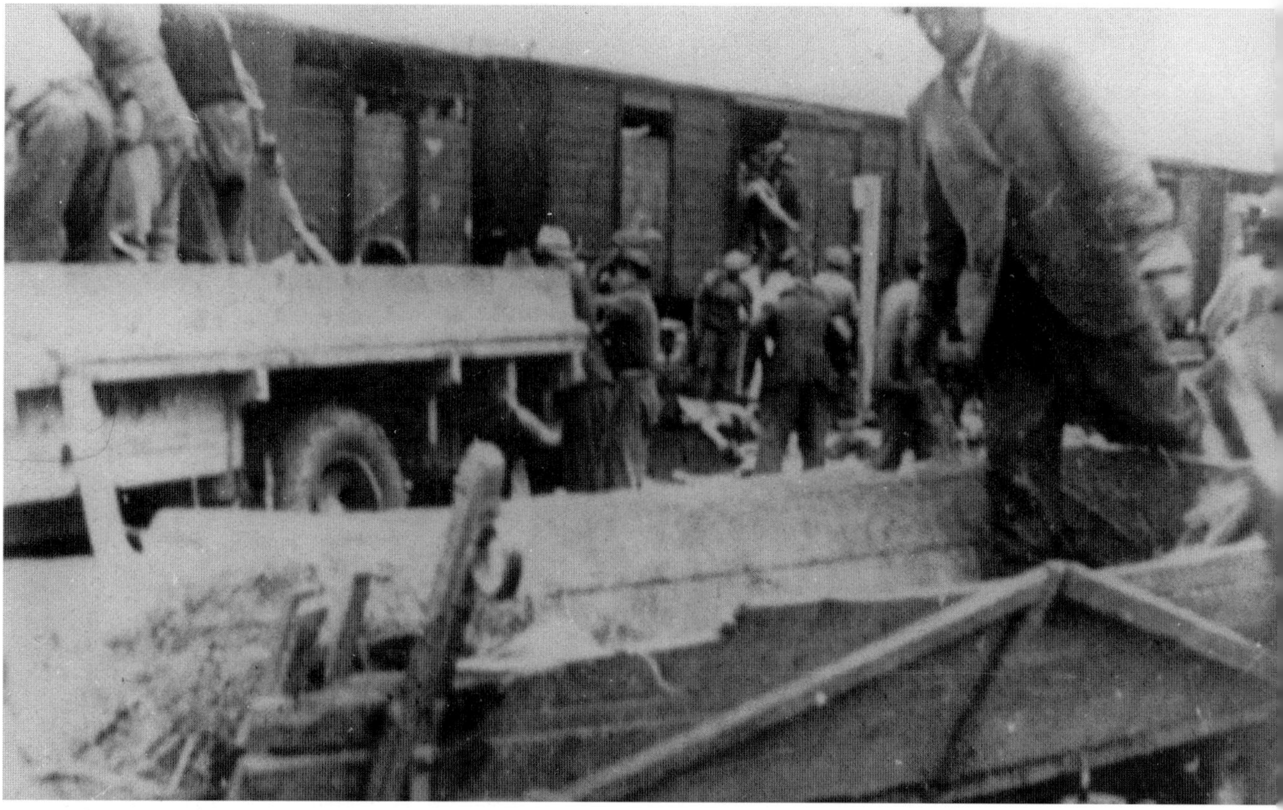

Six photographs taken in sequence showing the supervision and clearing of the dead from the Iași-Călărași death train. The deportees were crammed into the individual boxcars holding 120 people, which were then sealed and they set off very slowly. Some of those inside were so cramped they quickly died of dehydration and starvation during the journey, which took almost a week to complete. Some became so desperate for liquid they drank urine. *(USHMM)*

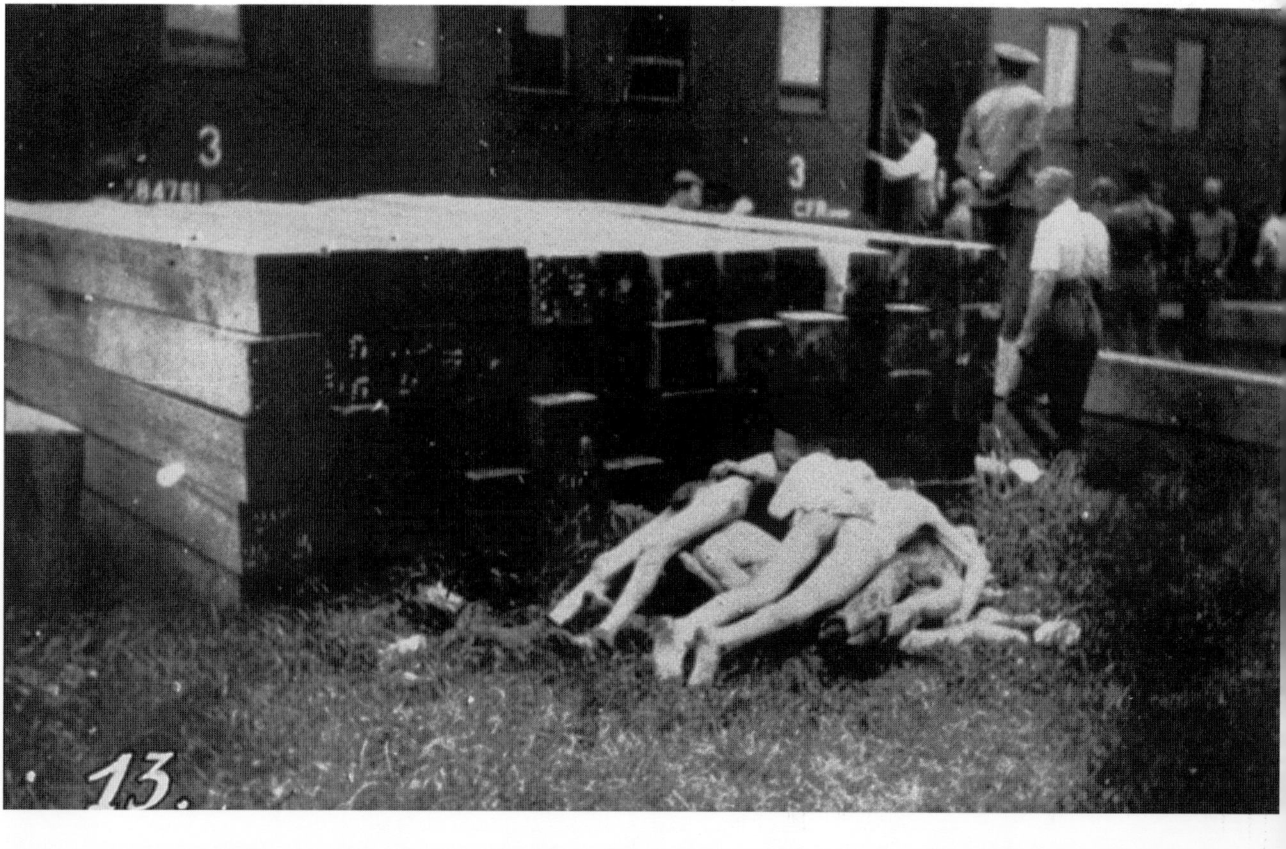
3
3
13.

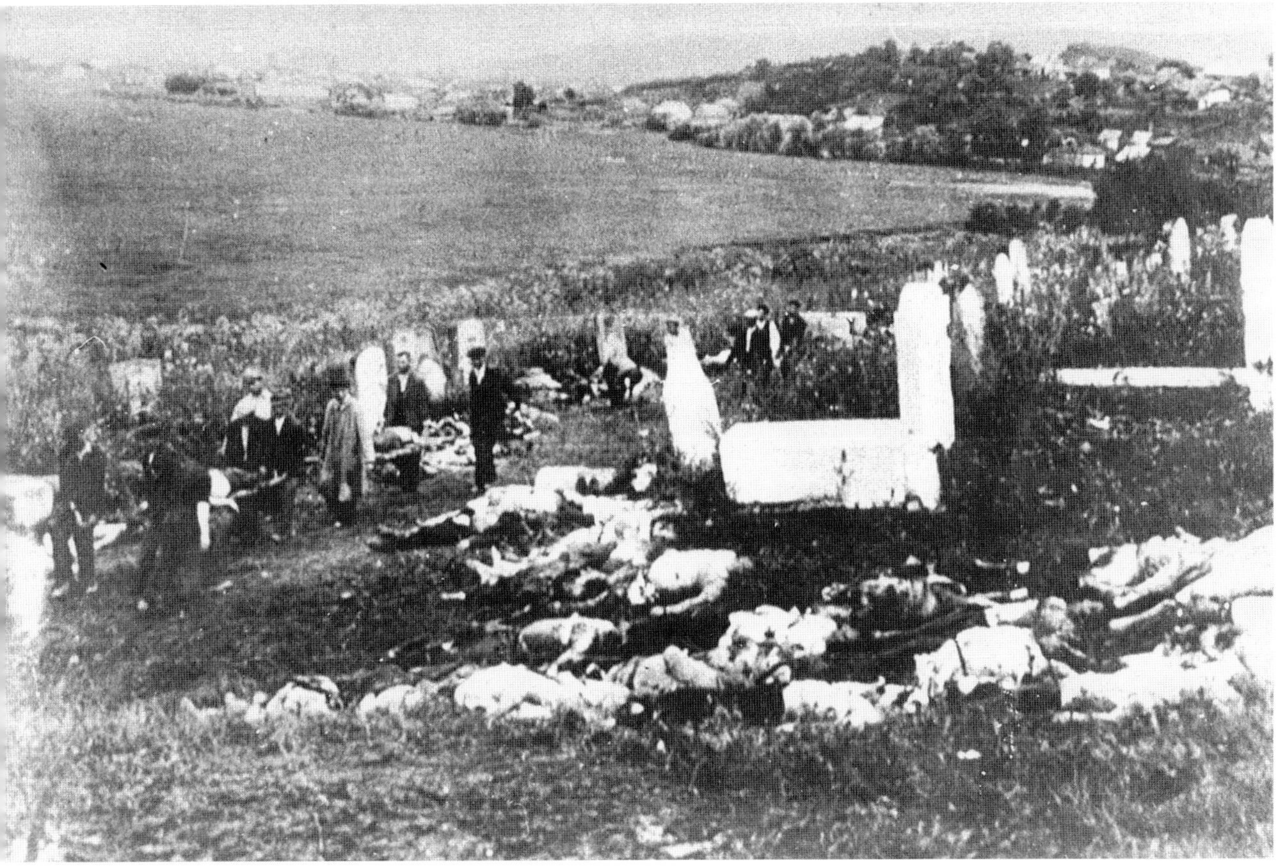

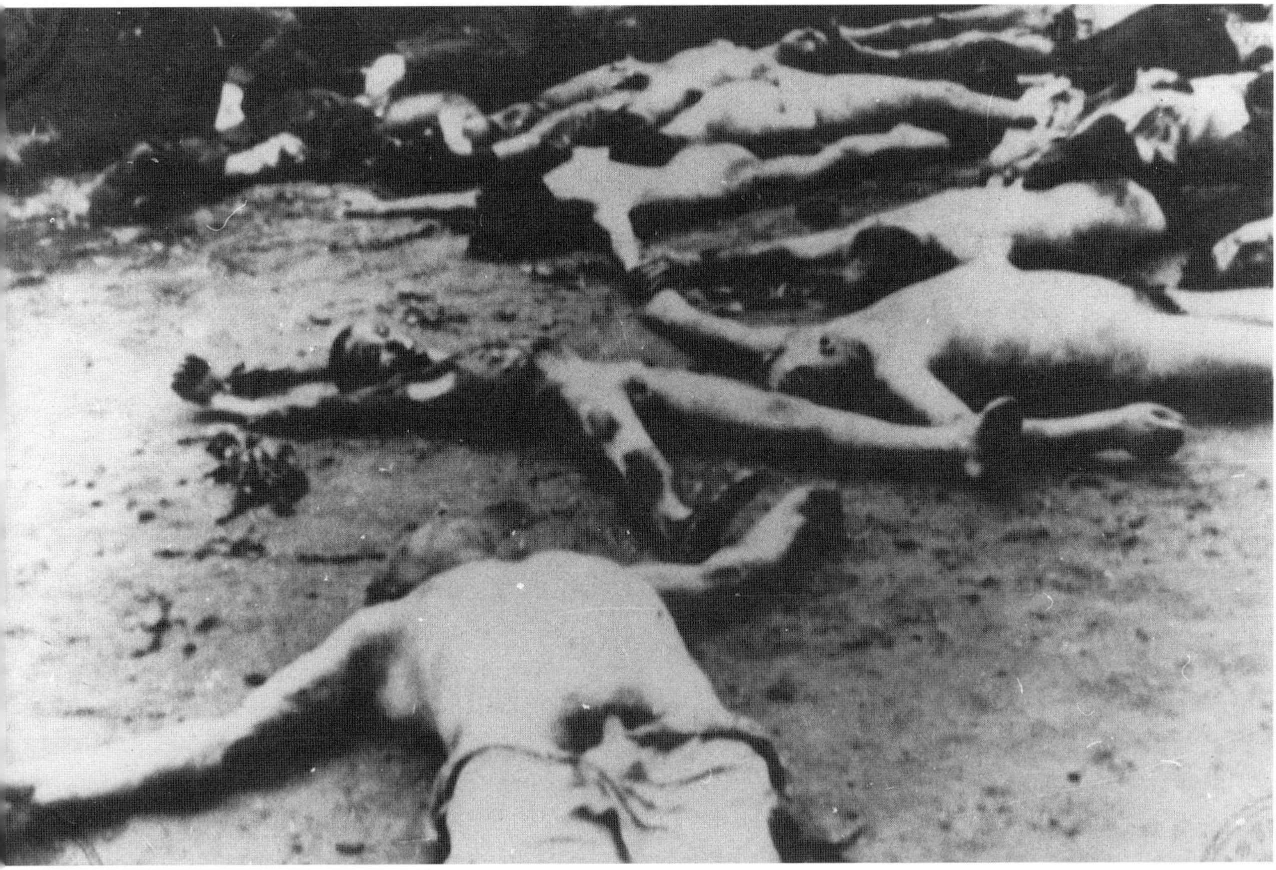

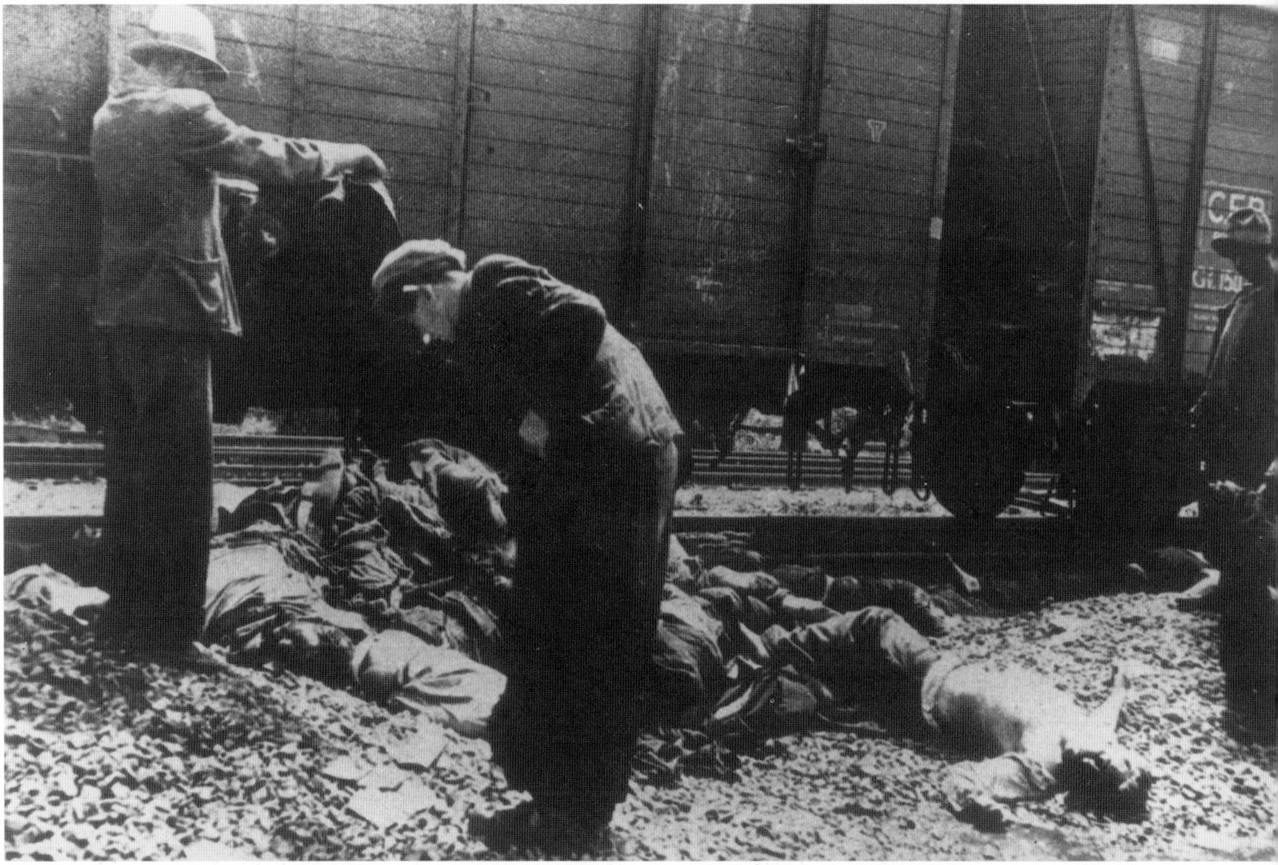

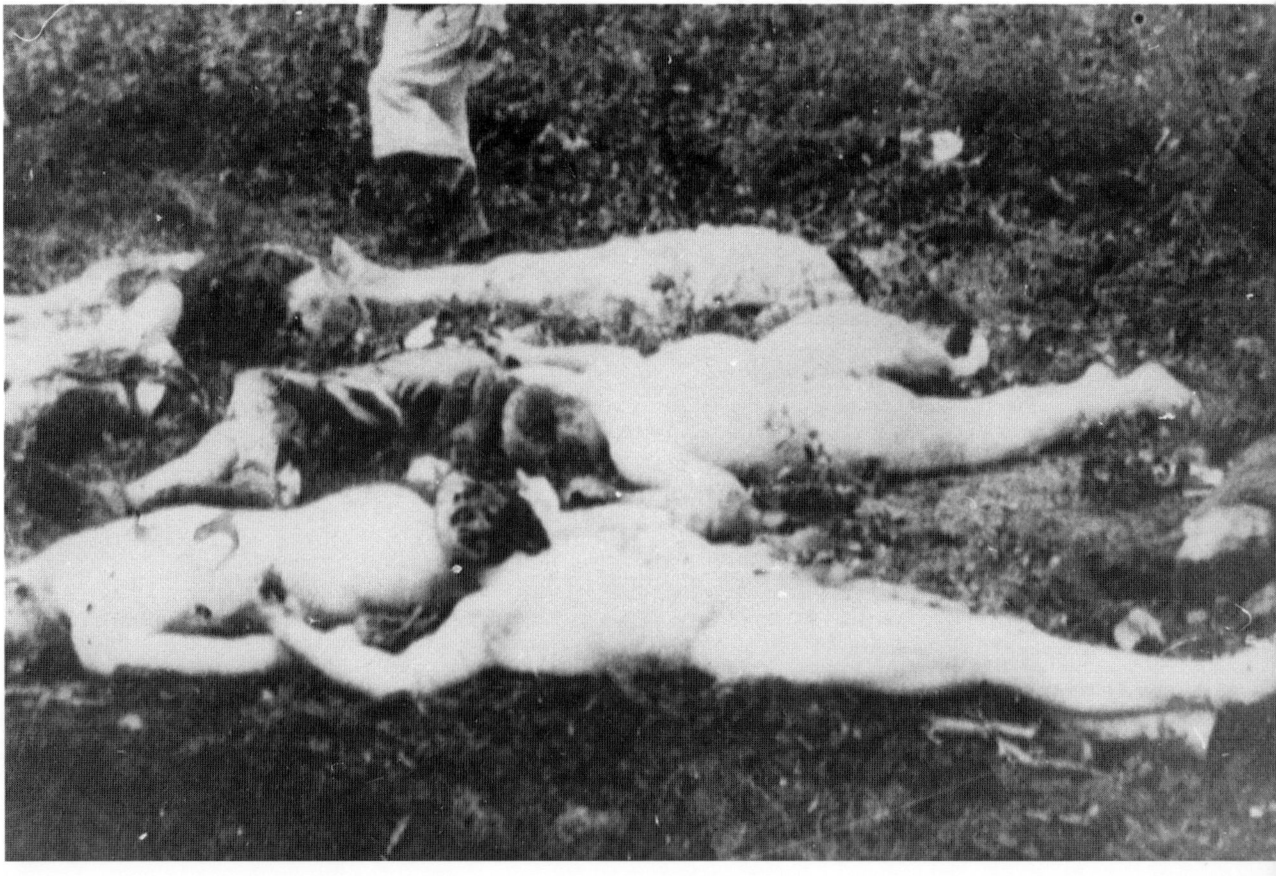

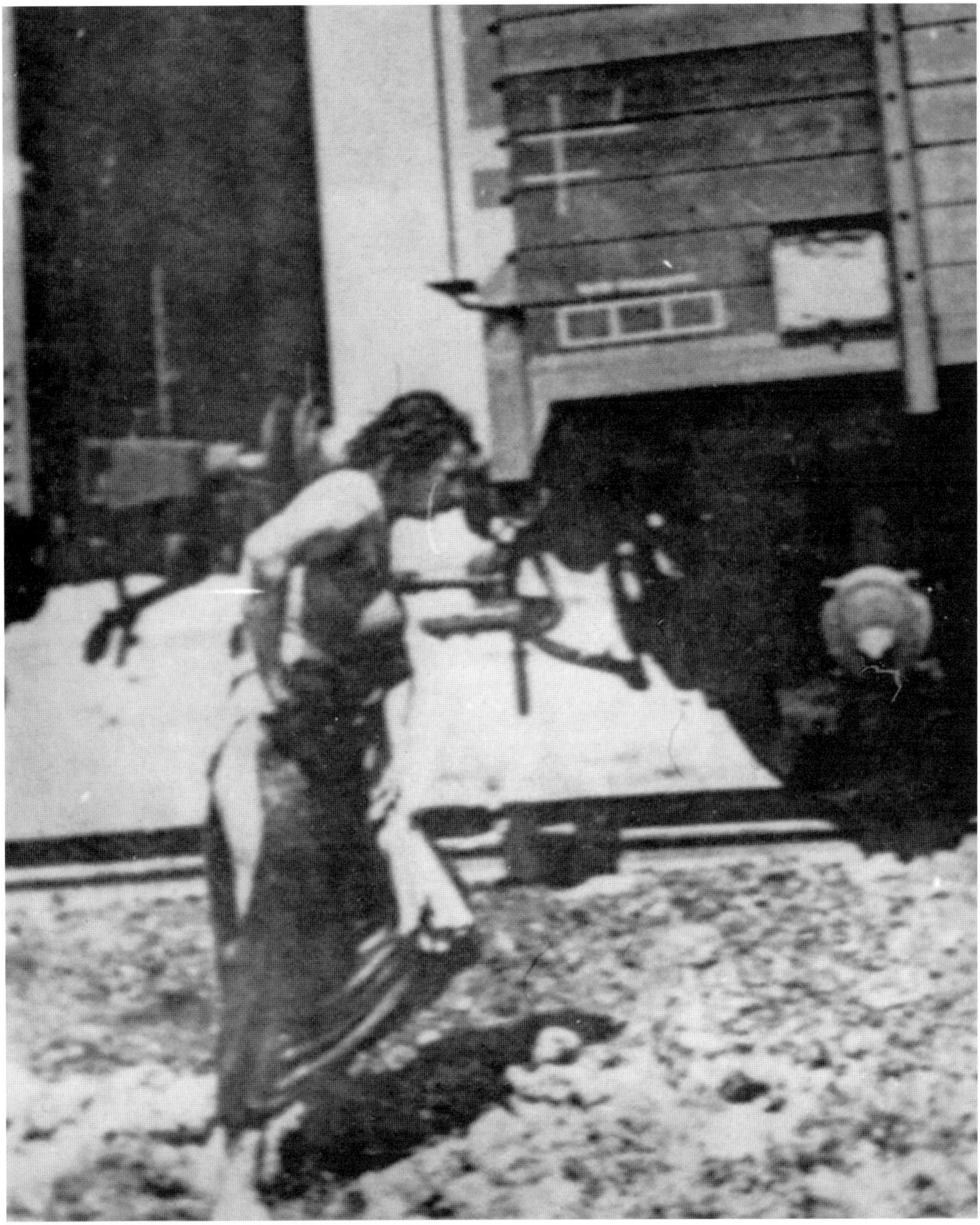

A partially-clothed Jewish woman who was a passenger on the Iași death train walks beside the train during a stop on the journey. *(USHMM)*

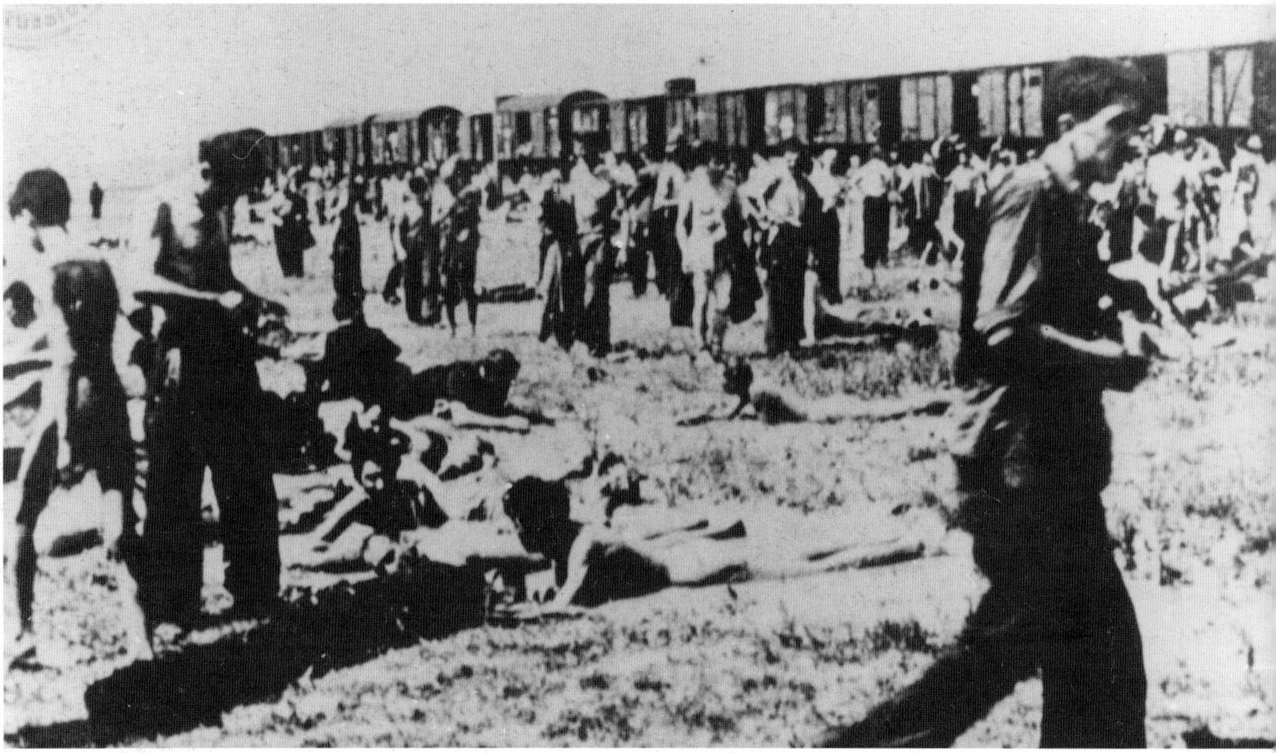

Jewish passengers on the Iași death train rest in a field beside the tracks during a stop on the journey. *(USHMM)*

A photograph of Auschwitz Station in 1939. The railway line to Auschwitz was a pinnacle of the success of the Germans in transporting large volumes of people through the General Government and other parts of Poland a year later in 1940. On 14 June 1940, the first passenger train steamed into Auschwitz station from Tarnów prison carrying 728 of what the SS termed political prisoners. An unloading ramp was built adjacent to the main Auschwitz camp and served the camp during the whole of its operation. It was here that the first transport of prisoners from Tarnów was shunted by train via the main railway line at Auschwitz and then unloaded at the new ramp. *(USHMM)*

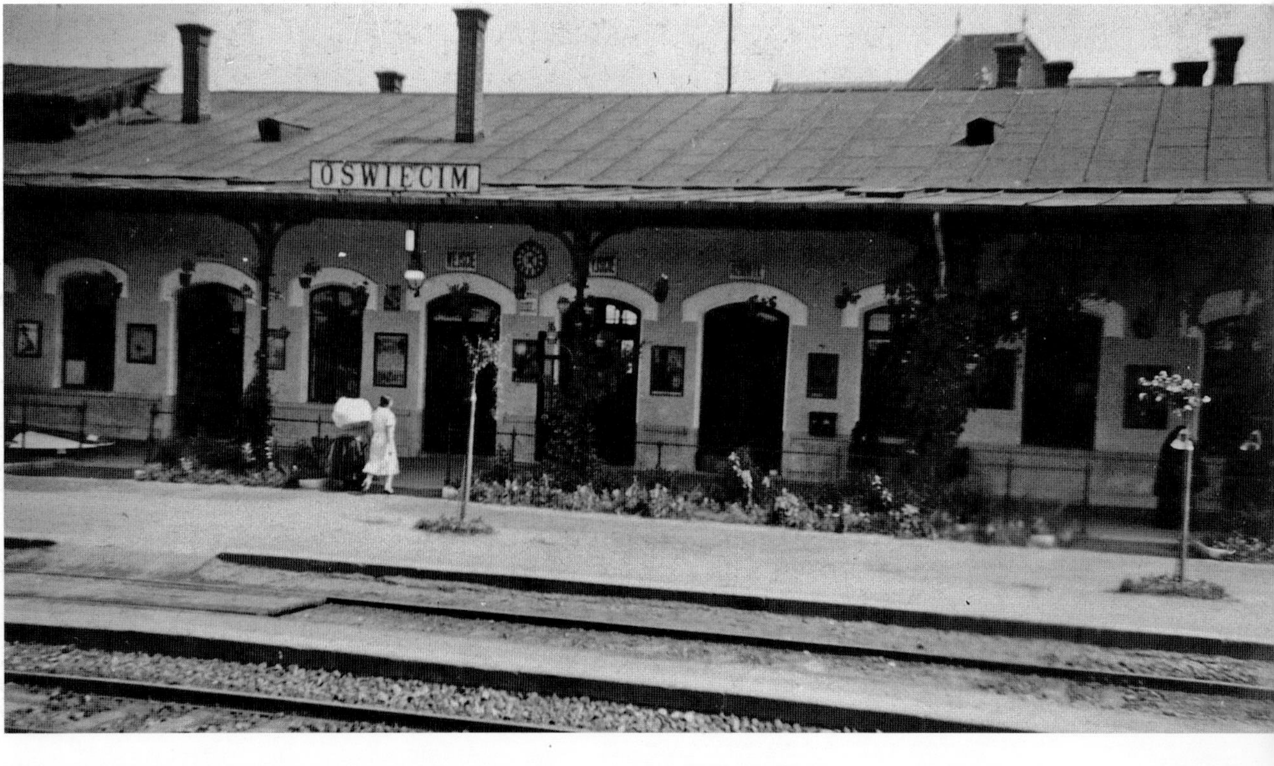
OSWIECIM

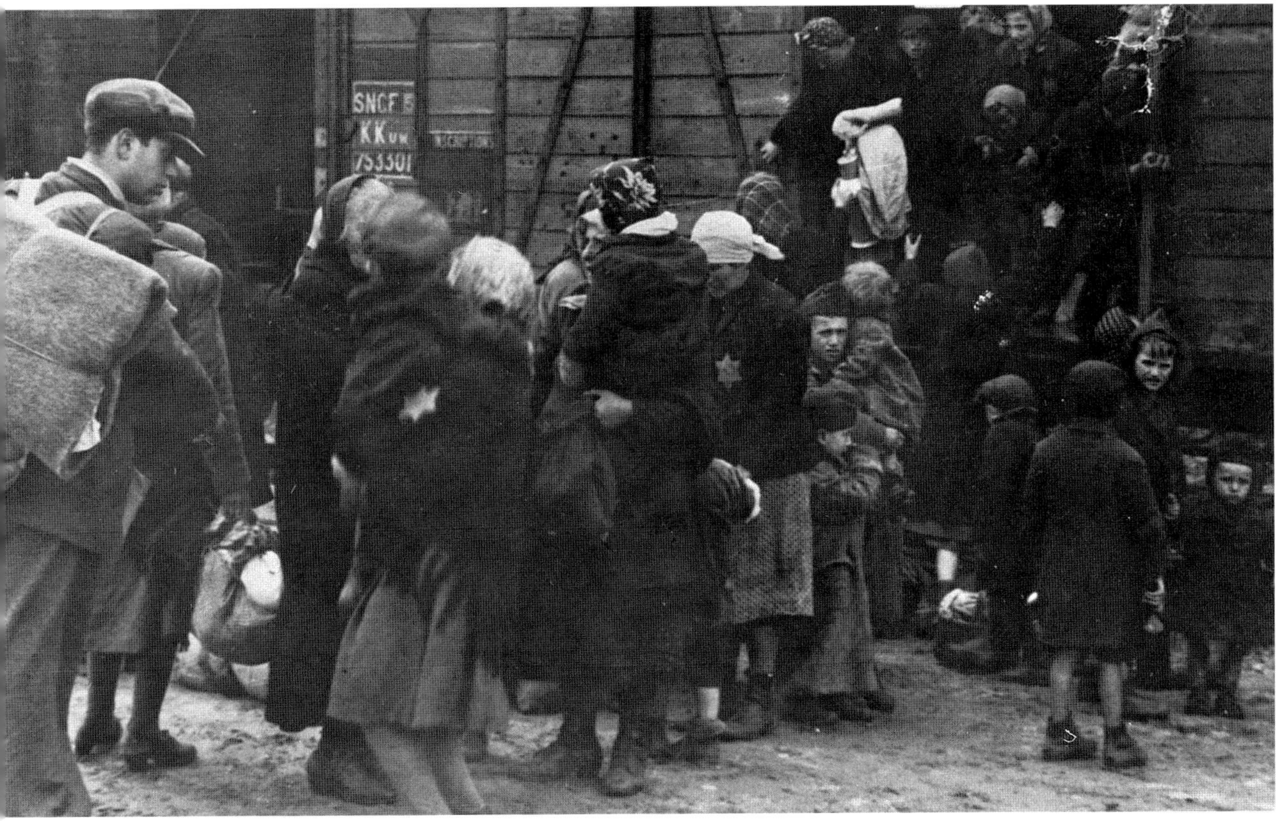
SNCF

A typical scene showing Jewish people being unloaded from a boxcar at their destination.

Following the train's arrival Ustaša guards in the Jasenovac concentration camp strip newly-arrived prisoners of their personal possessions. *(USHMM)*

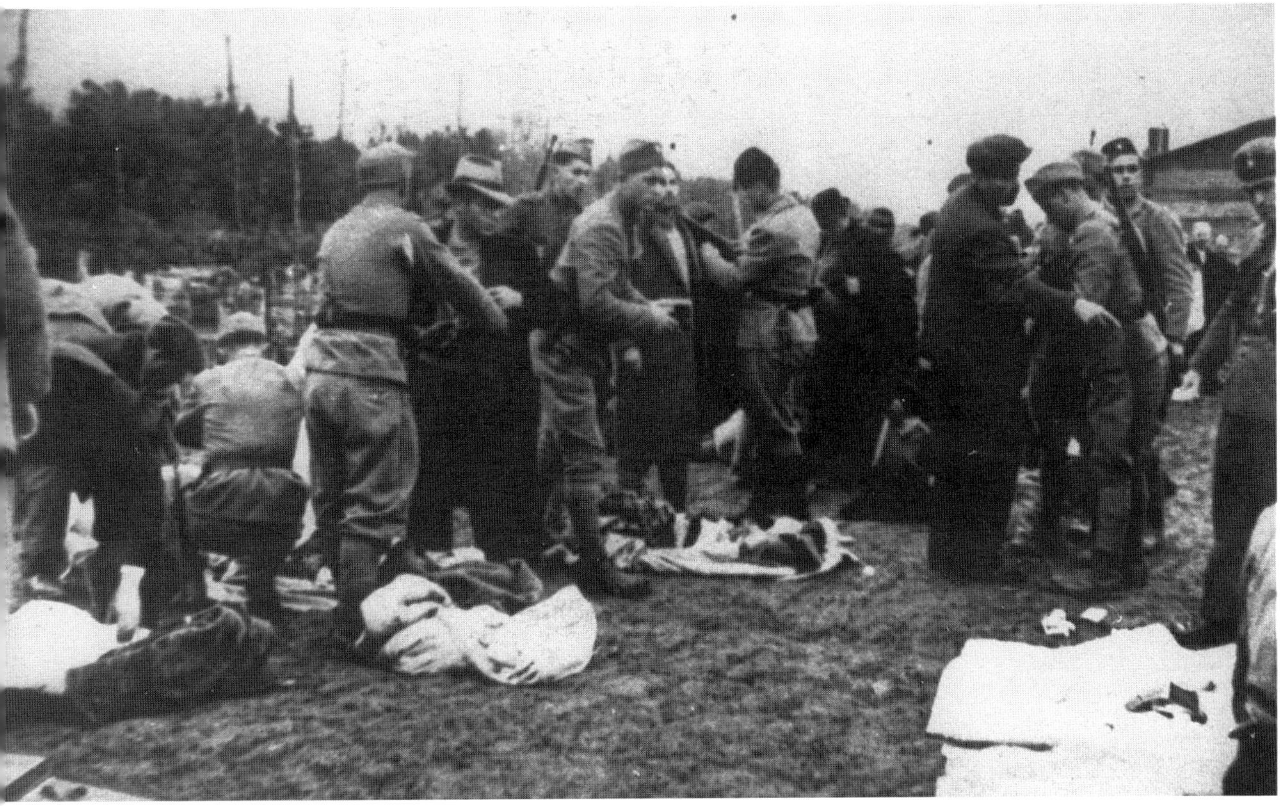

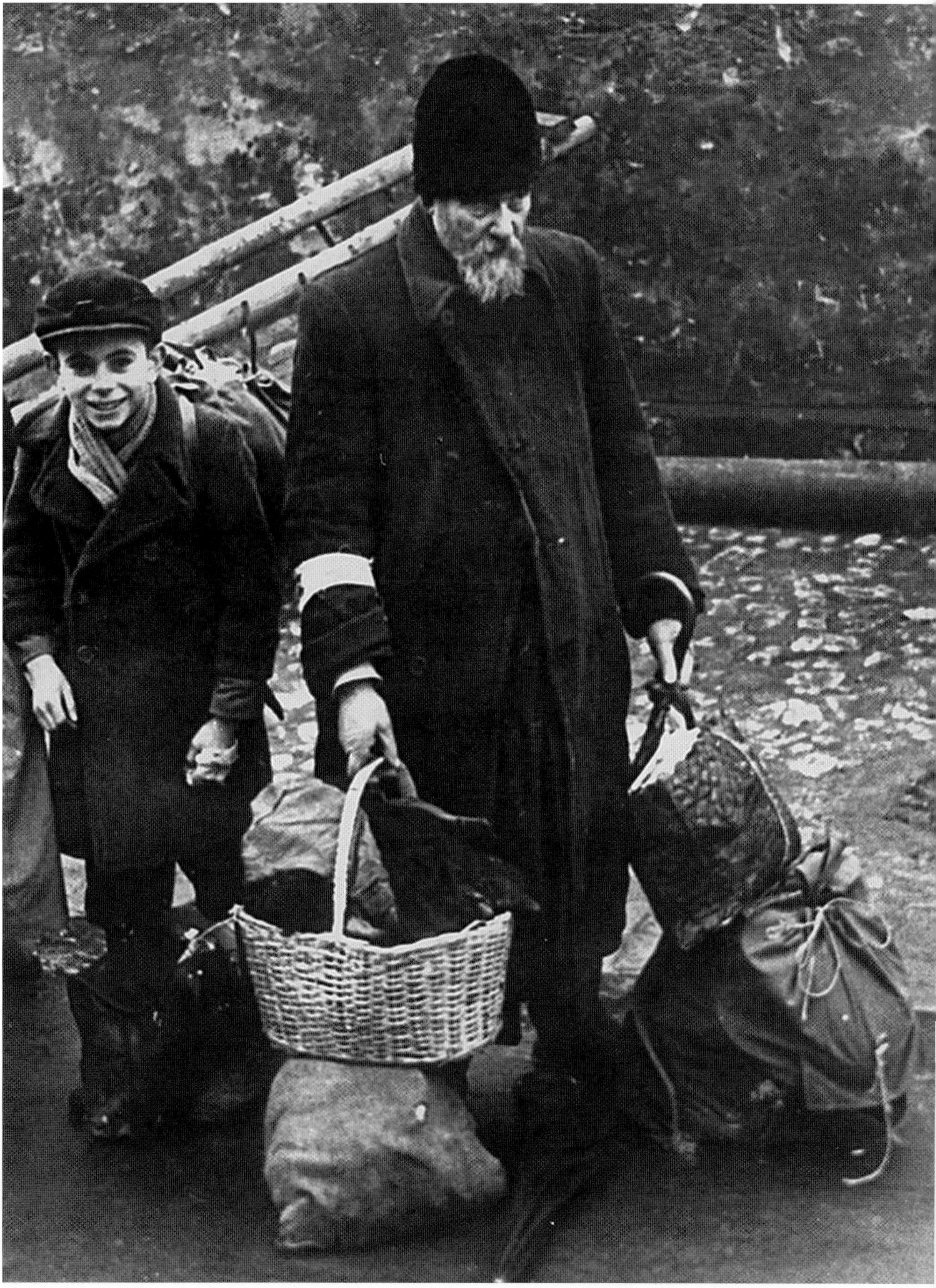

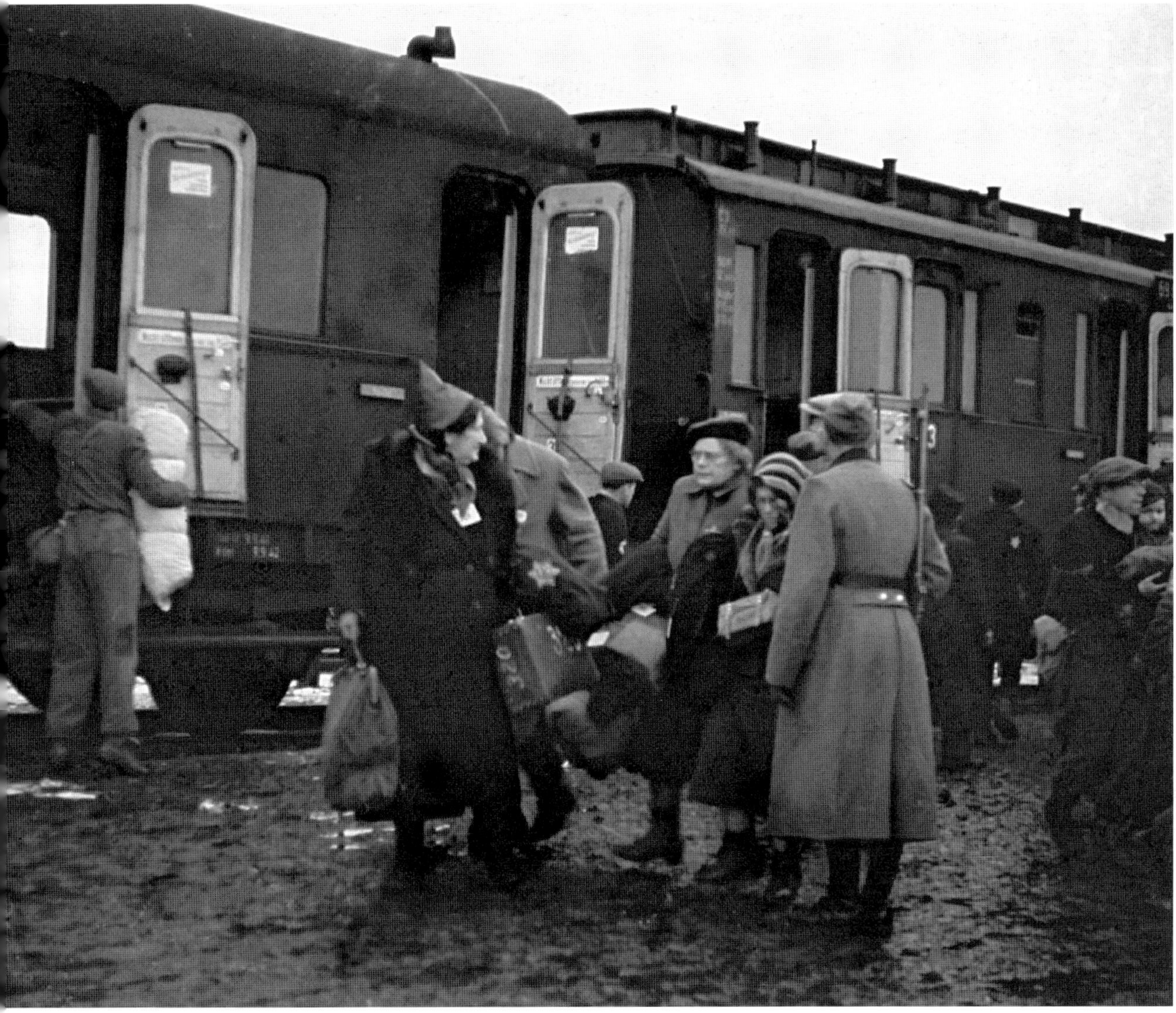

(**Opposite**) An elderly man and child who have been rounded up for deportation wait with their luggage at an assembly point in the Kraków Ghetto in 1942. *(USHMM)*

(**Above**) Jews arriving by passenger train at a railway siding for the Lodz Ghetto. They were unloaded from these trains and proceeded on foot in columns to the ghetto. Often they brought small bundles of belongings with them. Throughout 1940 and 1941 the resettlement of millions of Jews into the General Government continued. By the end of 1941 some 3.5 million Polish Jews had been segregated and ghettoized by Eichmann in his massive deportation action involving the use of hundreds of freight and passenger trains. Even by the time the Jews had arrived inside the confines of the ghetto, many were still under the impression that it would be short-term: a temporary stopover before their new life further east. They often had no idea that the German authorities had contained them inside a ghetto merely as a temporary measure to control and segregate them while the Nazi leadership in Berlin deliberated on their fate or their removal from life. They never had any idea that they would one day see their ghettos systematically destroyed, often barbarically, and be forced into nearby forests or fields and murdered, or transported by railway to various labour or death camps around Europe. *(USHMM)*

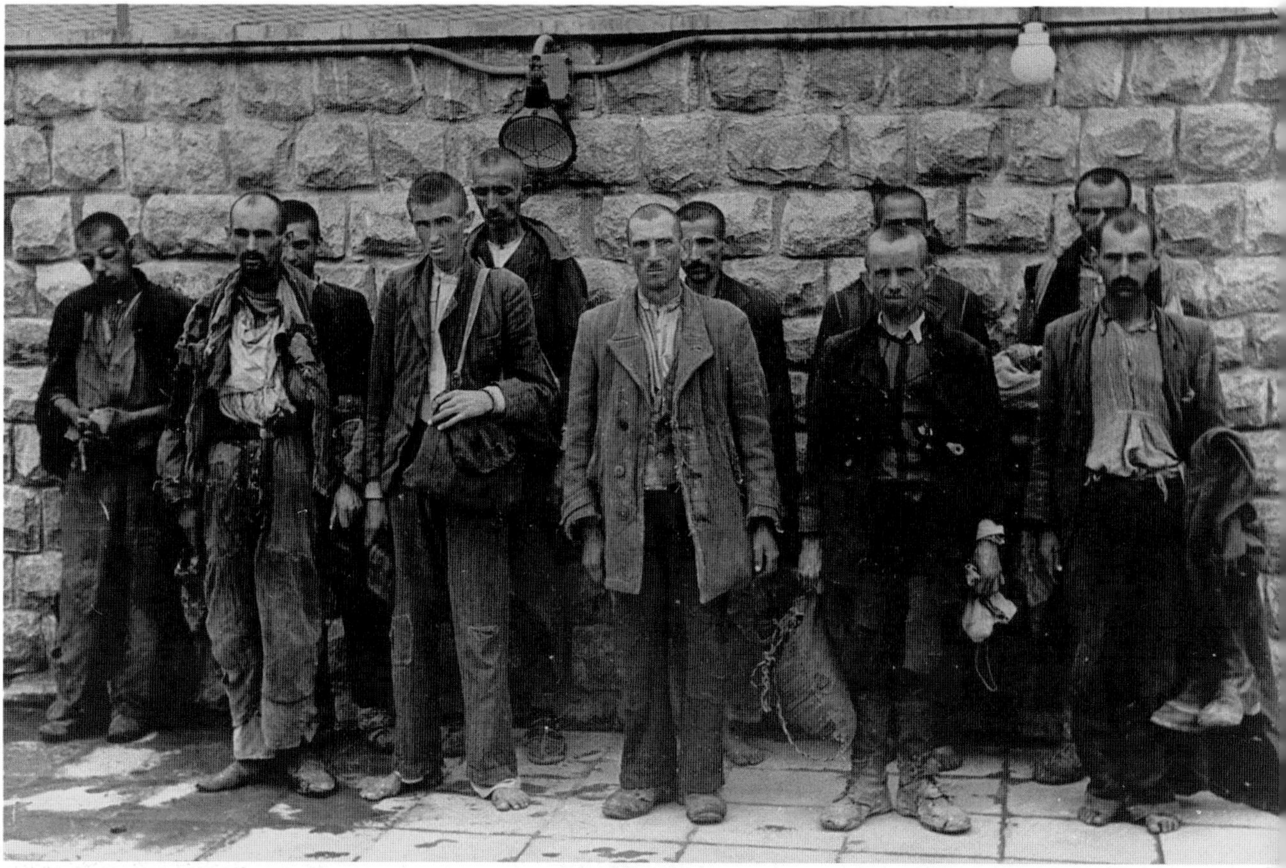

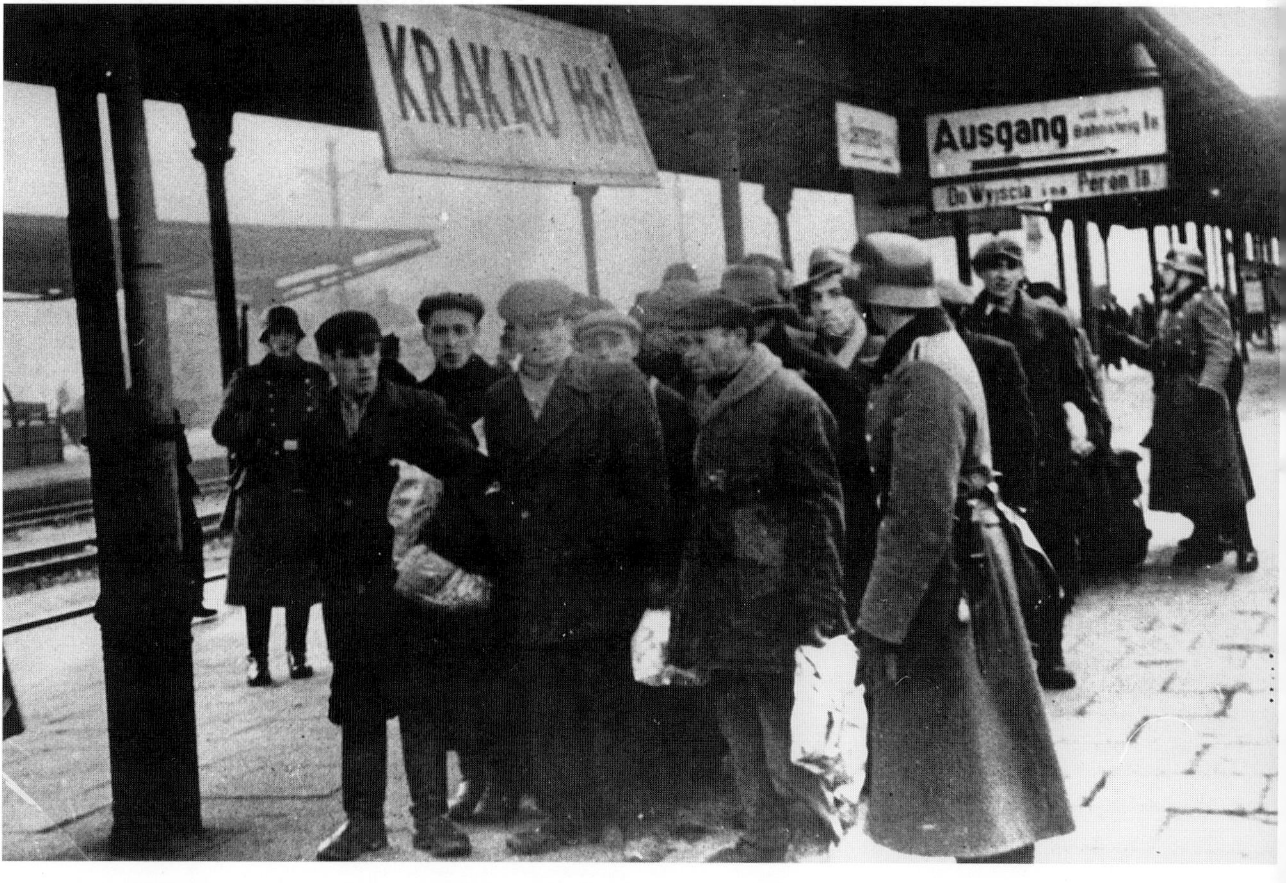
KRAKAU Hbf
Ausgang
Do Wyjscia
Peron Ia

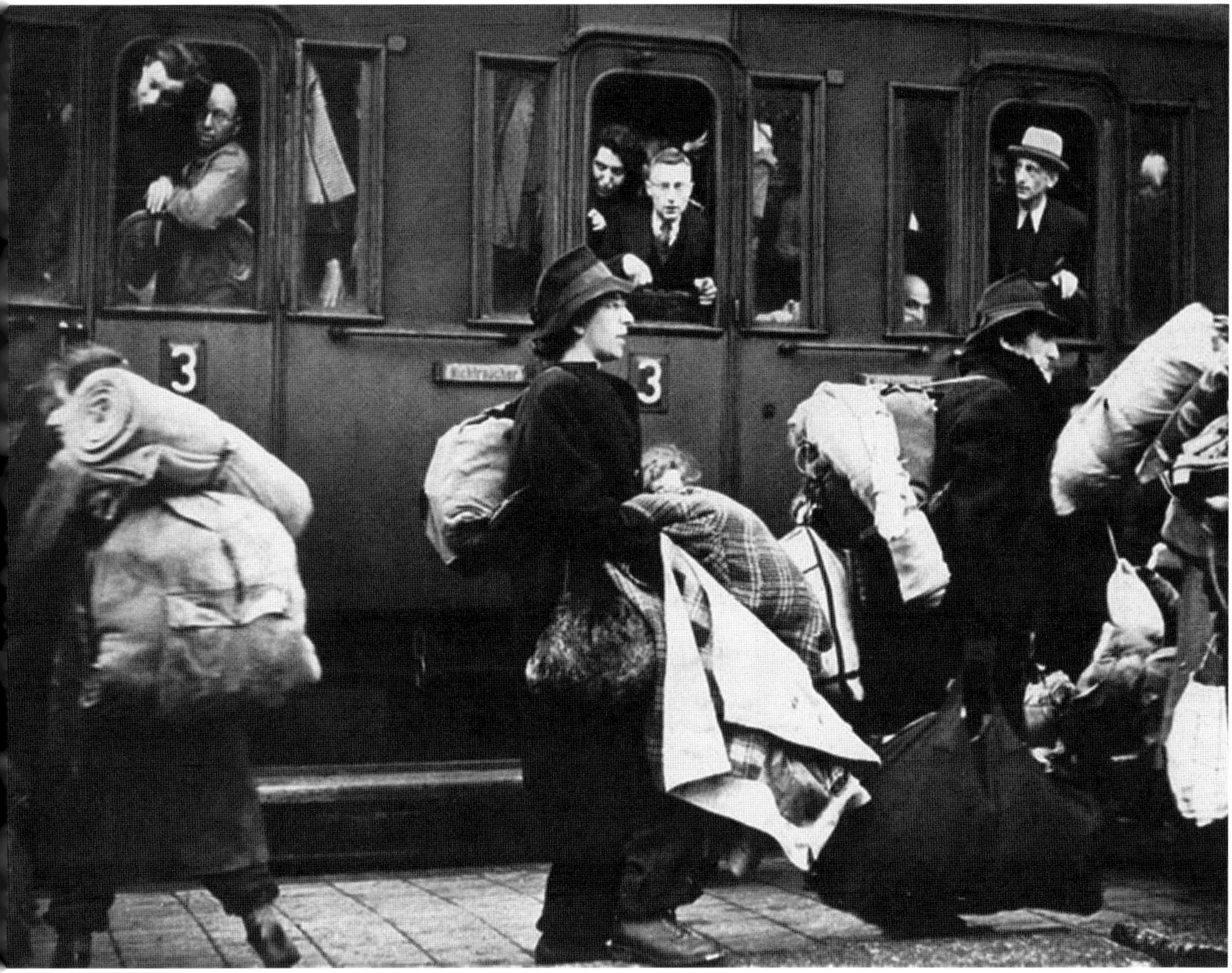

(**Opposite, above**) New arrivals at the *Klagemauer* ('Wailing Wall') after a week-long trip in open railway cars reach the Mauthausen concentration camp. Conditions on board the trains, especially the boxcars, were appalling. With no food or water, the boxcars were packed with 150 deportees, although 50 was the number initially proposed by deportation regulations. Often the boxcars had limited ventilation and this often resulted in many deaths from either suffocation or exposure to the elements. An average transport, especially those being moved to the General Government, might take four days. Often, when the trains arrived at their destination and the doors were opened, all those inside were already dead. Those that had survived the journey were removed from the trains under armed guard from the security service and either marched on foot or taken by transport vehicles to the camps. *(USHMM)*

(**Opposite, below**) Jews assembled for deportation wait on the platform at Kraków railway station for further transport in 1941.

(**Above**) A photograph taken on 13 December 1941 showing a deportation action of Jews from Bielefeld in Germany to Riga in Latvia.

Chapter Three

Destination:
The Reinhard Camps
(1942)

There were three camps built: Belzec, Sobibor and Treblinka. All were constructed with good rail connections. Belzec was located in the south-east of the district of Lublin and situated along the Lublin-Lvov railway line. The death camp had been constructed less than half a mile from the main Belzec railway station. A small railway siding was built to connect the camp to the station. The camp first went into operation on 17 March 1942 with a transport of fifty boxcars containing Jews from Lublin. Regional SS and police leaders coordinated and directed the deportations. The Order Police often rounded up and transported the Jews to the trains, while local auxiliaries or collaborators supported the operation. Those coordinating the transportation were told to lie to the Jews about their intentions by describing their train journey as a 'resettlement in the east'. However, in reality 'resettlement in the east' was a disingenuous term for transportation to the killing centres.

Between March and the end of April, dozens of trains containing thousands of Jews from the Lublin and Lemberg districts were transported to Belzec and those that had survived the journey were murdered.

In March while the first trainloads of Jews were being readied by train for Belzec, another Reinhard death camp was being constructed. It was near the small village of Sobibor in a wooded area on the Chełmno-Włodawa railway line a few miles south of Włodawa. The installation was an enlarged and improved version of Belzec with the same general layout. The camp incorporated a number of pre-war buildings including a forester's lodge, forestry tower, chapel and a Post Office. Railways tracks were built near the former Post Office and the SS adapted the railway line by adding an 800-metre rail spur into the camp itself. This railway line allowed regular transportation of boxcars straight into the camp where the Jews could be quickly unloaded at the railway platform. The victims were told they were in a transit camp and were forced to hand over their valuables. They were then separated by gender at the rail siding and told to undress, whereupon they were then all killed.

Between 16 and 18 May 1942, Sobibor became fully operational and within the first two months some 100,000 people were transported and killed there. Often the camp commandant *SS-Obersturmführer* Franz Stangl appeared at the unloading ramps dressed in his familiar white riding clothes watching as the Ukrainian guards unbolted the boxcar doors and chased the people out of the wagons with their leather whips. Instructions came from a loudspeaker: 'Undress completely, including artificial limbs and spectacles. Give your valuables up at the counter. Tie your shoes together carefully.' Then women and girls were herded into a building to be shorn of their hair, which was then put into potato sacks. The deportees were then moved along a path to their deaths.

While Sobibor and Belzec continued to operate at full capacity, a far bigger installation was being prepared for construction which would be intended to receive all transports from the Warsaw and Białystok ghettos. The site chosen was near the small village of Treblinka in the north-eastern part of the General Government. It was perfectly situated between a number of railway lines in a dense pine forest not far from the village of Małkinia. Planners had purposely selected the area because the woods naturally concealed the camp from both the Małkinia-Kosov road to its north and the Małkinia-Siedlce railway that ran to its west. Just to the south-west a railway line connected Treblinka station with a gravel quarry. The Germans improved the rail connections between these different areas by constructing a rail spur that led from the labour camp to the killing centre which also connected to the Małkinia station.

Initially, when Treblinka began to operate in July 1942, deportations to the death camp came mainly from the ghettos of the Warsaw and Radom districts in the General Government. The first transportations between Warsaw and Treblinka began on 22 July. A message to the camp commandant confirmed that the trains would have sixty closed cars each, and the 'cargo' would be transported deportees from the Warsaw ghetto. The trains would be unloaded and quickly turned around, and then sent back empty for more people.

The clearing of the Warsaw ghetto and organizing the transportation of the Jews to the death camps within Poland was an immense undertaking. The responsibility for the shipments from Warsaw in liaison with the railway authorities of the *Ostbahn* (Eastern Railway) was left in the hands of *SS-Hauptsturmführer* Hermann Höfle. The first transport of Jews from the Warsaw ghetto left Małkinia for Treblinka in the early morning of 23 July. The camp commandant *SS-Obersturmführer* Eberl instructed his SS personnel and Ukrainian guards to prepare for their first arrival. A large notice at the entrance to the camp was also erected. It read as follows:

Attention Warsaw Jews!

- You are now entering a transit camp from which you will be transported to a labour camp.

- To prevent epidemics both clothing and luggage must be handed in for disinfecting.
- Gold, cash, foreign exchange and jewellery are to be given up at the cash desk in return for a receipt. They will be later returned on presentation of the receipt.
- All those arriving must cleanse themselves by taking a bath before continuing their journey.

SS-Unterscharführer Lothar Bölitz and *SS-Unterscharführer* Ernst Gentz were the first SS men to receive the first batch of Warsaw deportees on the platform. They, like everyone else in the camp, had explicit instructions from the commandant that the process from unloading to murder had to be undertaken at high speed if they were to achieve the desired results. Rudolf Emmerich and Willi Klinzmann were in charge of overseeing the shunting of the trains. A Pole, Franciszek Ząbecki who was working at the camp, described the scene:

> Four SS men from the new camp were waiting. They had arrived earlier by car and asked us how far from Treblinka the 'special train with deportees' was. They had already received word of the train's departure from Warsaw … A smaller engine was already at the station, waiting to bring a section of the freight cars into the camp. Everything was planned and prepared in advance.

The first train comprising some sixty closed freight cars crossed the Bug River outside Treblinka during the morning of 23 July. Ukrainian guards that were outside the station announced its approach by firing a volley of rifle shots into the air. The train then came to a halt, and Emmerich and Klinzmann divided the train into three sections and each section was shunted separately into the camp. Franciszek Ząbecki recalled:

> The train was made up of sixty closed cars, crowded with people. These included the young and elderly, men and women, children and babies. The car doors were locked from outside and the air apertures barred with barbed wire. On the car steps on both sides of the car and on the roof, a dozen or so SS soldiers [which would have included Ukrainian guards] stood or lay with machine guns at the ready. It was hot, and most people in the freight cars were in a faint … As the train approached, an evil spirit seemed to take hold of the SS men who were waiting. They drew their pistols, returned them to their holsters, and whipped them out again, as if they wanted to shoot and kill. They came near the freight cars and tried to calm the noise and weeping; then they started yelling and cursing the Jews, all the while calling to the train workers, 'Tempo, fast!' Then they returned to the camp to receive the deportees.

The SS employed terror and speed as a means of ensuring the smooth processing of the Jews through their new murder factory. Another Jewish witness later recalled the scene:

> When the train arrived in Treblinka I can remember seeing great piles of clothing. Now we feared that the rumours really had been true. I remember saying to my wife more or less: this is the end.
>
> We were transported in goods wagons. The goods wagons were very over-crowded. We were able to take something to eat with us but got nothing to drink and that was the worst thing. When the train arrived in Treblinka a considerable number of people had already died of exhaustion. I can no longer remember how many there were. I would like to point out that one of the worst things about the transport was the lack of air. There was only a small window covered with a grill and there were no sanitary facilities. Anybody can imagine what that meant.
>
> I can remember the terrible confusion when the doors were pulled open in Treblinka. The SS and Ukrainians shouted 'Get out, out.' The members of the so-called Red Jewish Kommando also shouted and yelled. Then the people who had arrived began to scream and complain. I remember too that whips were used on us. Then we were told: 'Men to the right, women to the left and get undressed.' My little daughter was with me and then ran to her mother when we were separated. I never saw them again and could not even say good-bye. Then while I was undressing I was selected by a German to be a so-called work-Jew.

As the deportees were unloaded off the freight cars Ukrainian guards took up their positions around the reception area and on the surrounding roofs, while another group of well-armed Ukrainians and the SS took up position on the platform. At the unloading ramp there was a group of prisoners nicknamed 'Blue Kommandos'. They were given the task of carrying all clothes to the square adjacent to the ramp and clearing the wagons of the deportees including those that had died en route. Once everyone was removed from the cars they were hastily hosed down with water. After they had been cleaned the switching engine driver coupled the cars and shunted the empty carriages out of the camp in order to make room for the next delivery of cars.

On the ramp there was a hive of activity as the newcomers were crammed together. Most of them did not suspect anything. Nothing seemed to indicate the horror that was in store for them. Many believed that they had simply arrived at a quiet provincial railway station. As they stood assembled awaiting instructions, Eberl came through the gate flanked by his deputy *SS-Rottenführer* Max Biala and spoke to them. He told them calmly that they would soon be sent on their way further east, but had stopped at Treblinka because of their appalling hygienic conditions. They first were required to be disinfected, but prior to this were asked kindly to leave their luggage on the ramp and hand in all their money and other valuables. Everybody, he said, was to get a towel and soap, and he reminded them not to forget a deposit receipt. The speech was welcomed by many of the Jews for they were exhausted, hungry and very thirsty after spending hours crammed inside the freight cars.

For Eberl and his subordinates, this was the easiest and most practical means of duping the Jews, but the Jews' plight did not begin at Treblinka; it first began when they boarded the train bound for the camp. However, because the gas chambers were inadequate to deal with the numbers of people scheduled to be killed, there was a bottleneck of trains waiting to go through and as a result some trains were queuing around 7 miles away.

Debarkation at Treblinka was chaotic and disorganized to the point where Eberl could no longer cope with the number of arrivals. In the chaos that ensued over the next weeks very few men were selected from the transports, and the majority were simply unloaded from the dirty and cramped boxcars and sent straight to be killed.

Between October and the end of December 1942, Treblinka reached its peak. On occasions there were as many as six trainloads – 20,000 people – arriving daily. Initially these comprised mostly Jews from Warsaw, and then many started to arrive from Germany and other parts of Western Europe. They brought with them enormous quantities of food, money and jewels, plus there was a huge array of liquor taken from the new arrivals.

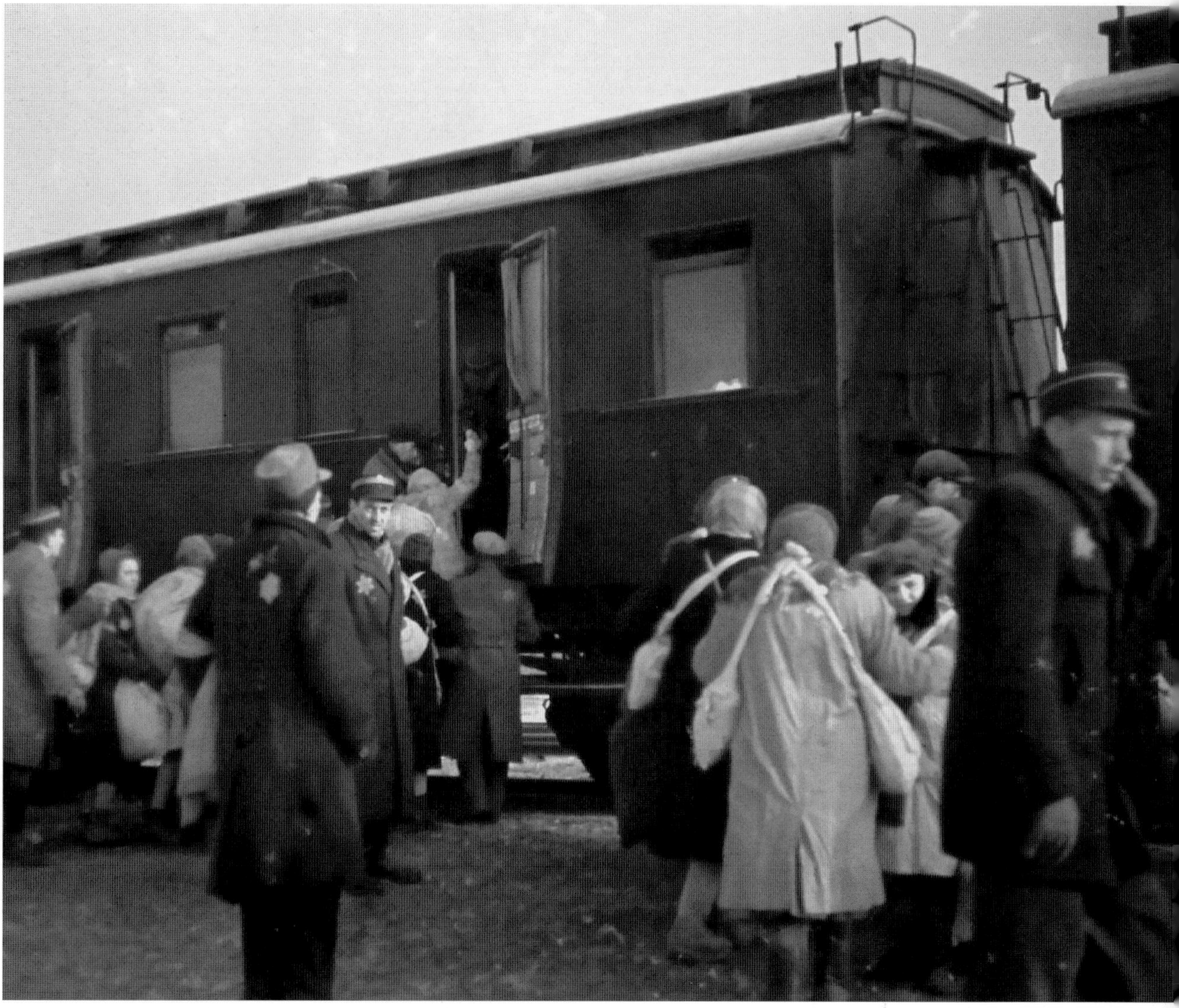

Five photographs showing Jews boarding a passenger train during a deportation action in the Lodz Ghetto. The photographs were taken at a railway siding in the Lodz Ghetto where Jews were preparing to board a passenger train during a deportation action from the ghetto. The majority of Jews that were transported like this in third-class passenger trains were actually forced to pay for their own deportation. This payment came in the form of direct money deposit to the SS and was known as a fare payment for 'resettlement to work in the east'. Adult Jews were often charged a full-price one-way ticket, while children under 10 to 12 years of age paid half-price. Children under the age of 4 travelled free of charge. Jews that had no money or had their finances confiscated for whatever reason were the first to board the trains. The original German caption of this set of photographs reads *Judenaussiedlung* ('Jewish Resettlement'), April 1942. By 2 April 1942, some 34,000 Jews had been deported by rail like this and sent directly to the Chełmno death camp. Although the German authorities had told the Jews that they would be resettled further east, there was already common knowledge of the mass executions and the deportation to labour or death camps. In fact, some parents fearing the inevitable committed collective suicide to avoid their children suffering at the hands of the Nazis. *(USHMM, courtesy of Robert Abrams)*

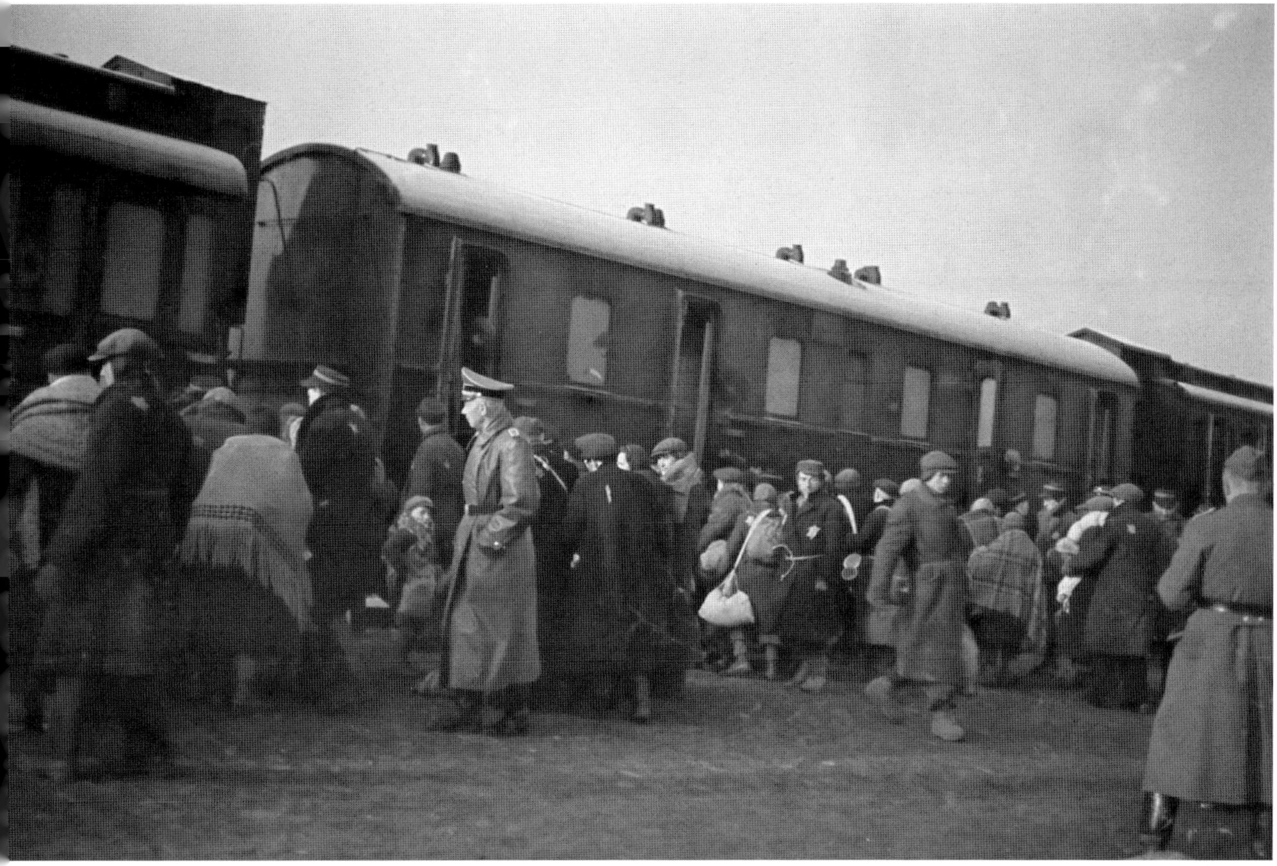

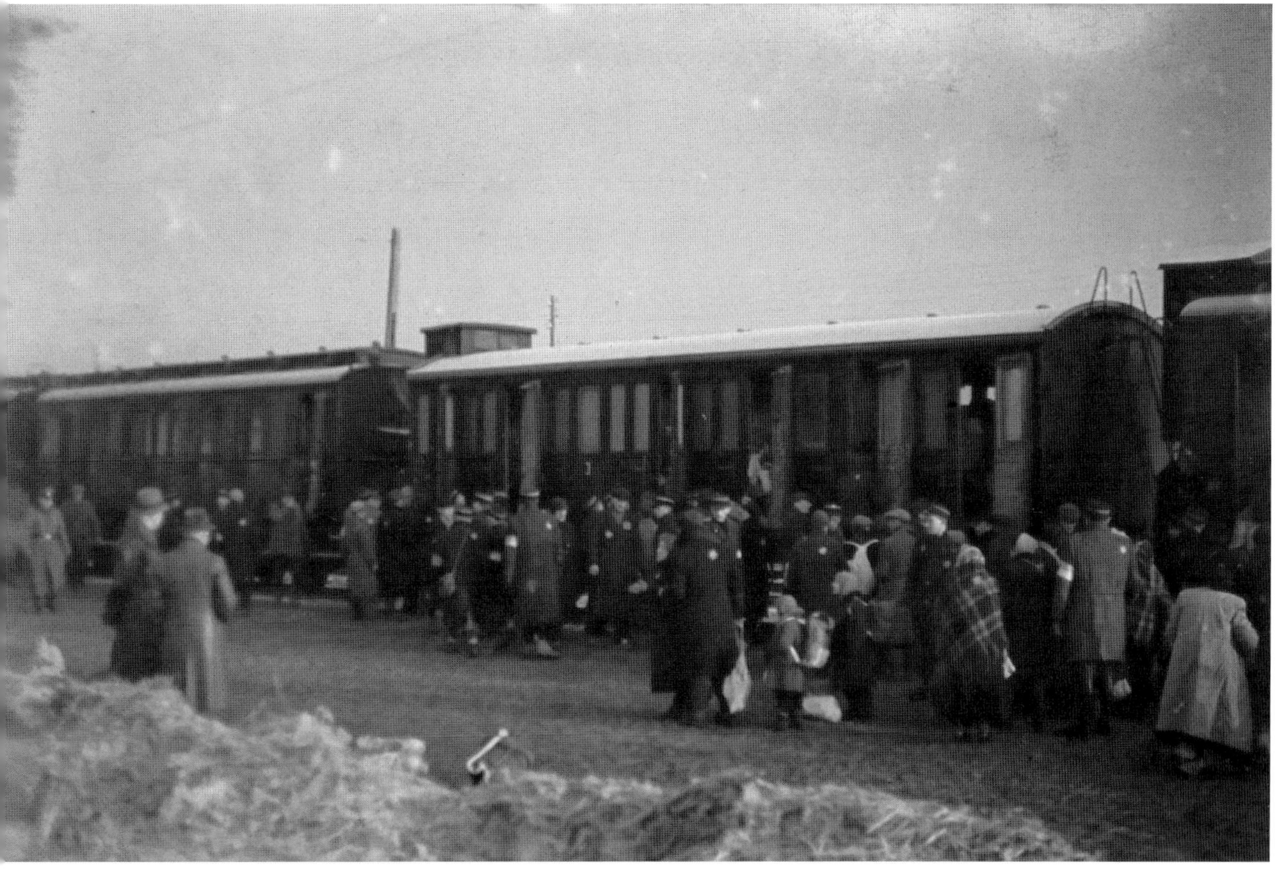

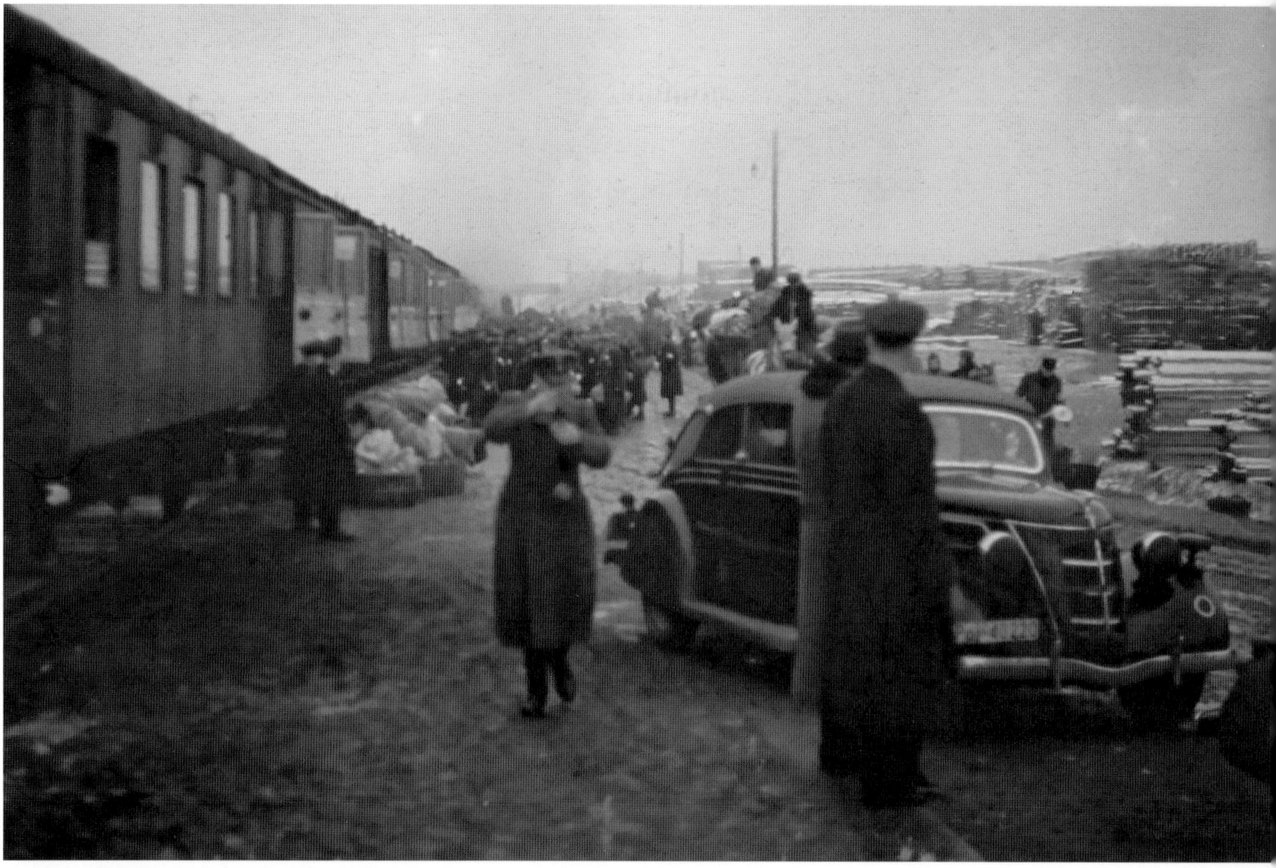

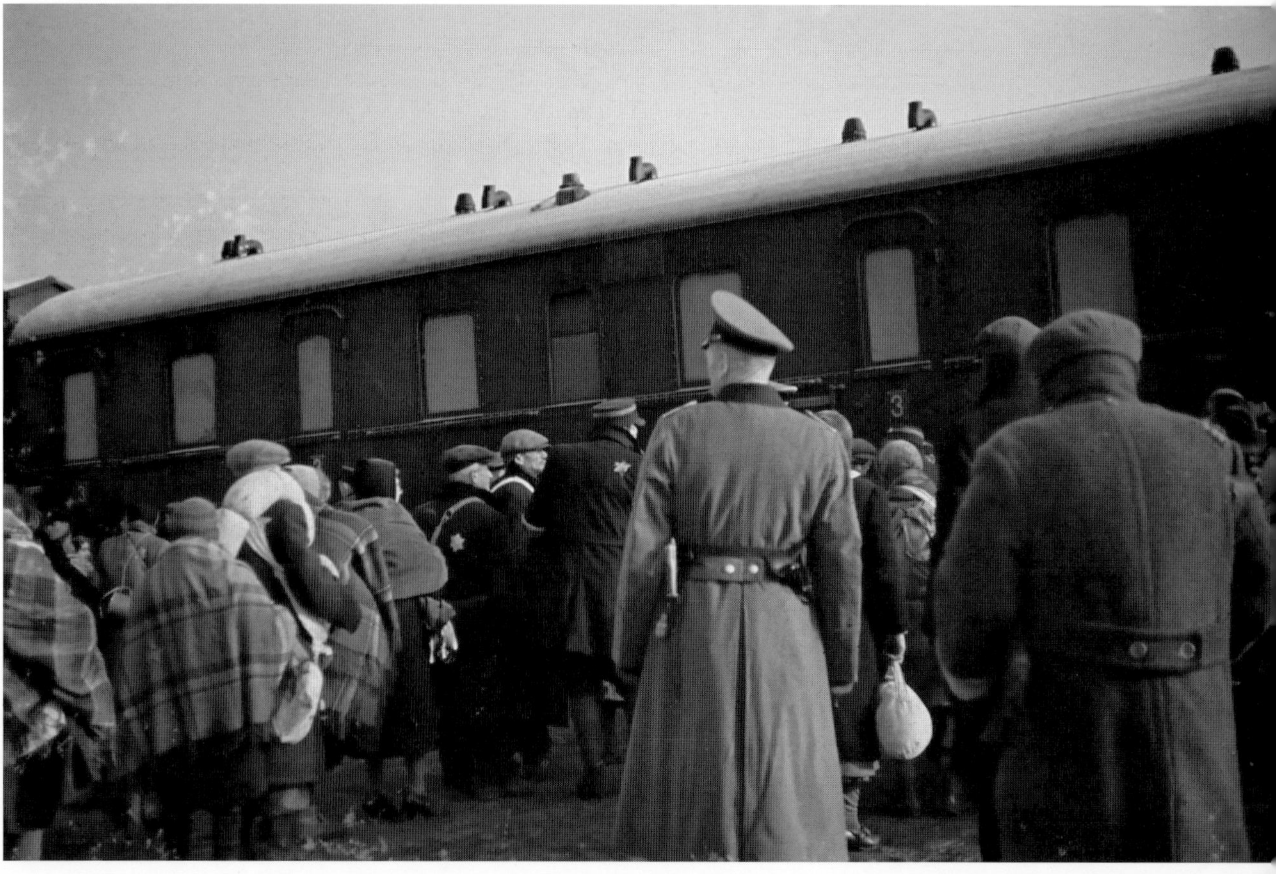
3

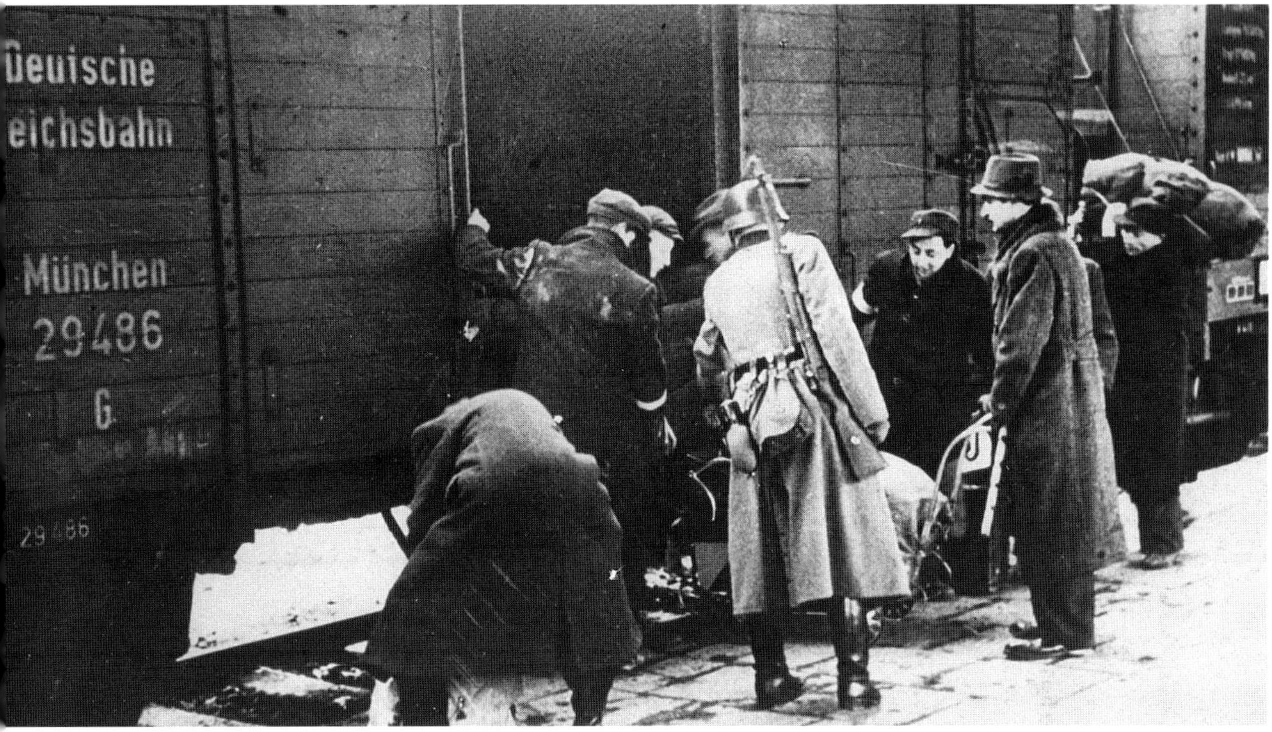
eichsbahn
München
29486
G

An SS guard supervises the boarding of Jews onto trains during a deportation action in the Kraków Ghetto. In the ghetto, due to its size, the liquidation was done in phases. The first transport consisted of 7,000 and the second 4,000 Jews, all of which were deported to the Belzec death camp in the summer of 1942. It was not until March 1943 that the final liquidation of the ghetto was carried out. Those deemed unfit for labour, numbering around 2,000, were rounded up and either murdered in the streets of the ghetto or transported to Auschwitz. The 8,000 Jews that were left were transported and forced to work in the Plaszów labour camp. *(USHMM)*

Jewish deportees from the Lodz Ghetto who were being taken to the Chełmno death camp were transferred from a closed passenger train to one of open cars at the Koło railway station. *(USHMM)*

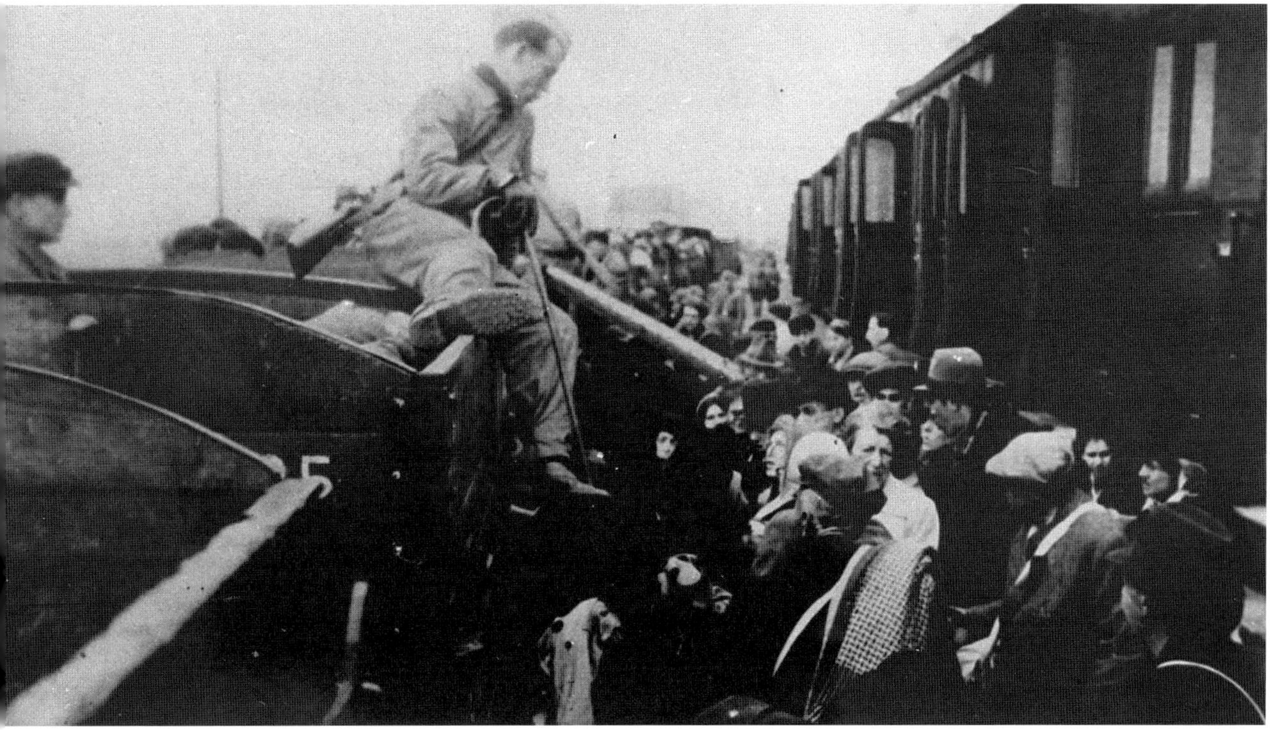

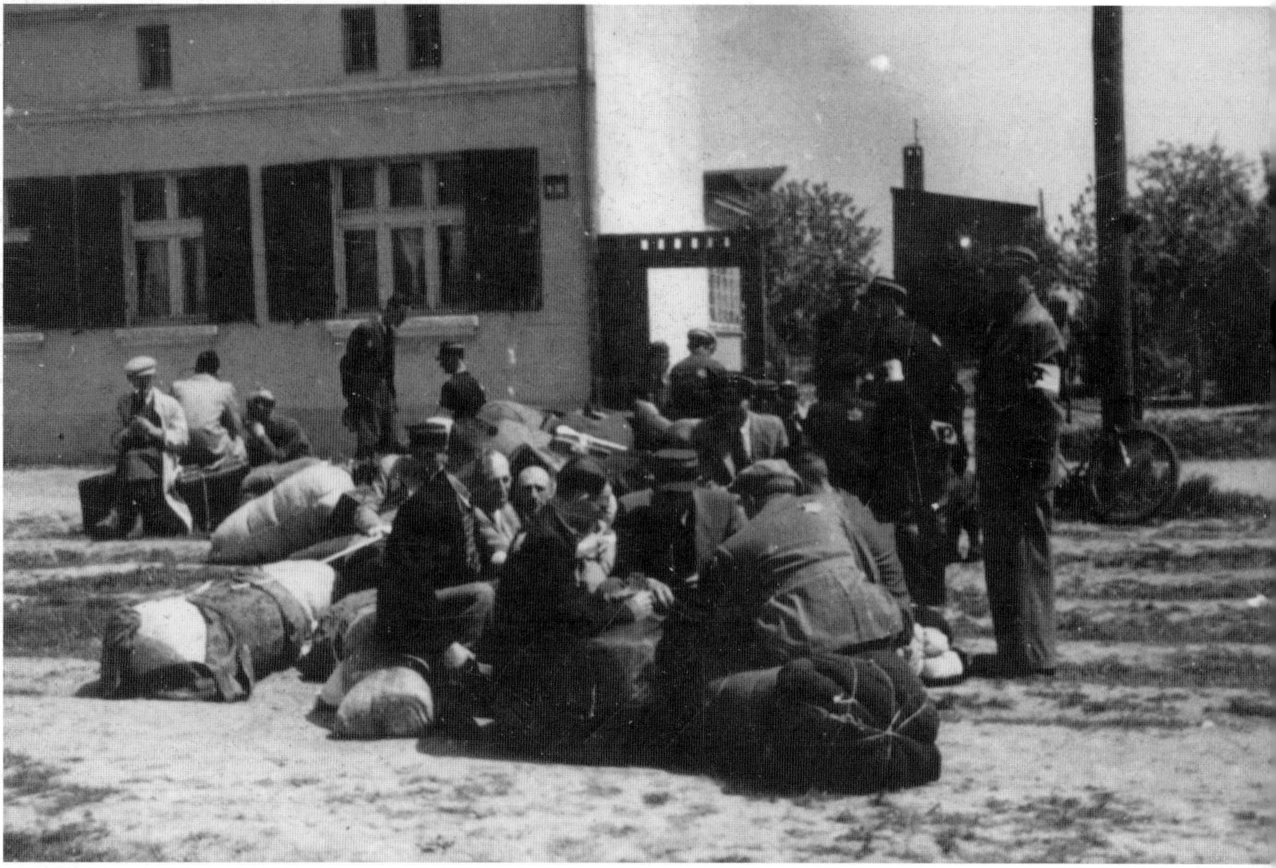

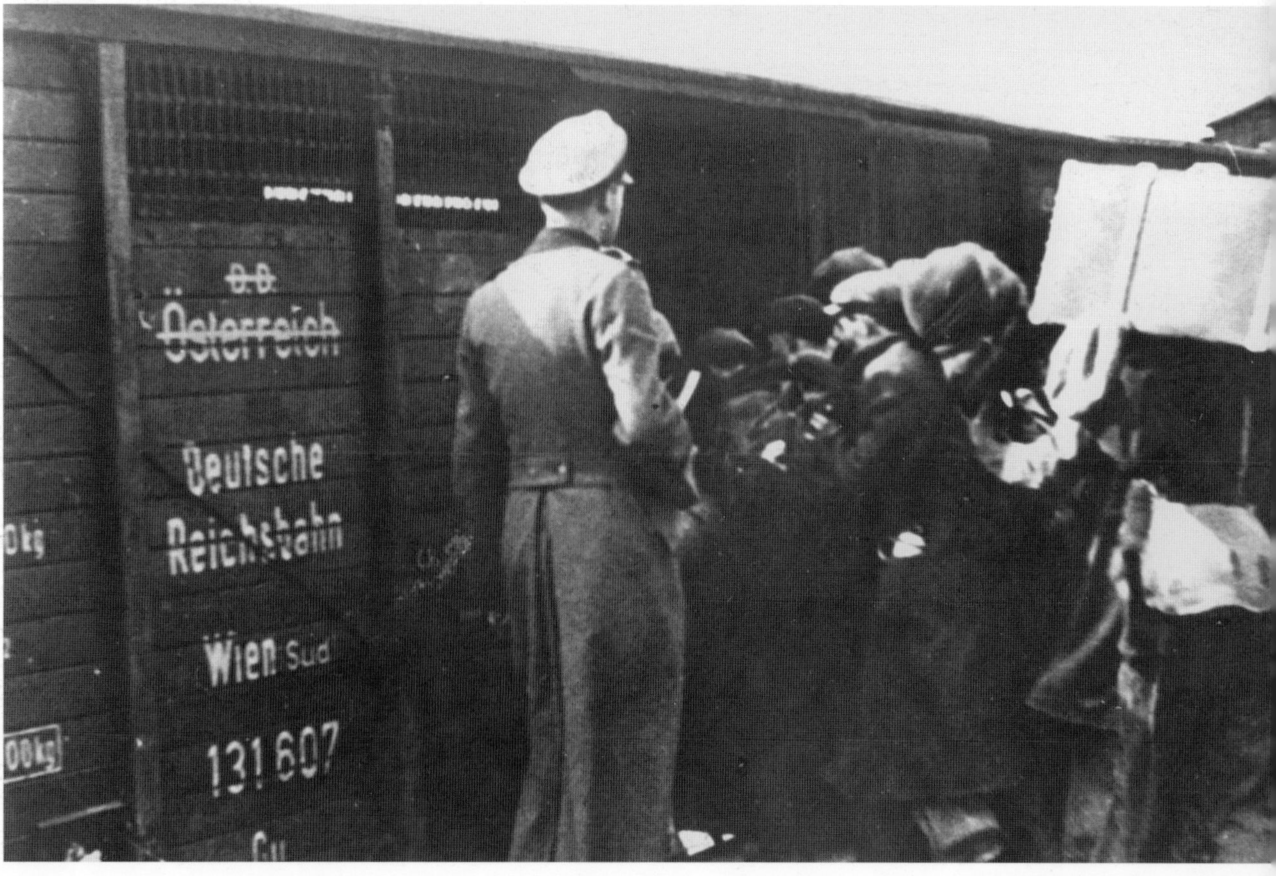
Österreich
Deutsche
Reichsbahn
Wien Süd
131 607

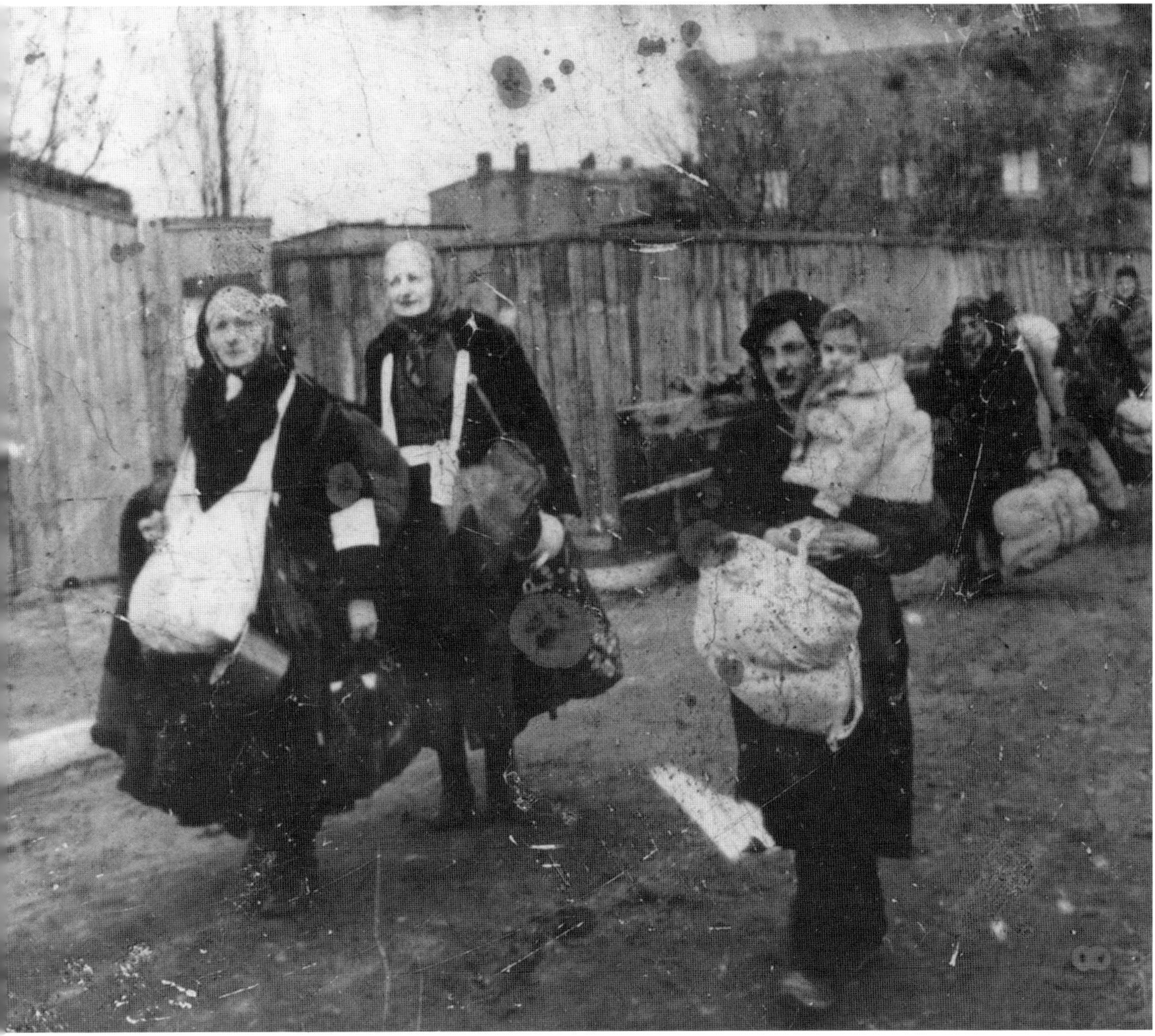

(**Opposite, above**) Jewish police guard a group of central European Jews who have been assembled for deportation in the central prison of the Lodz Ghetto.

(**Opposite, below**) Jews in Lublin being forced onto a deportation train to Belzec. Between mid-March and mid-April 1942, during the Lublin Ghetto's liquidation more than 30,000 Jews were sent to Belzec and an additional 4,000 to Majdanek by train where they were subsequently murdered. *(Yad Vashem)*

(**Above**) Elderly women carrying young children and bundles of personal belongings trudge along a street in the Lodz Ghetto towards the assembly point for deportation to Chełmno. The first liquidation actions of the Lodz Ghetto began in early 1942, transporting Lodz residents by rail to their death at the Auschwitz and Chełmno extermination camps. It was the last ghetto in occupied Poland to be liquidated, and during its establishment some 210,000 Jews had been forced to live or die there. When the Russians arrived in the ghetto in August 1944, only 877 Jews were found alive hiding in buildings and cellars. *(USHMM)*

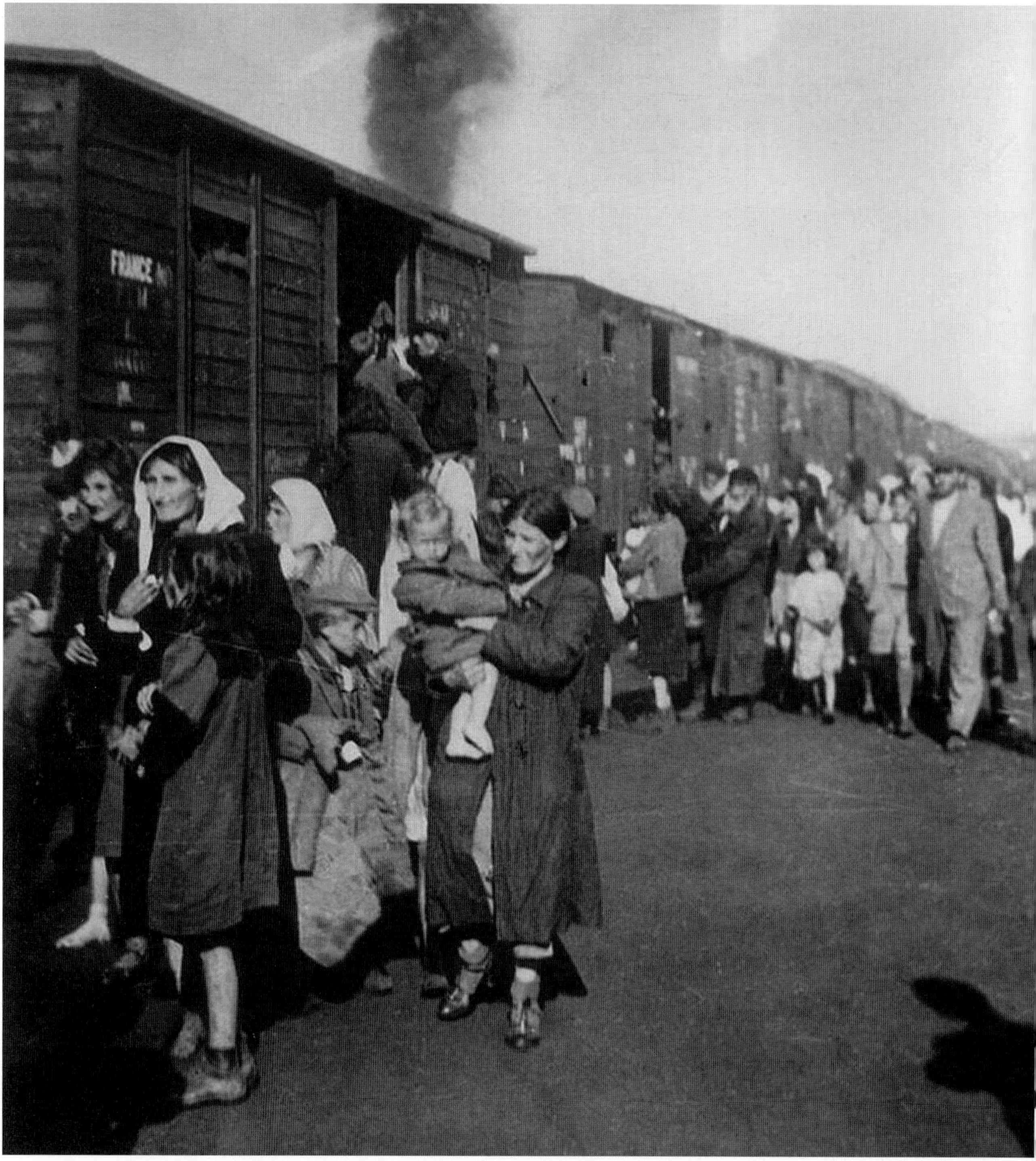

A deportation action to Treblinka from the Siedlce Ghetto in 1942. These Jews were being led through the streets of the town on their way to the railway station. On 22 August 1942, orders were given for the ghetto to be liquidated and some 10,000 Jews were forced into the square on 22 August. Of these people, 500 were selected for work detail, while the remainder were either murdered in pits outside the city or deported to Treblinka by rail cars. By late November the remaining workers were shot. *(USHMM)*

A posed photograph of Rudolf Gockel, Belzec camp station master, standing in front of the locomotive shed. Belzec was built purely for logistical reasons. The Belzec railway station, for instance, was connected to the railway line centre in Rawa Ruska, some 10 miles from Belzec. The main railway lines from Lvov, Stanisławów in the east and from Rzeszów, Przemyśl, Tarnów and Kraków in the south-west all passed through Rawa Ruska. The Belzec death camp was built on a railway siding in close proximity to the Belzec village railway station and only 50 metres east of the main Lublin-Lvov railway line. (*Tregenza Photo Collection, ARC*)

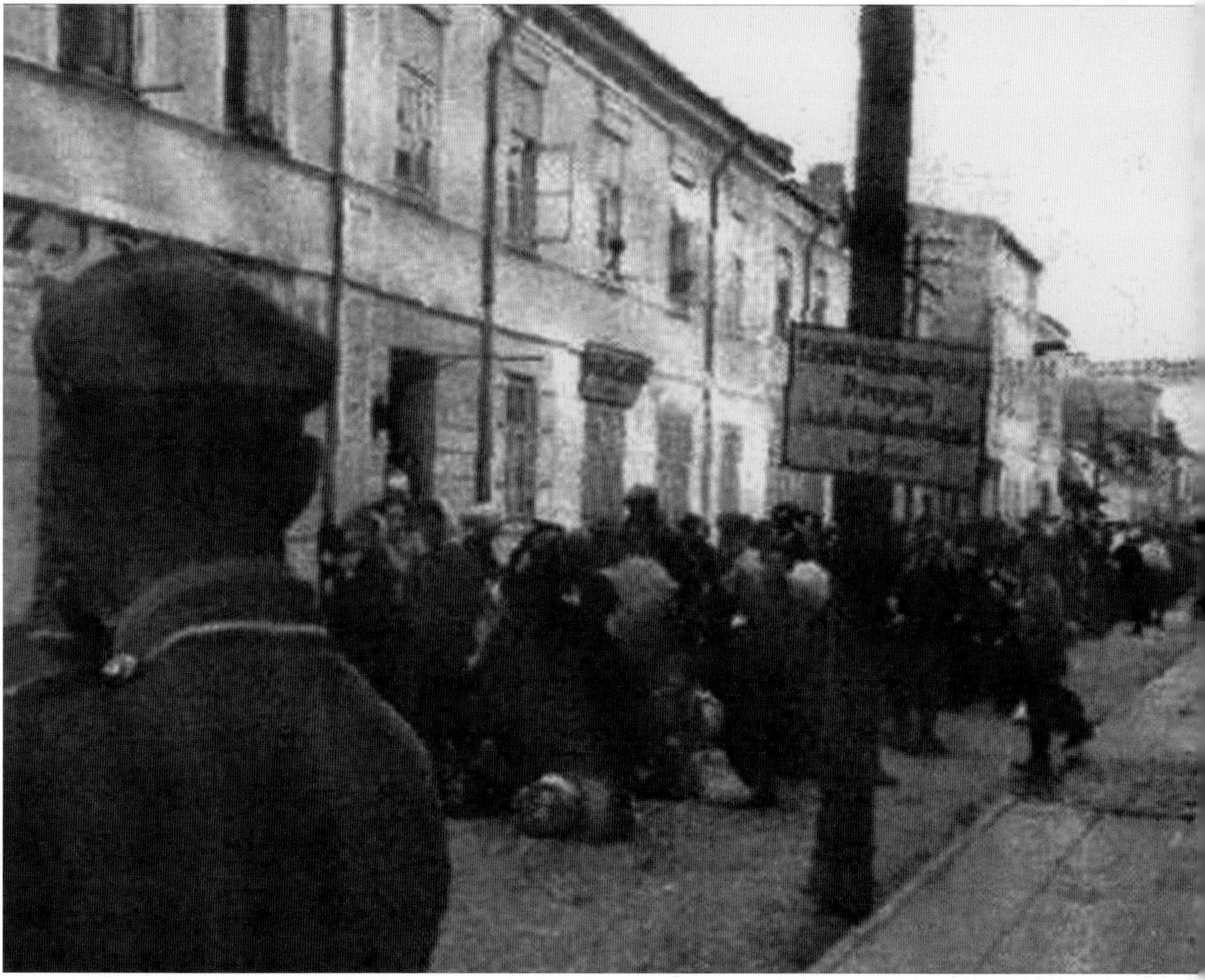

(**Above**) Jews from the Biała Podlaska Ghetto being escorted on foot to board trains. On 10 June 1942, some 700 Jews guarded by Jewish police and members of the *Sonderdienst* were escorted to the railway station. The next day they were loaded into boxcars and transported to the Sobibor death camp. In total 3,000 Jews from Biała Podlaska were deported to their deaths in Sobibor on that day.

(**Opposite, above**) *SS-Oberstgruppenführer* Odilo Globocnik observing the railway siding, probably in 1942. Note the boxcars behind the SS officers. Globocnik was appointed the commander of the Reinhard operation. He was a ruthless and fanatical SS officer who believed wholeheartedly in the Nazi vision. From his office he planned and gossiped with his associates about the future SS colonization of the East and the task of preparing for the extermination of the Jews in the General Government. *(ARC / BA)*

(**Opposite, below**) Three German railway personnel pose for the camera in front of Sobibor station. The Sobibor death camp was constructed near the small village of Sobibor in a wooded area on the Chełmno-Włodawa railway line a few miles south of Włodawa. The installation was an enlarged and improved version of Belzec with the same general layout. Again, the railway line was vital to the success of the operation and the station was used to deceive the incoming deportees. *(ARC)*

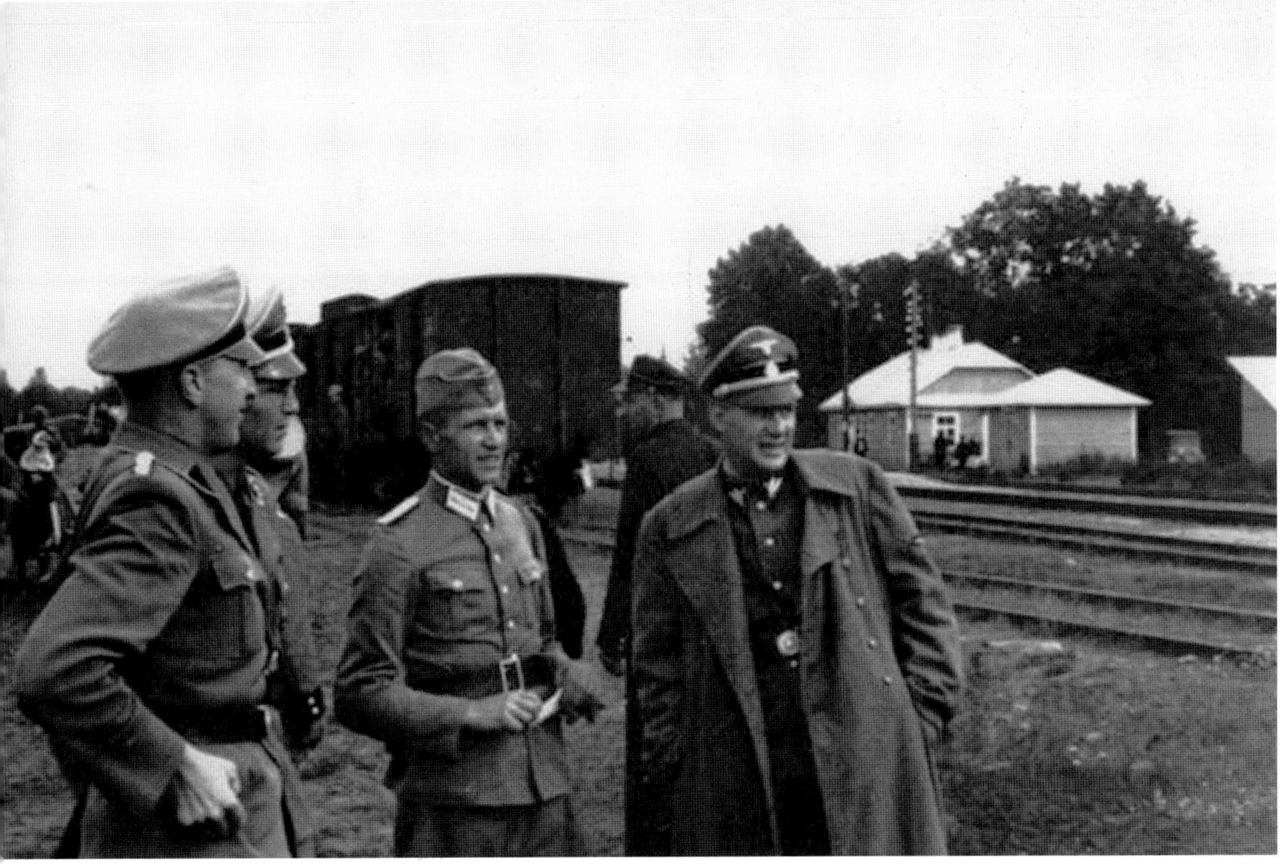

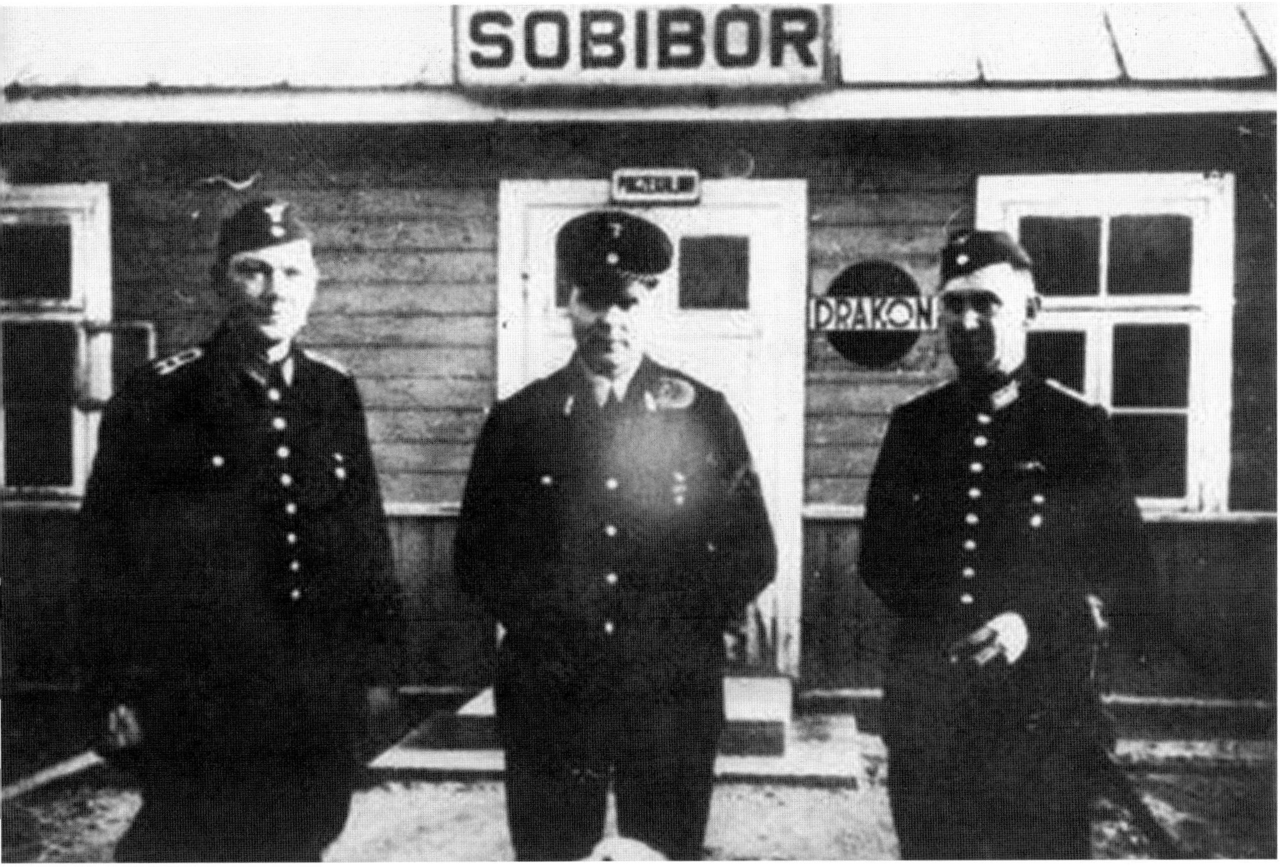
SOBIBOR
DRAKON

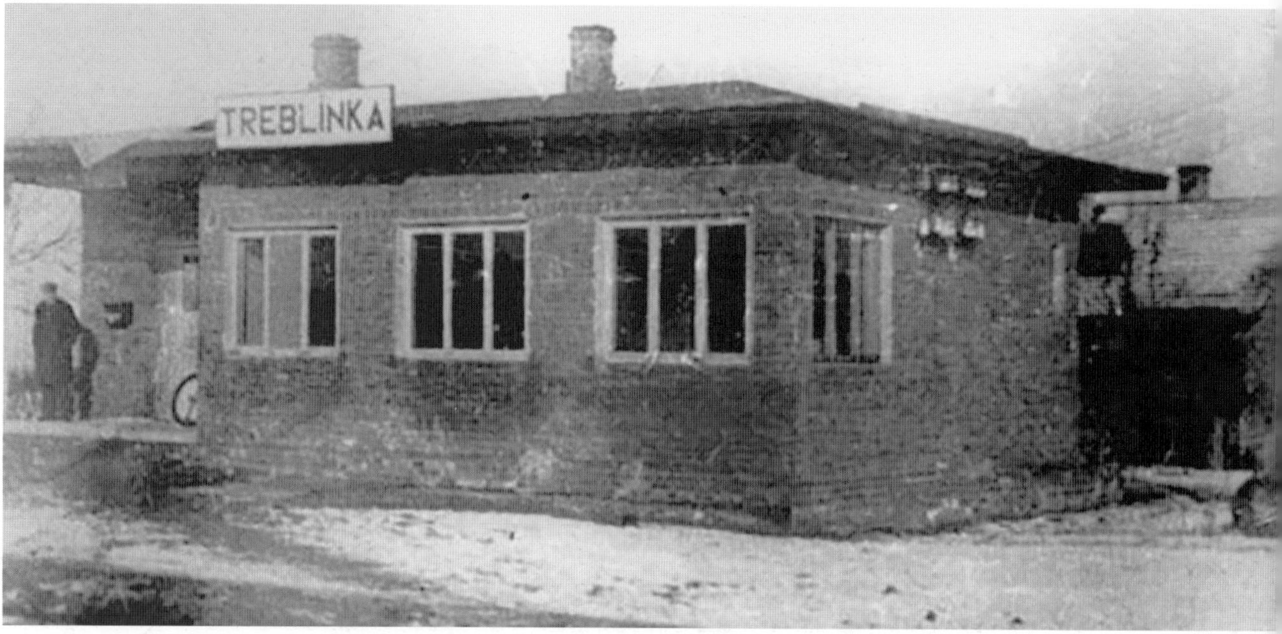
TREBLINKA

Two photographs showing Treblinka station. The second image shows SS and Ukrainian guards posing for the camera outside the fake Treblinka station in the early spring of 1943. At Christmas Commandant Stangl had ordered the construction of a fake railway station. Stangl wanted to enhance the illusion and deception in order to fool the new arrivals into believing they had arrived at a genuine station to a transit camp. There was a clock painted with numerals and hands that never moved, a ticket-window was constructed and various timetables and arrows indicating train connections to Warsaw, Wolwonoce and Białystok were plastered on the walls of the sorting barracks. There were fake doors and windows installed, a waiting room, information telegraph office, a station manager and rest rooms, and there were also many trees and flowerbeds. The station was well-connected with a railway line. While constructing the site, planners had purposely selected the area because the woods naturally concealed the camp from both the Małkinia-Kosov road to its north and the Małkinia-Siedlce railway that ran to its west. Just to the south-west the main railway line connected Treblinka station with a gravel quarry. Later, outside the camp, another railway line was built from Siedlce to Małkinia. At the station a double-track railway line was laid and another bridge across the Bug River was constructed. For weeks gangs of labourers worked every day inside the camp and along the railway lines leading to the Treblinka station. The SS were aware that in order for the camp to function it depended on new transports, and new line was one way of ensuring that the camp remained in operation. *(ARC)*

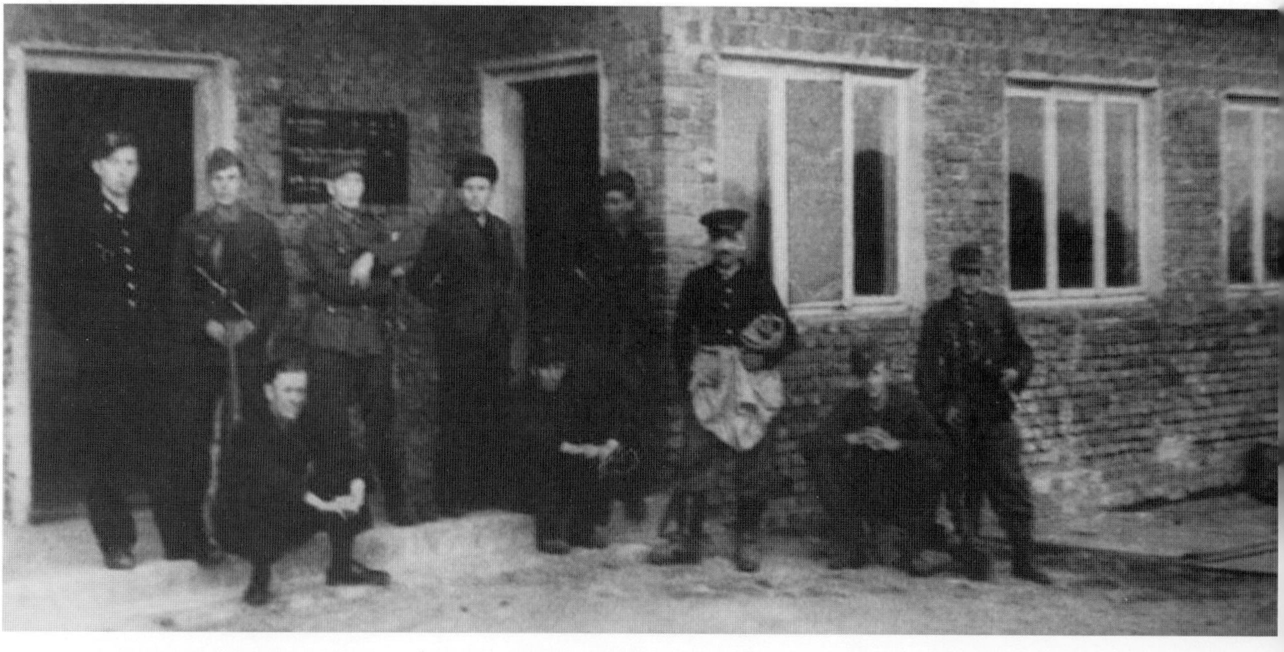

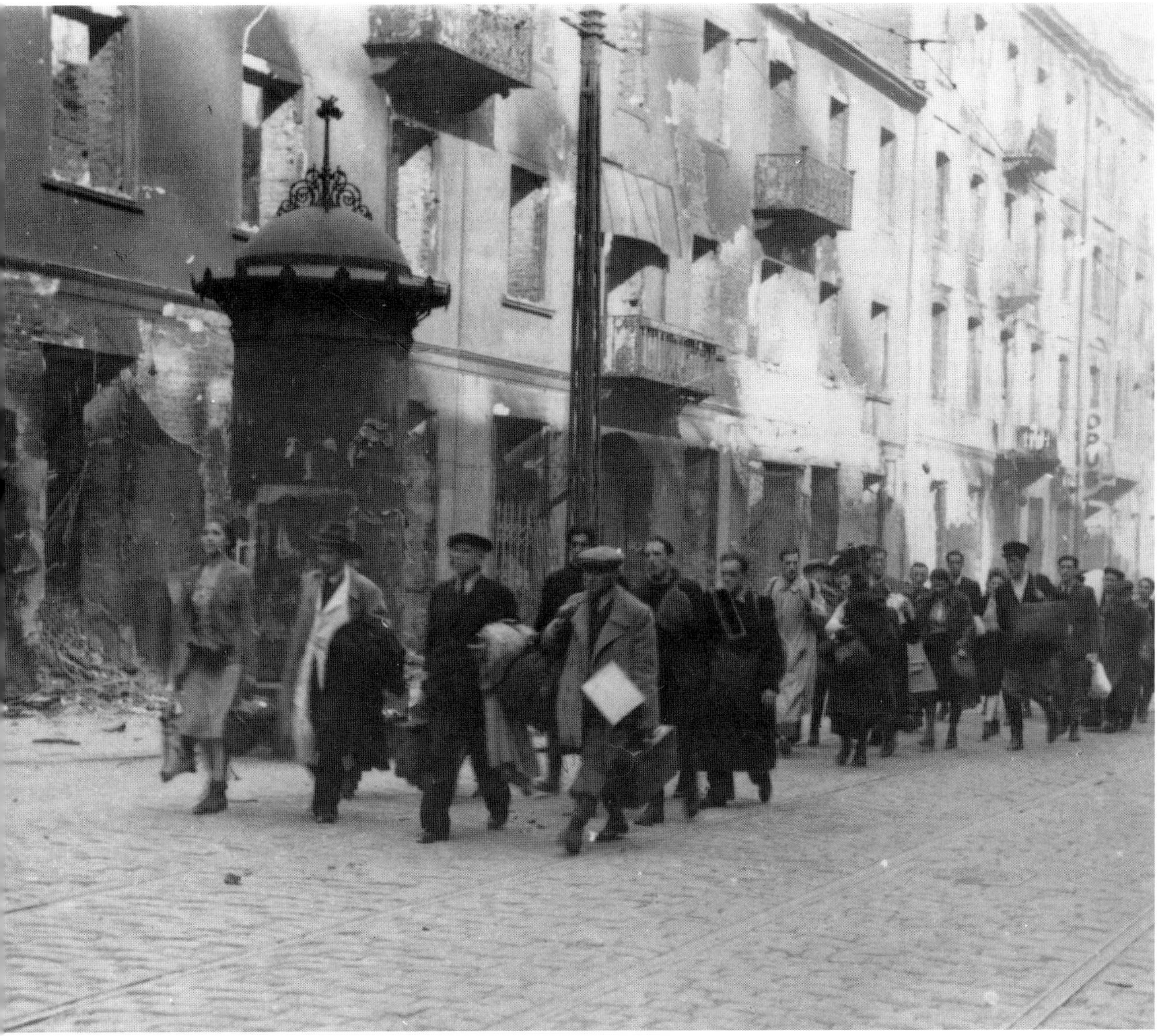

The first of two photographs showing Jews being escorted along a decimated street in Warsaw following the end of the Warsaw Uprising in May 1943. The cause of the uprising was the liquidation of the Warsaw Ghetto which was a massive deportation action comprising some 265,000 ghetto residents being sent to the newly-opened Treblinka extermination camp with some 20,000 being sent to labour camps. This process took some eight to twelve weeks to achieve, and it soon became apparent to the Jews left inside the ghetto that these deportations were to death camps. What followed was a ghetto uprising in April 1943 during which approximately 13,000 Jews were killed. Of the remaining 50,000 residents, most were captured, rounded up and marched out of the smouldering ruins of the ghetto destined for the Treblinka death camp. When the first trainload arrived at Treblinka from Warsaw, the SS personnel noticed that the boxcars were in a terrible condition. According to one of the soldiers accompanying the train to the death camp, some prisoners inside the car, fearing what would happen to them, frantically attempted to escape by pulling apart the wooden flooring and other internal fixings. It seemed that, even after capture and during their transportation to their final destination, some of the Jews were still determined to try to evade being sent to their deaths. *(USHMM/NARA)*

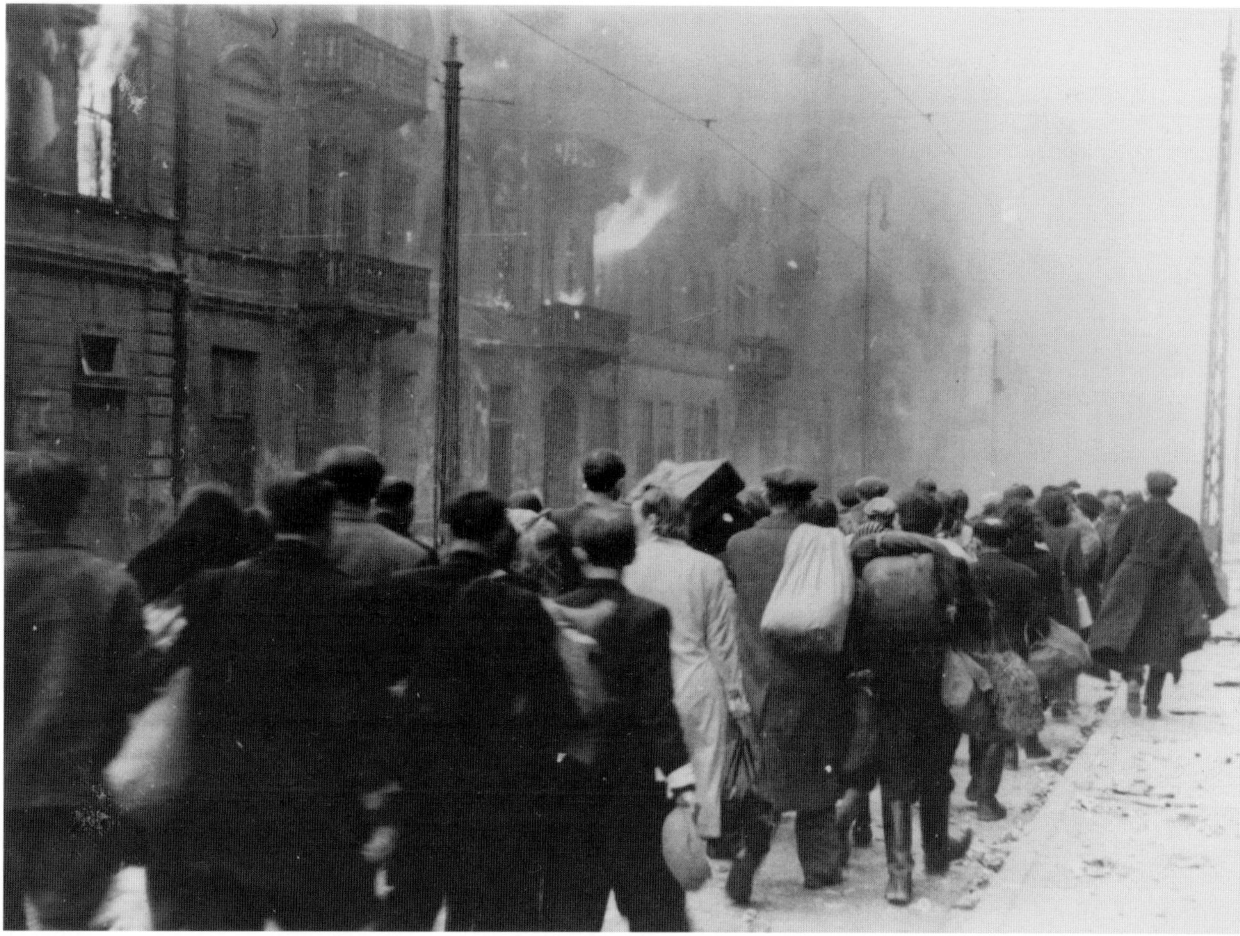

A photograph showing the outcome of an air-raid on Belzec station on 5 July 1944, in which a Russian plane hit an ammunition train in the station. *(ARC, Tomaszów Lubelski Regional Museum)*

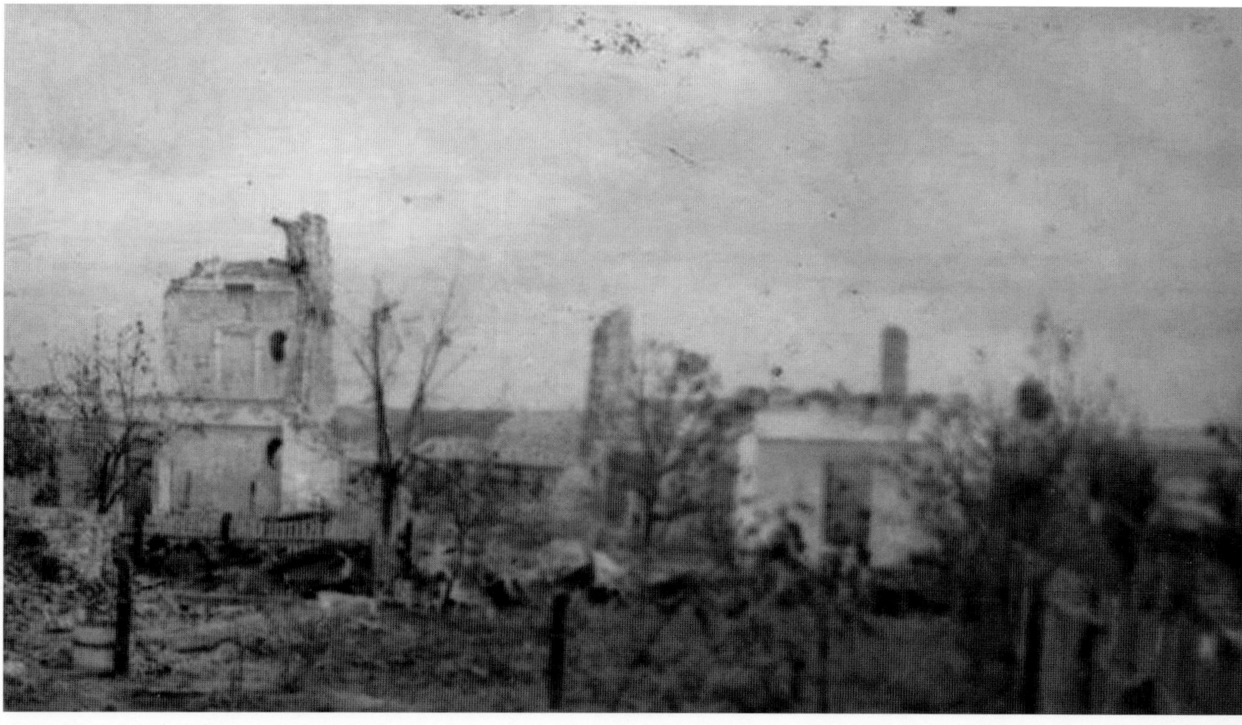

Chapter Four

Transports across Europe

Apart from the Reinhard camps, there were other main killing centres built such as Chełmno, Majdanek and Auschwitz. The Chełmno camp was specifically intended for no other purpose than mass murder and operated from 8 December 1941 to 11 April 1943. The first shipments of people transported to the camp were the Jewish and Romani populations of Koło, Dąbie, Sompolno, Kłodawa, Babiak, Izbica Kujawska, Buhaj, Nowiny Brdowskie and Kowale Pańskie. The victims were transported from all over the region to Koło by rail with the last stop in Powiercie. From the railway siding they were then moved in overcrowded trucks to the camp. They were often forced to leave all their belongings at the siding.

In January 1942 some 10,000 Jews were rounded up from the Lodz ghetto and transported from the Radegast train station to Koło railway station, which was about 6 miles north-west of Chełmno. Under the strict supervision of SS and police personnel the victims were transferred from both freight and passenger trains to a narrow-gauge railway line that took them to the Powiercie station near the camp. Throughout 1942 rail transports continued their journey to Chełmno. The shipments varied between victims from Bohemia-Moravia and Luxembourg, including 5,000 Roma gypsies from Austria.

All across Poland trains were now transporting deportees directly to the concentration camps. However, there were numerous camps that did not have railway platforms. Often those that arrived had to walk miles to their destination. Majdanek camp, for instance, had no platform so trains arrived at the main railway station or the Flugplatz labour camp in Wronska Street. From there, the deportees were forced on foot into the camp.

As these killing facilities continued to receive large numbers of Jews by railway, there was one camp in Poland that would 'outshine' any other site in terms of its murder rate: Auschwitz. The camp had initially condemned just the sick and disabled, but huge plans were put together, producing a factory-like killing installation that was capable of removing anyone deemed a threat to the Reich or unfit for slave labour.

In November 1942 the Auschwitz camp commandant Rudolf Höss was called to Eichmann's office in Berlin. Here in the Reich capital he chaired a meeting with Eichmann, his deputy, various leaders from Belgium, Holland, France, Slovakia and

Hungary including *SS-Hauptsturmführer* Theodor Dannecker, Alois Brunner, Franz Novak, *SS-Sturmbannführer* Hermann Krumey, Hans Günther, his brother Rolf Günther and Rudolf Jaenisch. The meeting was convened purely to discuss the various difficulties of transportation of the Jews, the numbers of them that had already been delivered into the camps and how many could still be expected. The seizure and deportation of thousands of Jews to the concentration camps had not been an easy task. There had been problems with railway lines and railcars moving across Europe to the east and the killing process was still being refined. The SS men that gathered around the table all collectively discussed the best ways to overcome the logistical problems and spoke at length about the much-expanded programme of genocide. Those fit for labour were still to be profitably used, but many Jews would continue to be deported by rail to the extermination camps and killed immediately. The unexpected military setbacks on the Eastern Front had presented a number of difficult circumstances for the rolling stock, but Eichmann told his audience that the war would not influence the successful outcome of the 'Final Solution'. At Auschwitz the transports would arrive on a large scale. Initially, prisoners arrived by rail at a siding at the nearby Auschwitz station where they were force-marched to the main camp.

By the summer of 1940 an unloading ramp was constructed adjacent to the camp. Later transports of Poles also arrived here and from 1942 trainloads of Jews began arriving. It was also at this ramp, during the years 1941 and 1942 before the building of the Buna sub-camp, that the prisoners were used to construct the Buna-Werke, which was the I.G. Farbenindustrie plant. It was here that they boarded trains that transported them to construction sites and disembarked on their return to the camp. Another unloading ramp was built in 1942, known as the *Alte Judenrampe*. It was constructed at the Auschwitz freight station, between the Auschwitz main camp and the newly-constructed Birkenau camp. It would be here between 1942 and 1944 that the majority of deportees arrived by train. A third ramp was also planned inside Birkenau. Drawings were submitted outlining that a spur off one of the main lines should run directly through the main gate and run the full length where the newly-built gas chambers and Crematoria II and III were under construction. However, due to typical German bureaucracy and numerous other logistical and official problems, it was not completed until May 1944.

All three ramps also served as embarkation areas for prisoners transferred from Auschwitz to the various sub-camps and other concentration camps in the area. Throughout 1942, the *Deutsche Reichsbahn* was in full operation across the railway network, planning, scheduling, transporting and perfecting its part in the Holocaust. Speed in what the SS termed 'processing' was of great importance, and for this reason constructing railway lines directly to the camps was considered favourable. Numerous camps and sub-camps had lines built. Places like Dachau had their own sidetrack that led from Dachau railway station to the camp. The SS sometimes transported prisoners to the site in boxcars. The newly-arrived prisoners passed through the western entrance of the camp and on to the barracks area where the deportees could be quickly dealt with.

The drastic requirement for slave labour also ensured that an intricate system of railway lines was either built or existing lines operated on. One old concentration camp known as Mauthausen was extensively operated by the *Deutsche Reichsbahn* for the transportation of a slave labour force. In 1941 alone some 18,000 new transportees arrived at Mauthausen, including the camp's first group of Jews, who came in May from the Netherlands. Other new arrivals included many new Spanish and Czech political prisoners, and more than 4,000 Russian prisoners of war.

In 1942, more trains began operating from the Netherlands, Russia, Czechoslovakia and Yugoslavia. Later shipments were made from France, Belgium, Greece and Luxembourg. In 1943 there were some 21,000 people transported to Mauthausen alone arriving from all over Europe with only a few that were Jews. In fact, Belgium became the first country in Western Europe to deport immigrating Jews. The Mechelen transit camp served as a holding-point to gather Belgian Jews and Romani before they were transported to concentration and extermination camps in Eastern Europe. It was run by the Belgian National Railway, and Eichmann saw this rail system in Northern Europe as pivotal to the success of his transport operation. The main destination for the Belgian Jews was Auschwitz. However, smaller numbers of trains transported Jews to Buchenwald and Ravensbrück concentration camps, as well as the Vittel internment camp in France.

In France the French national SNCF railway company operated by the Vichy Government also played a prominent part in the 'Final Solution'. Some 76,000 Jews were deported and sent to various concentration and extermination camps.

The Netherlands was yet another country that saw thousands of Jews being transported by rail to Westerbork transit camp from the Amsterdam ghetto. The transports were operated by the state-owned *Nederlandse Spoorwegen* or NS (Dutch Railways). The NS was forced by the Germans to construct a railway network to the Westerbork transit camp. Some 100,000 Jews died. Between July 1942 and 1944 every Tuesday a transport of boxcars was assembled and operated from Westerbork destined for the Auschwitz-Birkenau, Sobibor, Bergen-Belsen or Theresienstadt camps. Only 5,200 survived, mainly those from the Theresienstadt camp.

In occupied Norway it was not until 1942 that the SS with the support of the Norwegian police began transporting its Jews from Oslo. The small Jewish community of 770 Norwegian Jews were put on a ship and taken to Hamburg. From there, a train deported them directly to Auschwitz-Birkenau.

Italy was another country that would eventually see its Jewish community rounded up and sent mainly to Auschwitz-Birkenau via rail routes through Austria and Switzerland.

Greece was also forced to send 45,000–50,000 Salonika Jews crammed in eighty boxcars on the long rail journey to Auschwitz-Birkenau between March and August 1943.

In Bohemia and Moravia the newly-established *Böhmisch-Mährische Bahn* (BMB) sent trainloads of Jews from the Theresienstadt Ghetto mainly to Auschwitz-Birkenau.

The Bulgarian government also assisted in transporting some of their Jewish community, predominantly by passenger trains to Treblinka. These shipments began on 22 February 1943 and over a four-day period some twenty overcrowded transports took the deportees to their deaths. Conditions were so bad in the boxcars that each transport had to stop and undertake a daily body dump of Jews that had died during the previous twenty-four hours.

Shipments like this were not uncommon. The Romanian railway, which was heavily involved in transporting Romani people to concentration camps in Bessarabia, Bukovina and Transnistria, transported their Jews in appalling conditions. Jews were forcibly loaded onto the boxcars with planks hammered in place over the windows and they travelled for a number of days without food or water. The majority of the deportees died en route.

In late 1941 the Slovak government also began shipping its Jewish community of 89,000 Jews. In fact, the Slovak People's Party paid 500 Reichsmarks per Jew on the understanding that the deportees would never return to Slovakia.

Between early 1942 and mid-1943 hundreds of thousands of Jews were being transported from all over Europe to either work or be murdered in the camps. The *Deutsche Reichsbahn* remained crucial to the operation and was paid to transport Jews and other victims on the rail networks of occupied territories and Germany's allies. Although the logistics and operations varied from country to country, they all had one sole purpose: to victimize these hapless people and send them to their deaths.

(**Opposite**) The first of six photographs taken in sequence showing prisoners from the Buchenwald concentration camp building the Weimar-Buchenwald railway line during forced labour. In the spring of 1943, inmates from the same camp were ordered to construct a 7-mile stretch of railway track between Weimar-Schöndorf and Buchenwald over a period of three months. The line initially served the supply needs of the armament factory. In early 1944, some 100,000 people were transported on these tracks, and many of them in open freight were transported directly to Buchenwald concentration camp from all over Europe and transferred from there to one of the sub-camps for forced labour. (*USHMM*)

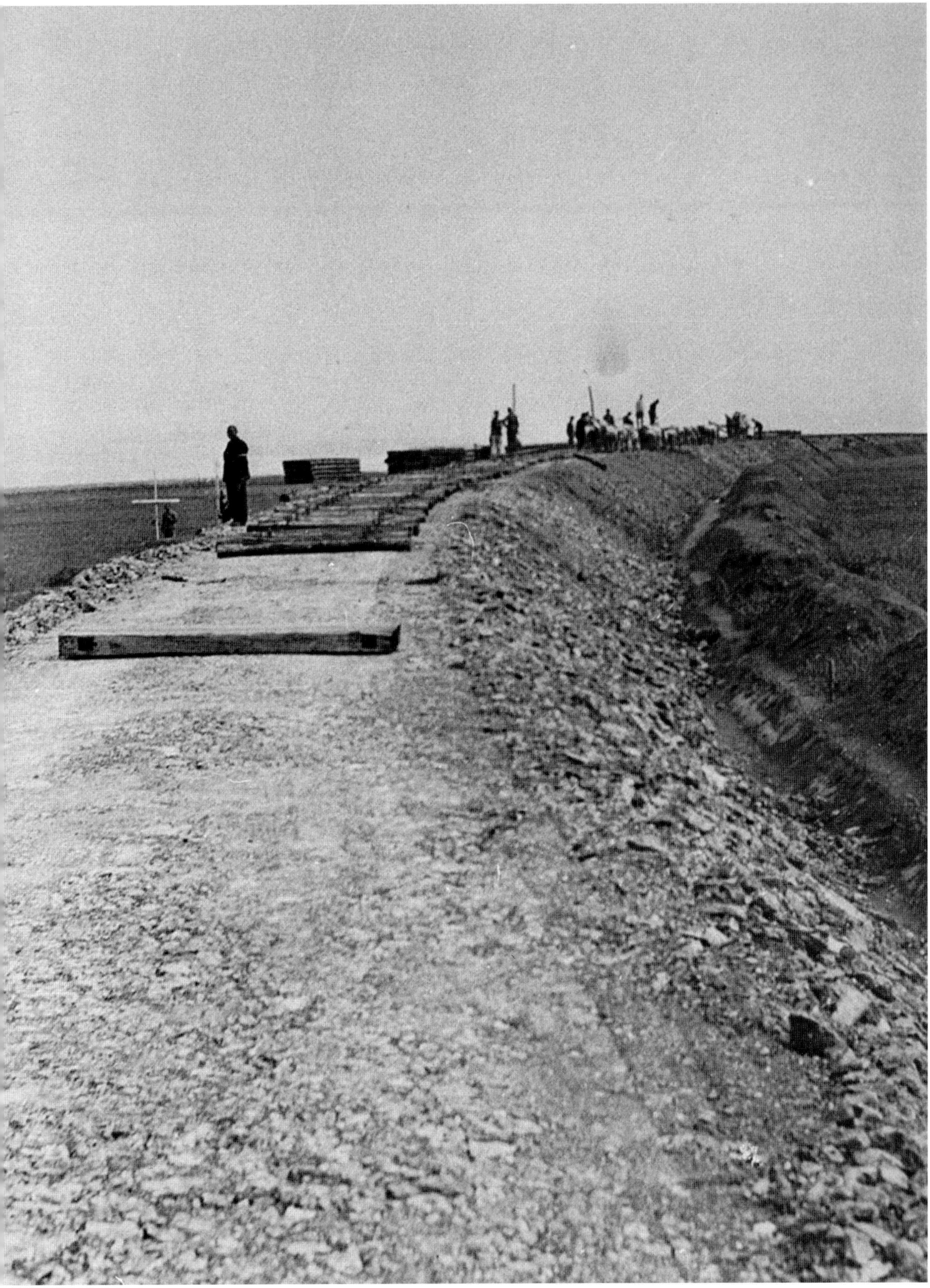

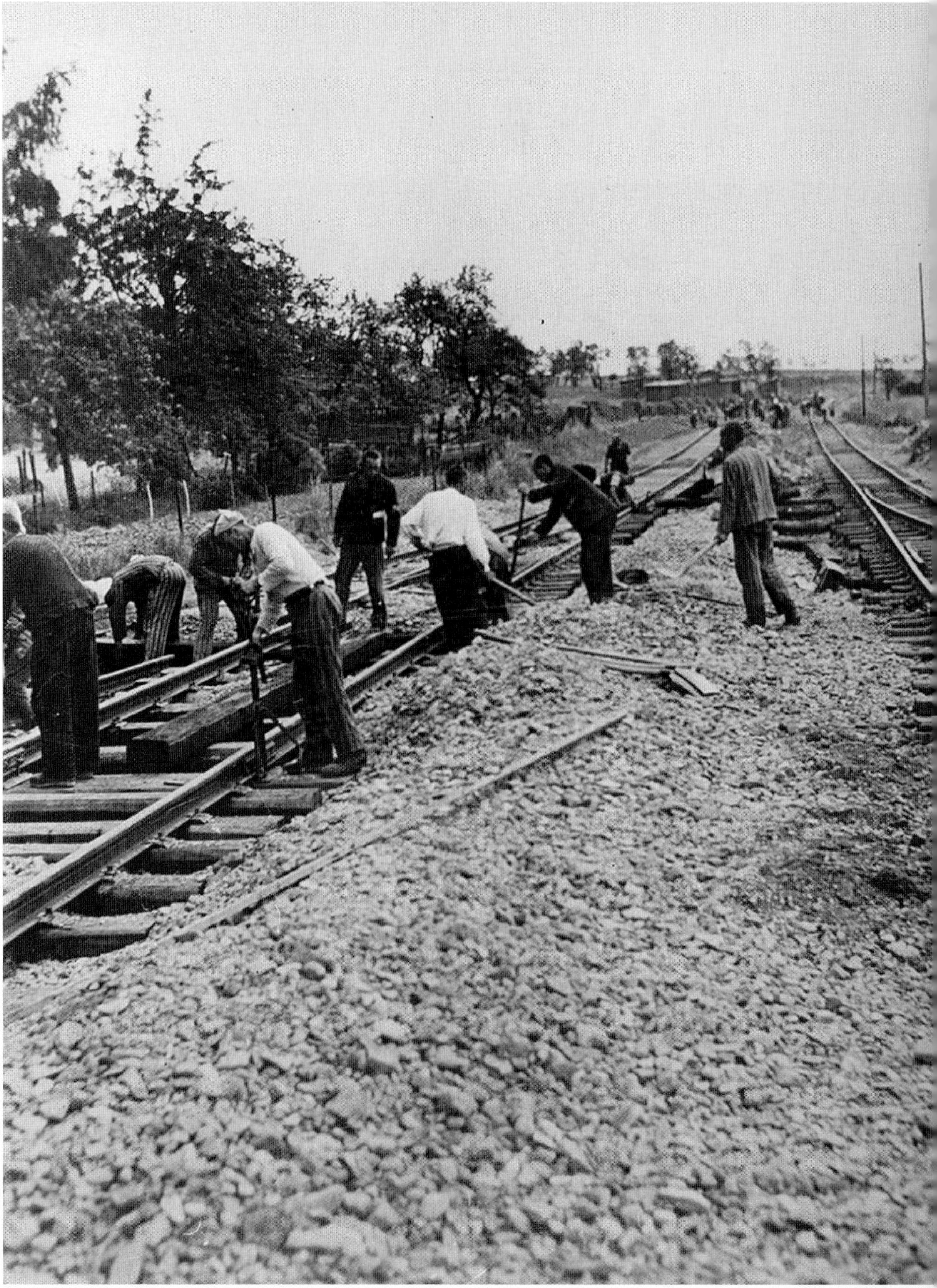

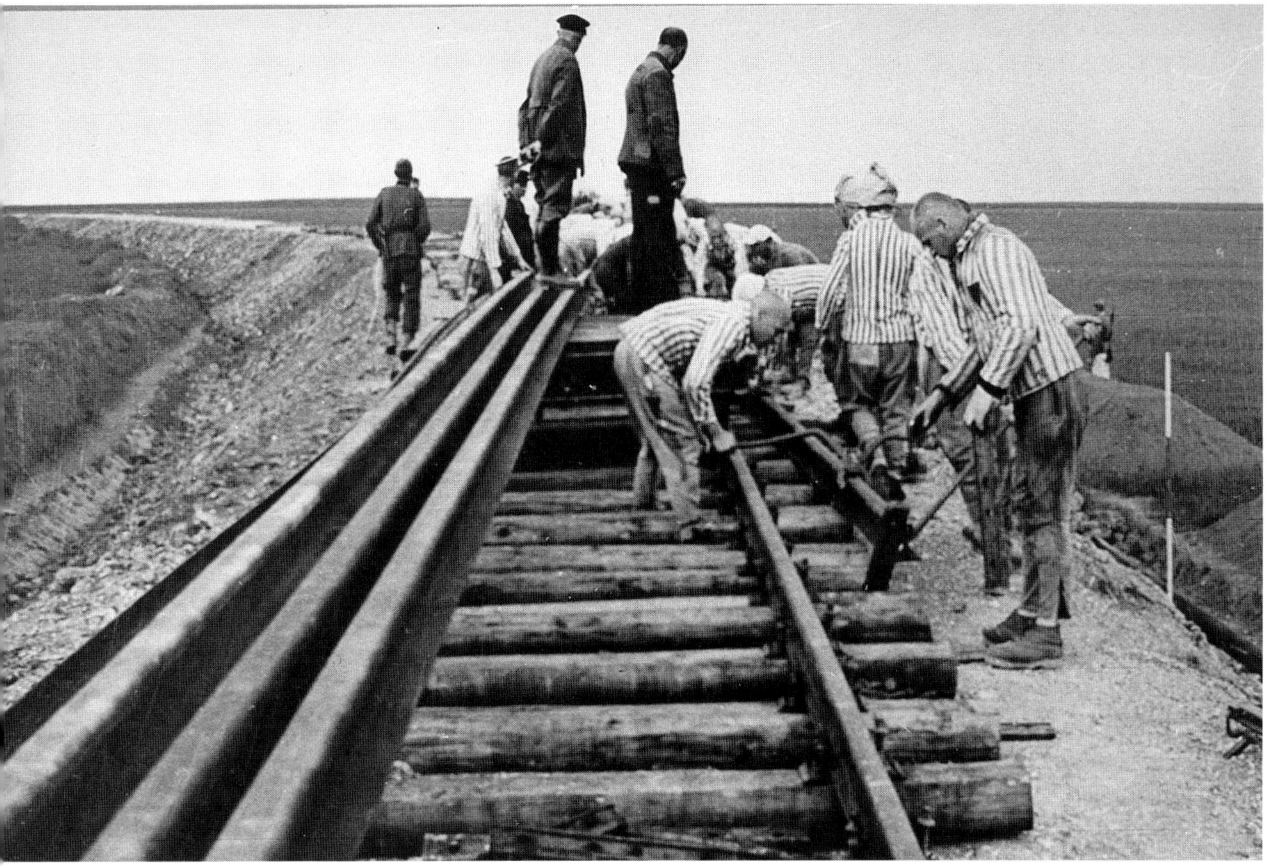

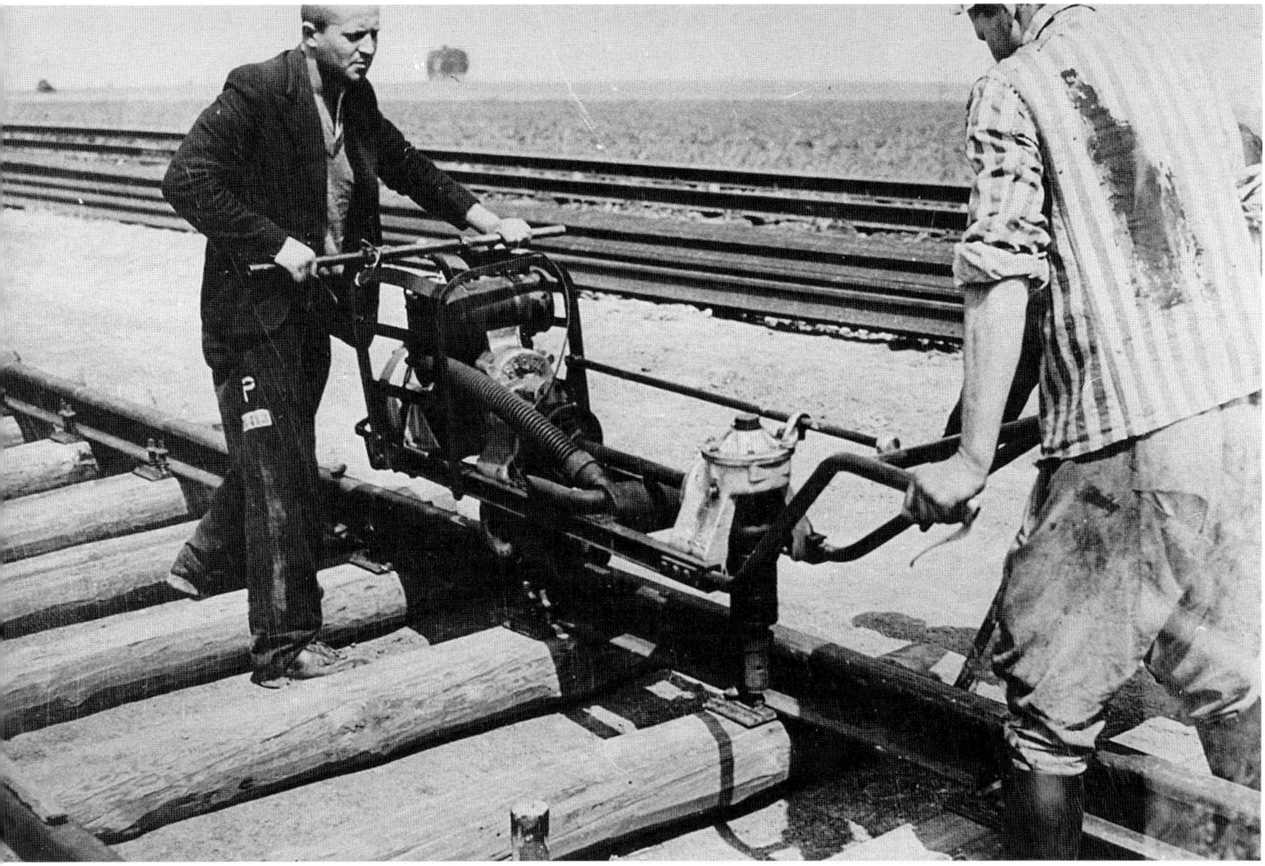

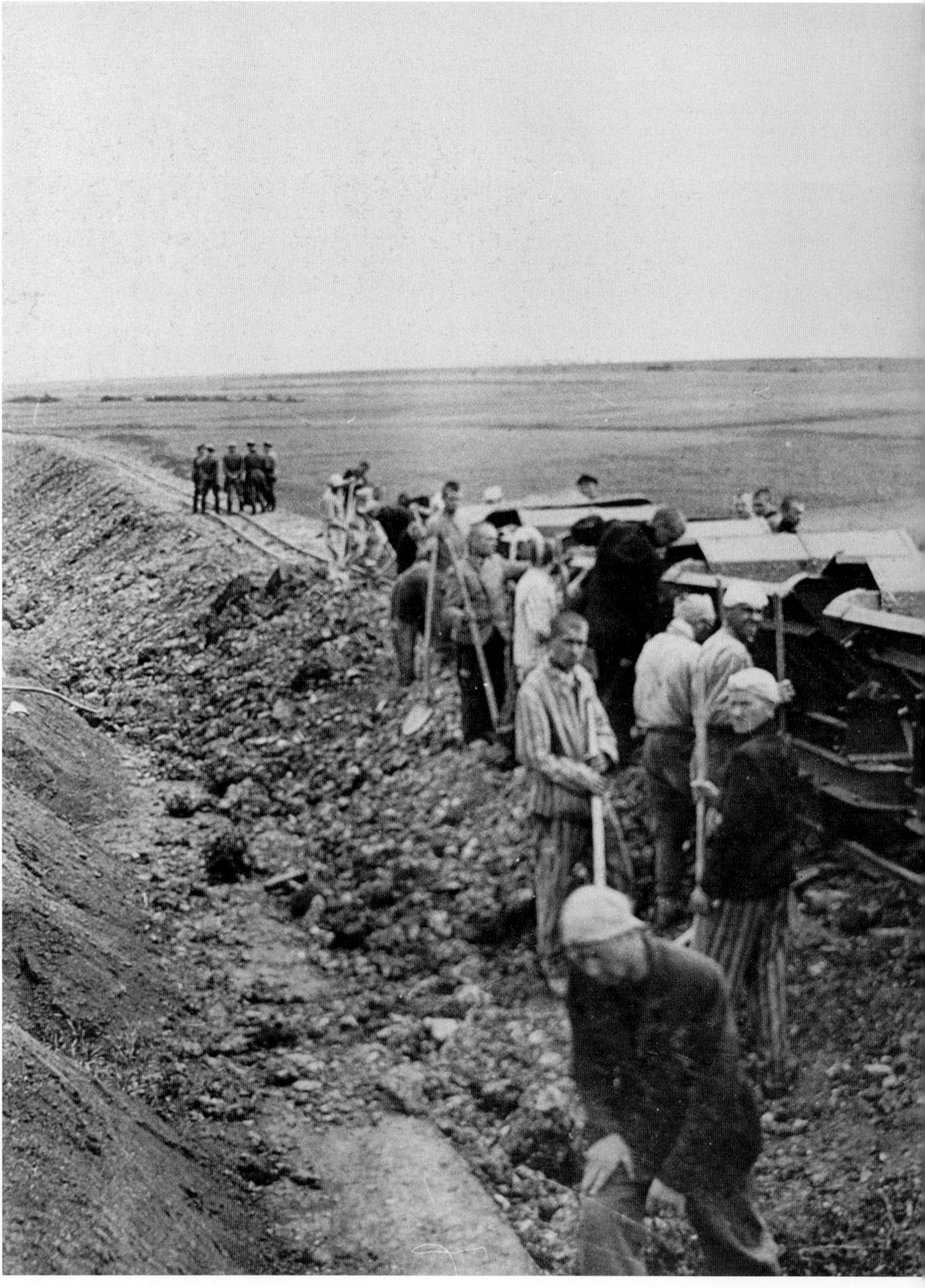

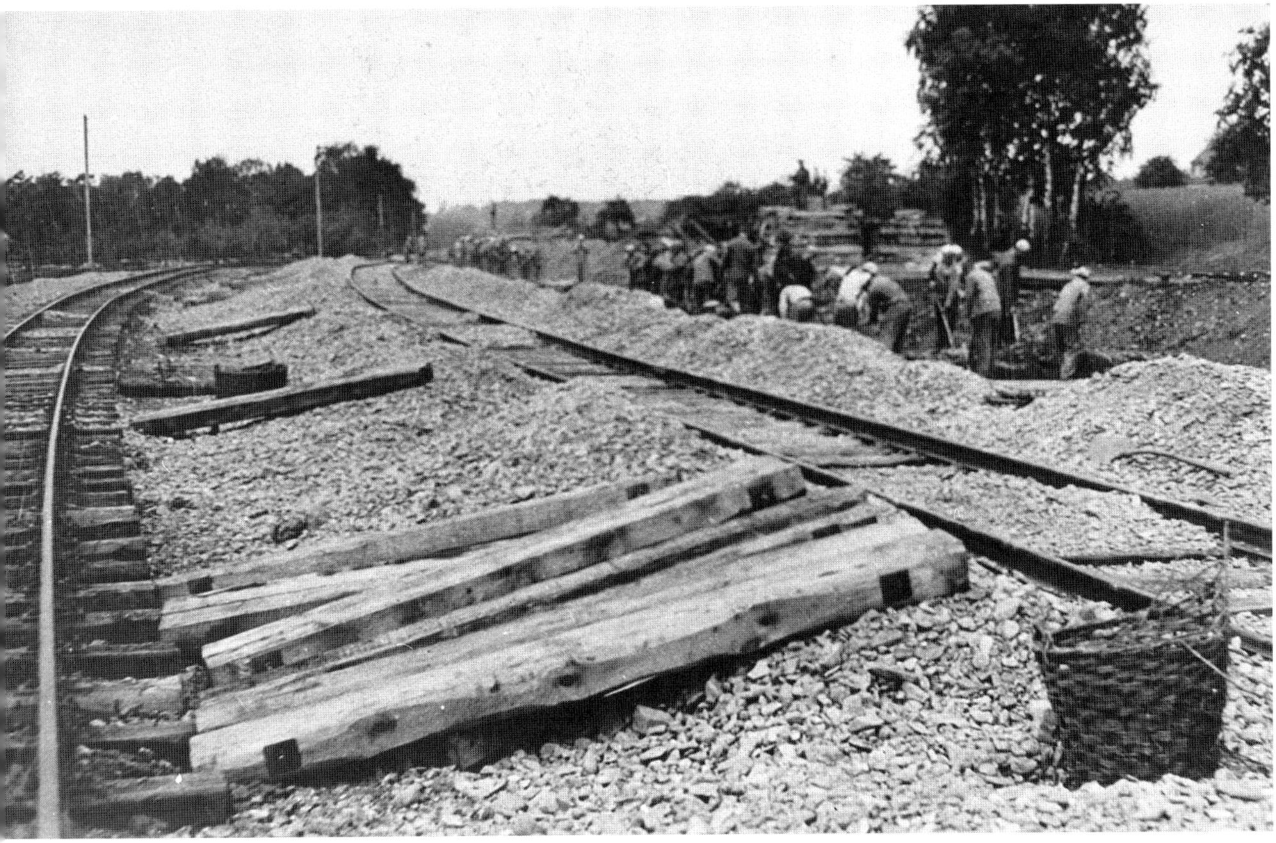

The first of two photographs showing a locomotive driver and fireman preparing their engine for transportation. The *Deutsche Reichsbahn* remained crucial to the operation and was paid to transport Jews and other victims on the rail networks of occupied territories and Germany's allies. (*NARA*)

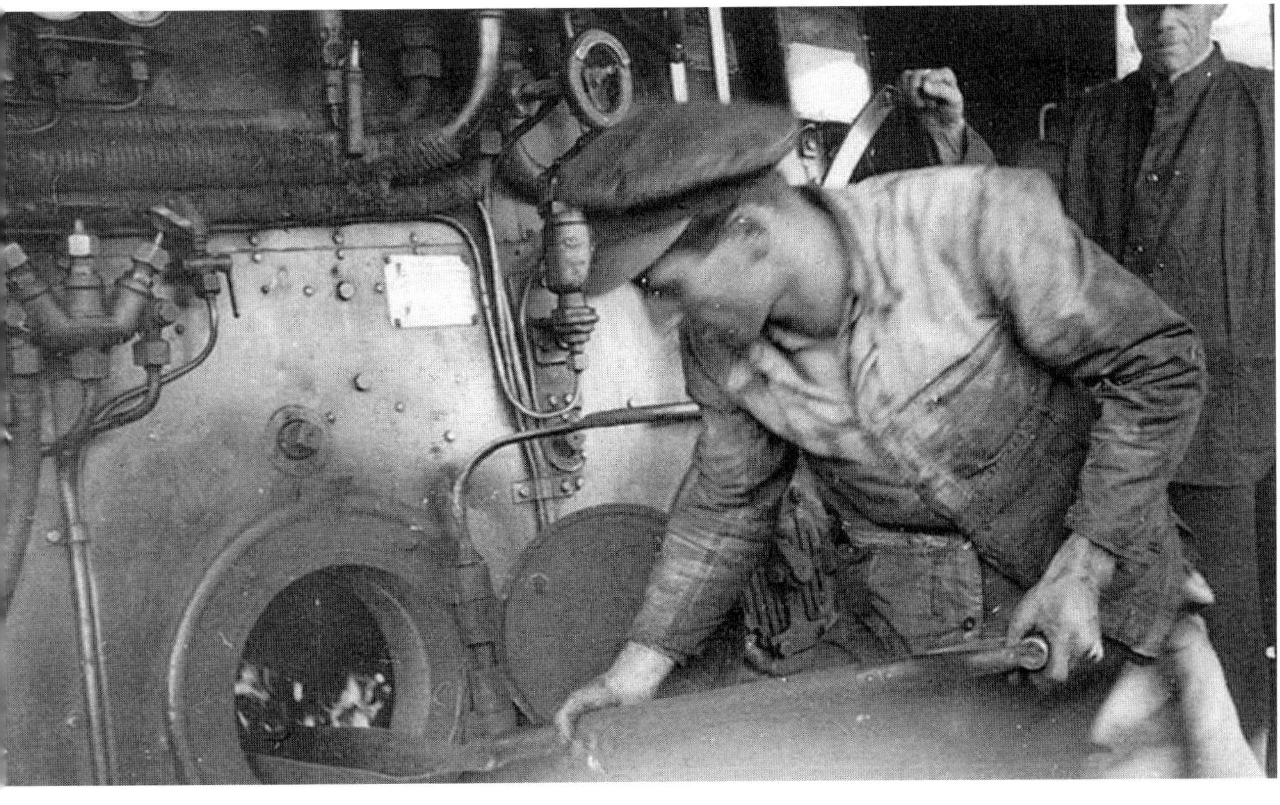

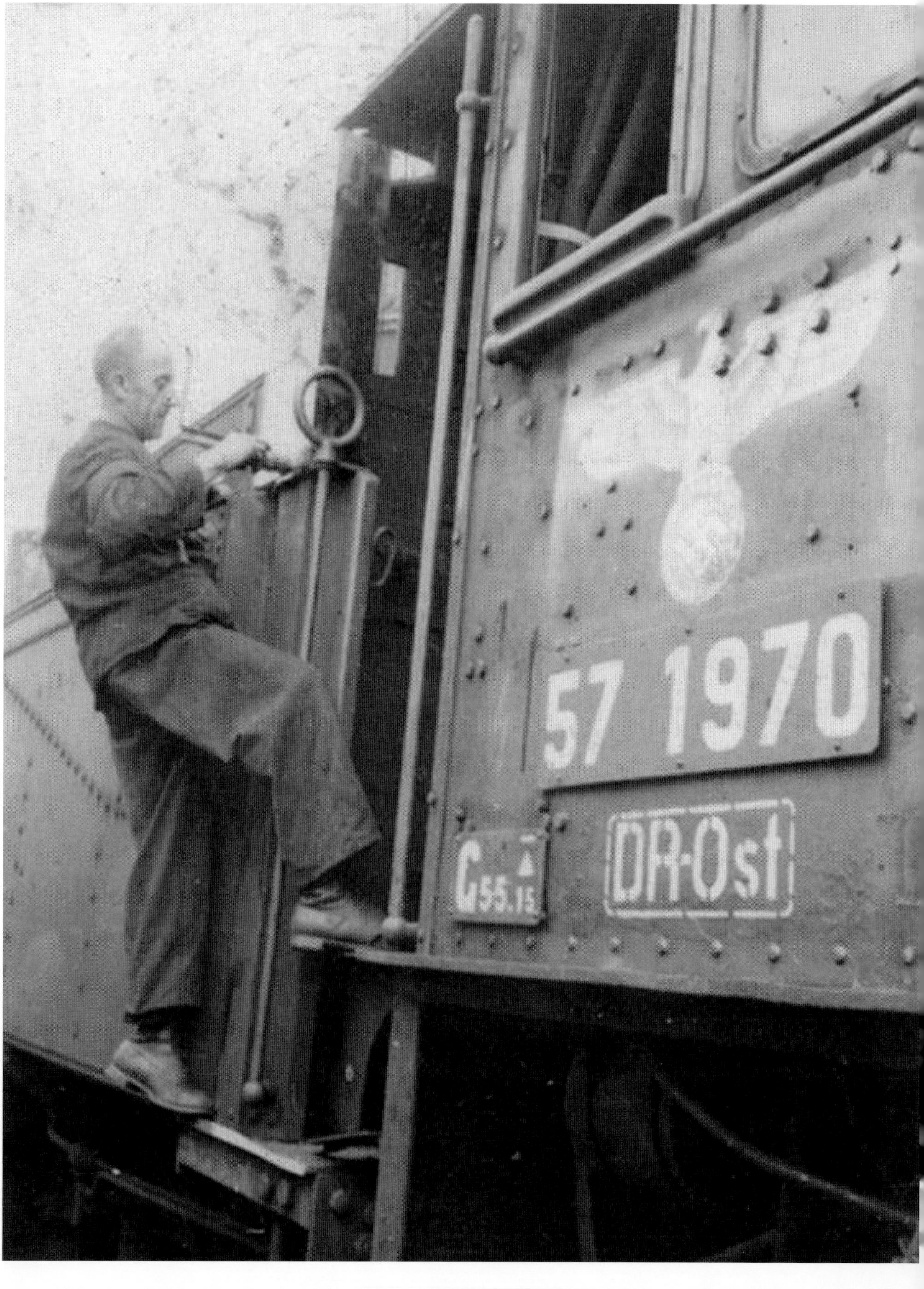
57 1970
DR-Ost

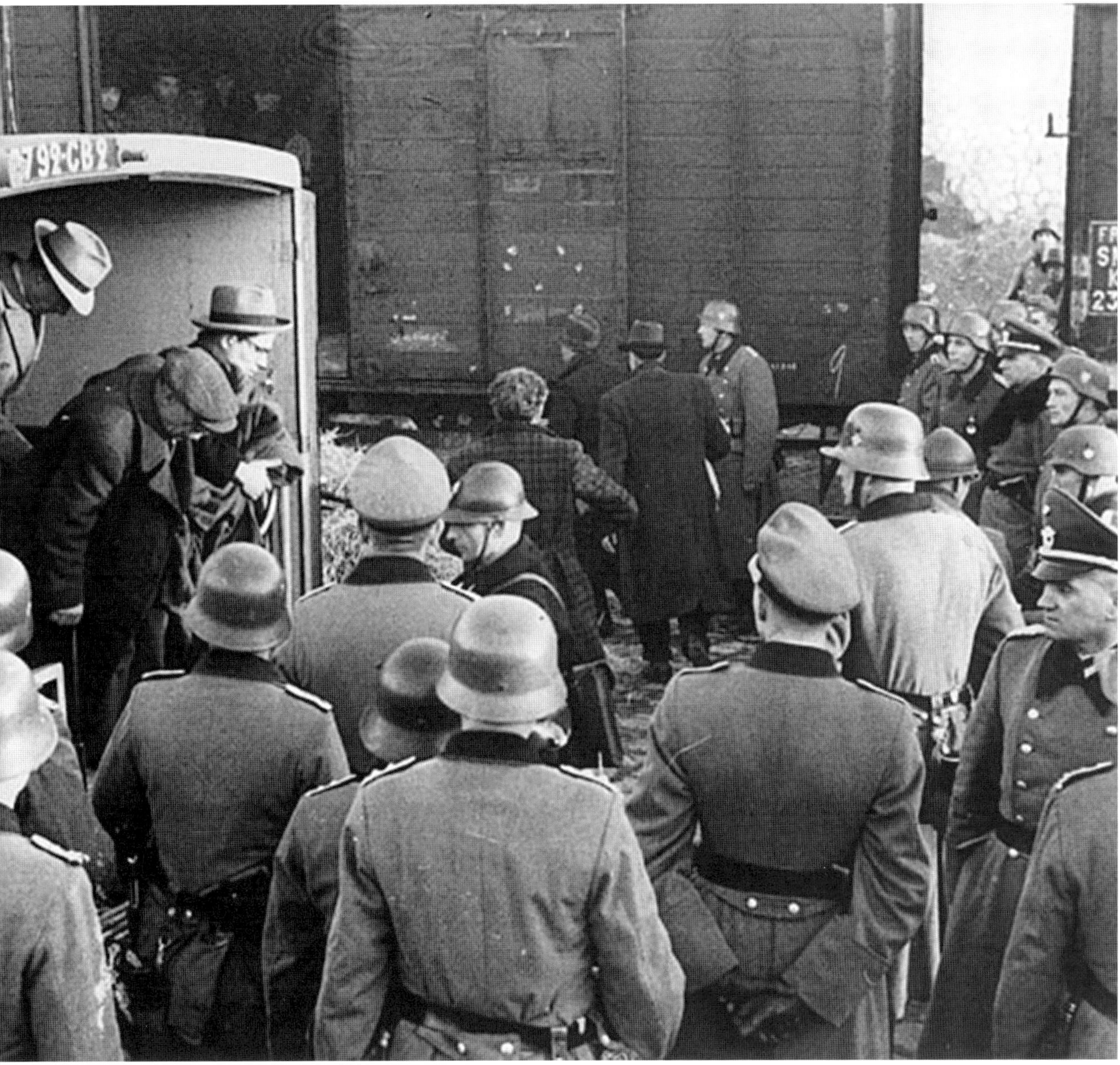

French Jewish men being unloaded from a vehicle at a railway siding in preparation for deportation, probably to a forced labour camp somewhere across Europe.

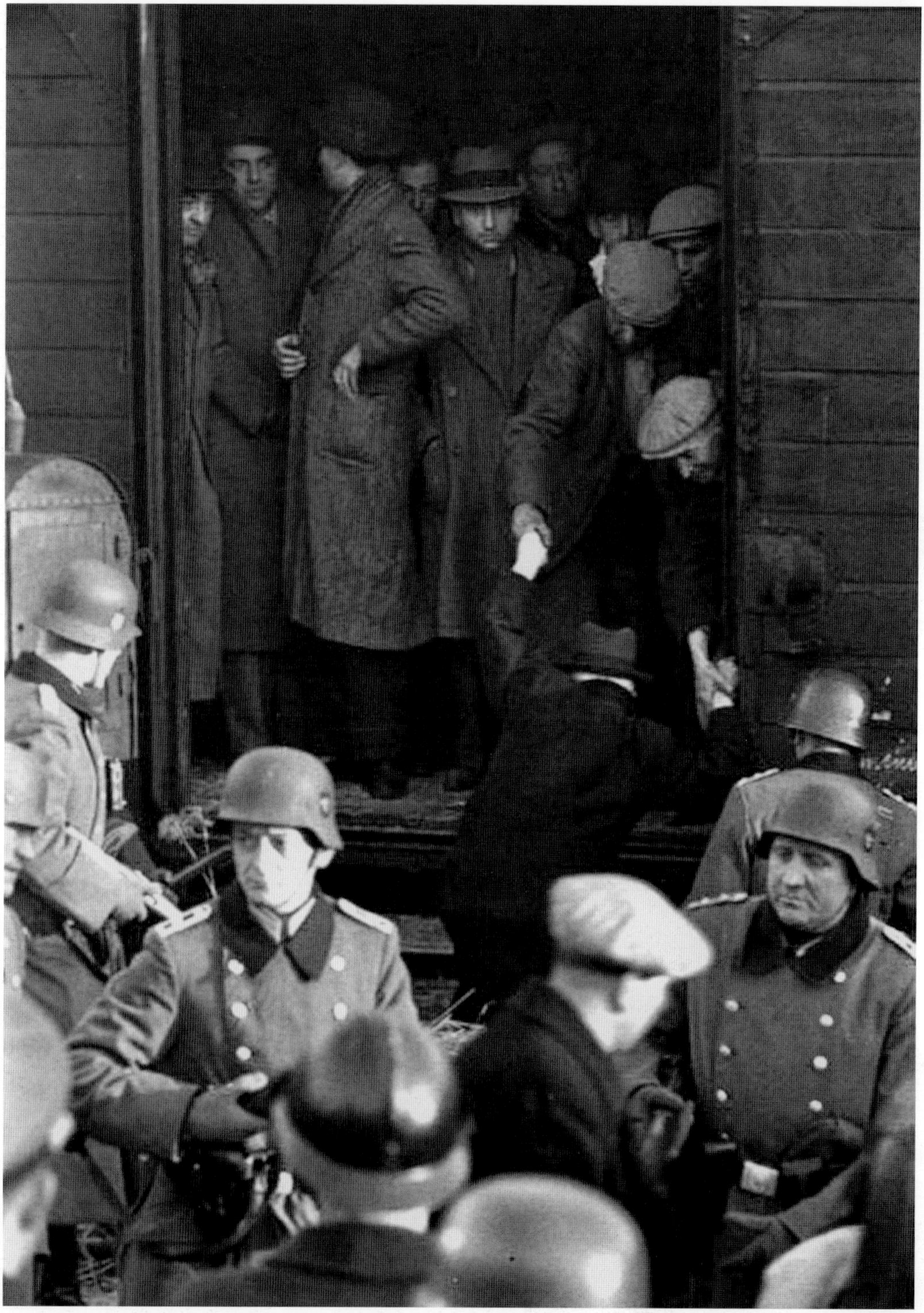

A deportation action of French Jews from Marseille between 22 and 24 January 1943. Of the 40,000 people deported, the operation saw 2,000 Jews transported first to Fréjus, then to the camp of Royallieu near Compiègne in northern France and then to Drancy internment camp, which was the last stop before being transported by rail directly to the extermination camps in the east.

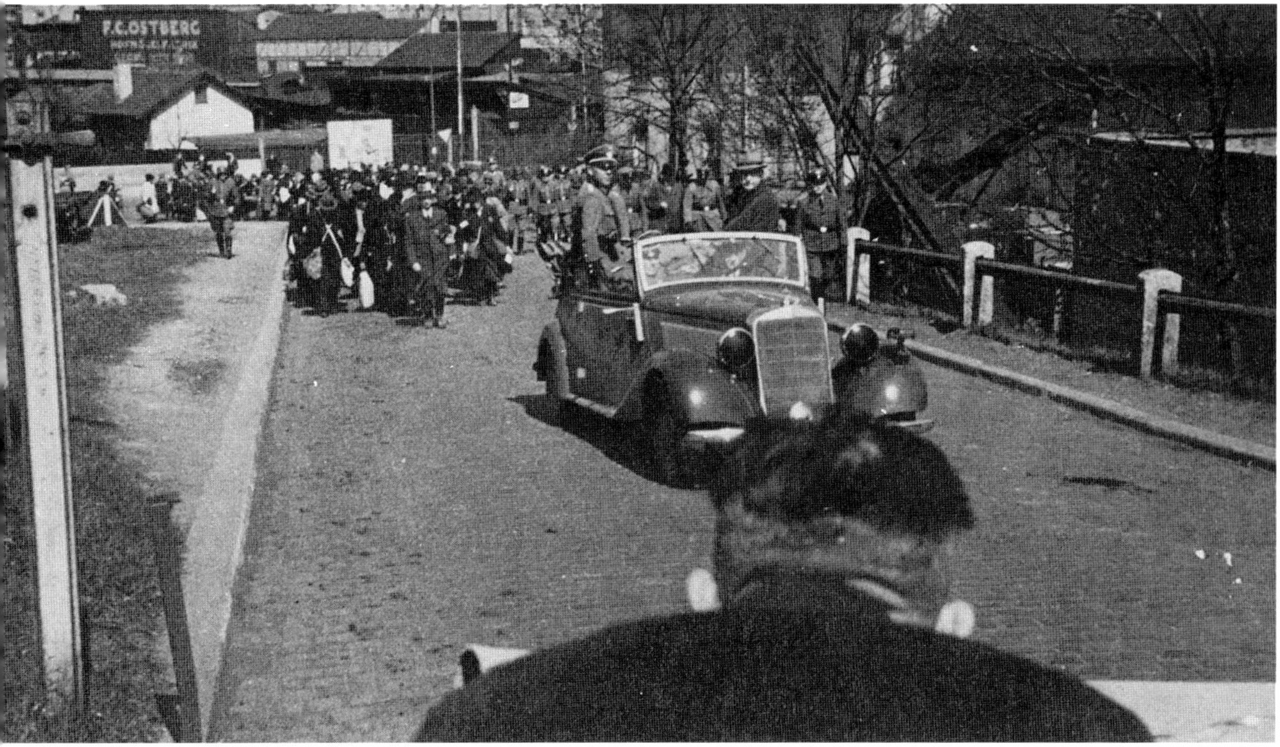
F.C.OSTBERG

Jewish deportees carrying bundles and suitcases march through town towards the railway station behind Nazi officials riding in an open car. *(USHMM)*

Jews arriving at the Gare d'Austerlitz railway station during a deportation action from Paris. Some 5,000 foreign-born Jewish men between the ages of 18 and 40 had been ordered to report to the various assembly points in May 1941, mainly comprising Czechs, Austrians and Poles. They were then transported by bus to the Gare d'Austerlitz railway station where they boarded four special trains destined for the internment camps of Beaune-la-Rolande and Pithiviers located in the Loiret near Orléans. *(USHMM)*

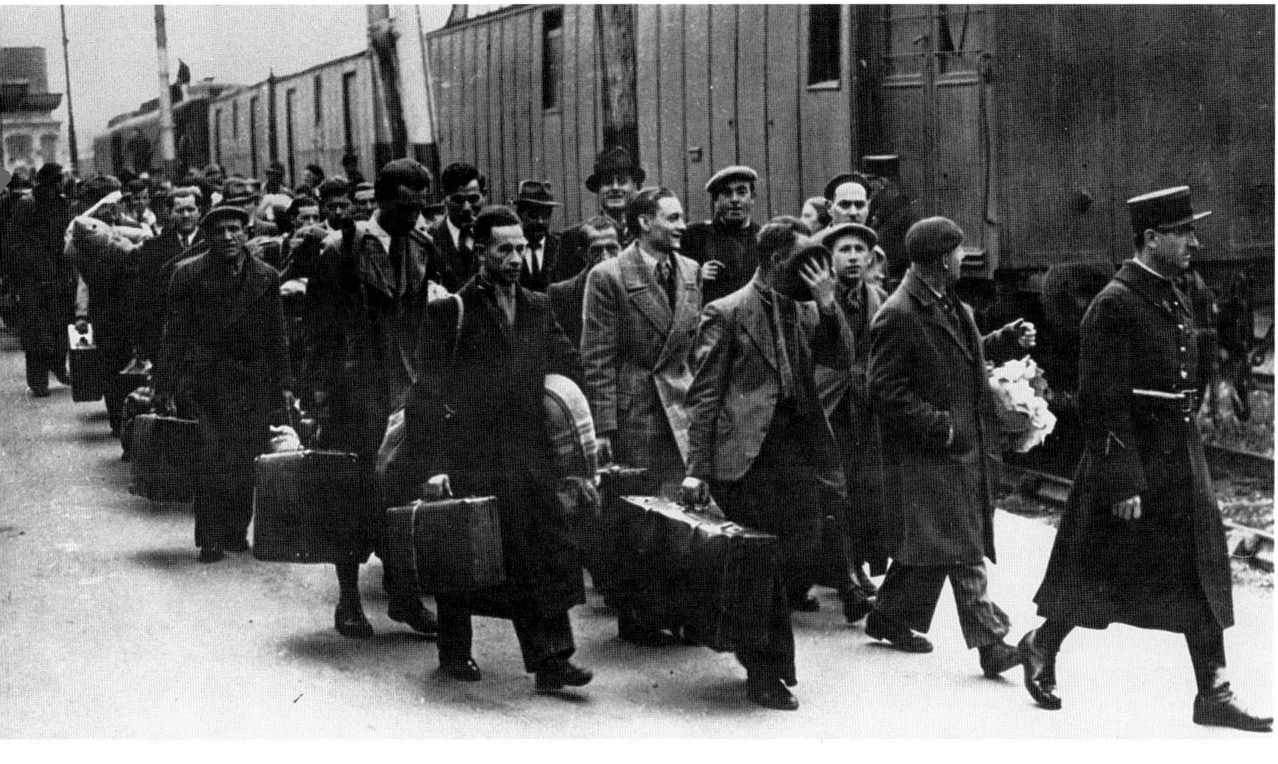

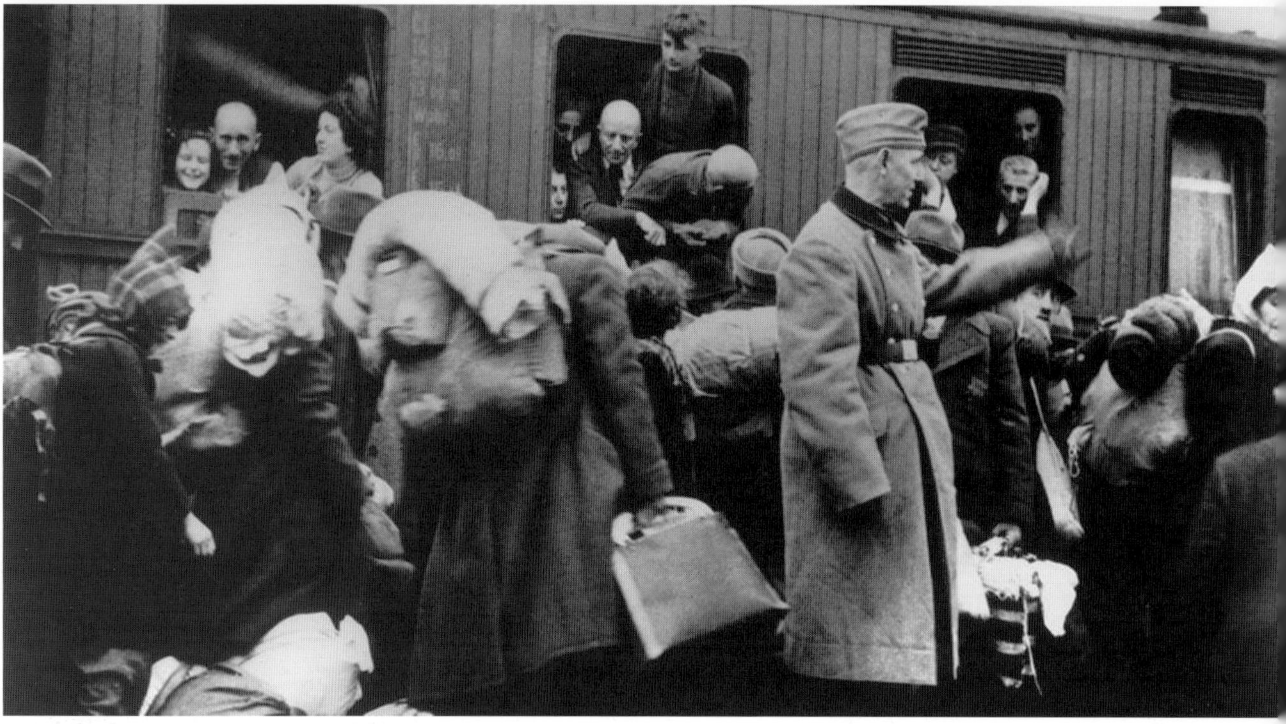

(**Above**) Jews being deported from a station in Germany.

(**Opposite**) Railway station in the Westerbork camp. Westerbork operated in the Netherlands between 1942 and 1944. The Netherlands was another country that saw thousands of Jews being transported by rail to Westerbork transit camp from the Amsterdam ghetto. The transports were operated by the state-owned *Nederlandse Spoorwegen* or NS (Dutch Railways). The NS was forced by the Germans to construct a railway network to the Westerbork transit camp. Some 100,000 Jews died.

(**Below**) Jews boarding a deportation train at Westerbork transit camp in the Netherlands. In early 1942, the Germans began preparations to deport Dutch Jews to killing centres in the east. For this operation Dutch Jews were to be concentrated in Amsterdam. They also decided to intern all non-Dutch Jews in Westerbork. There were some 20,000 non-Dutch Jews living in the Netherlands, most of them refugees from Germany.

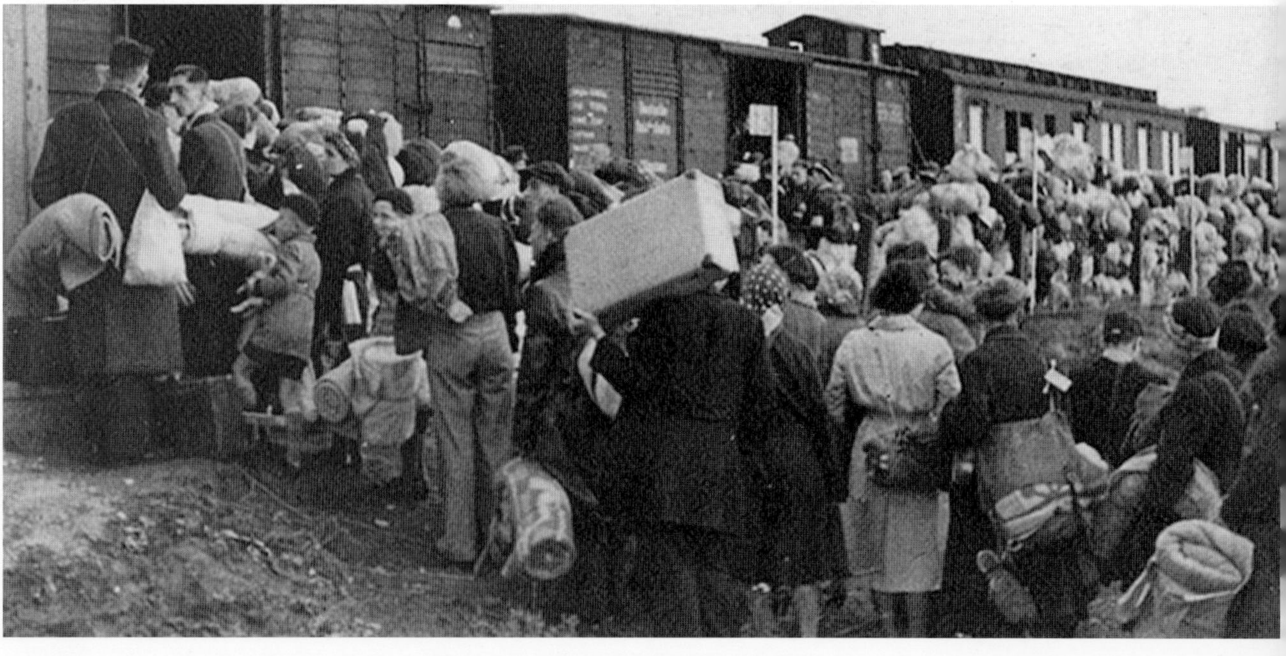

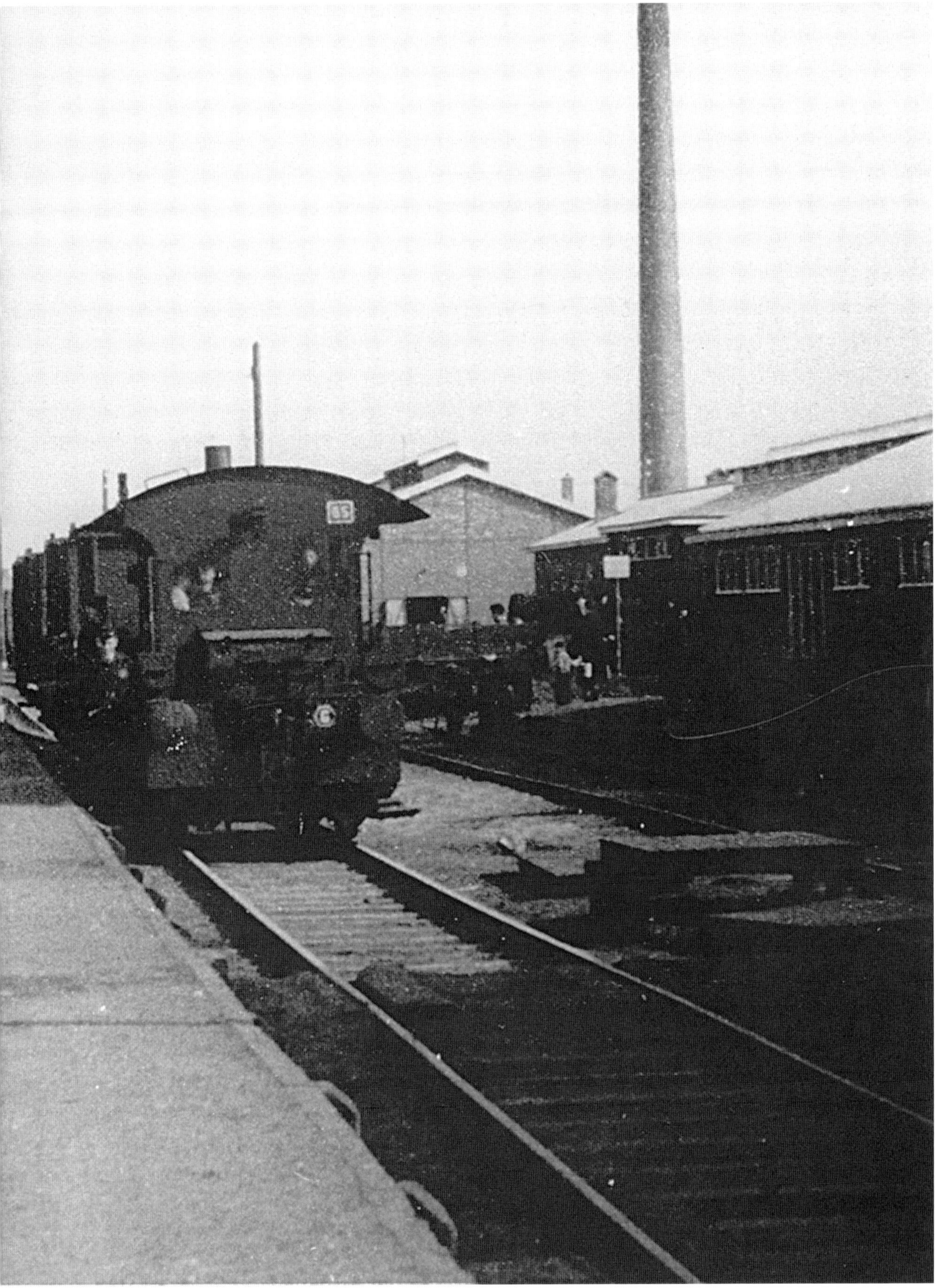
65

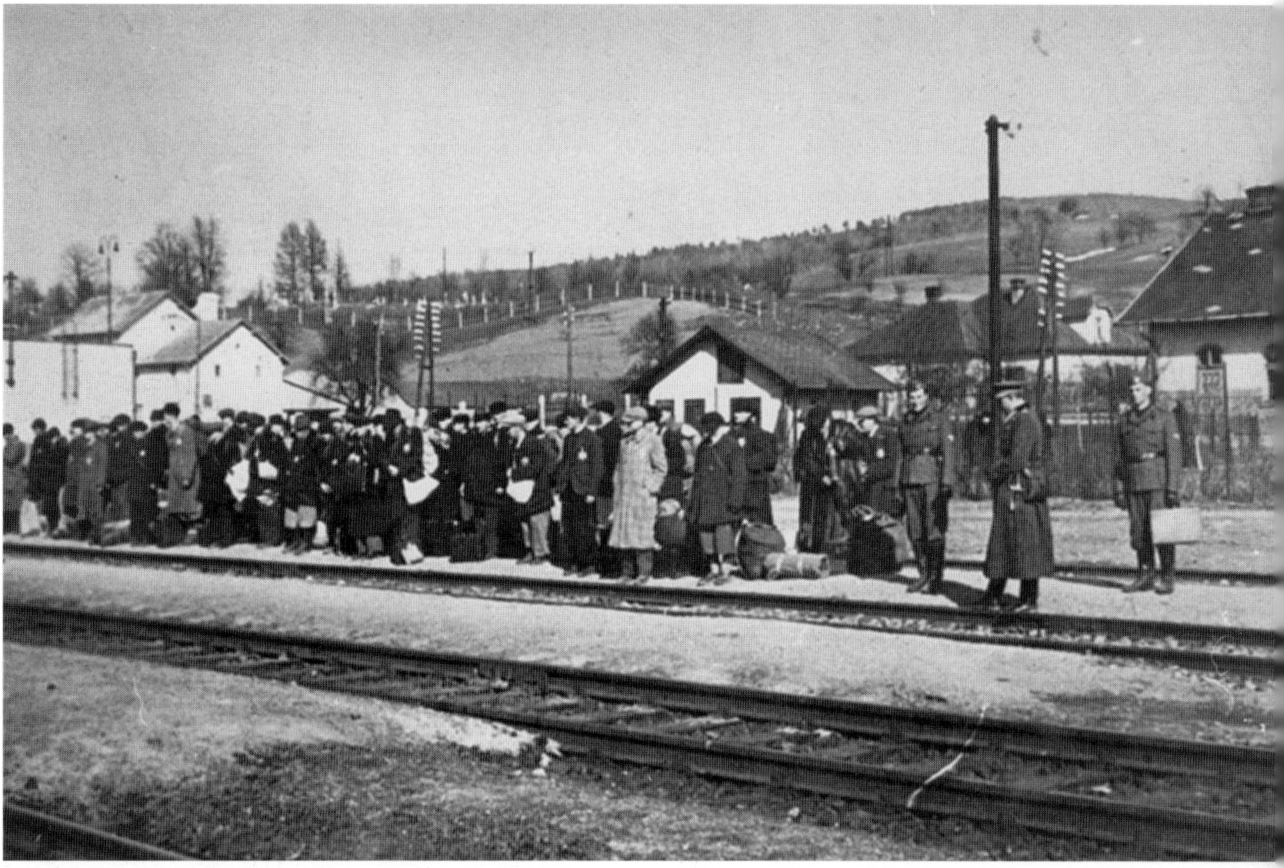

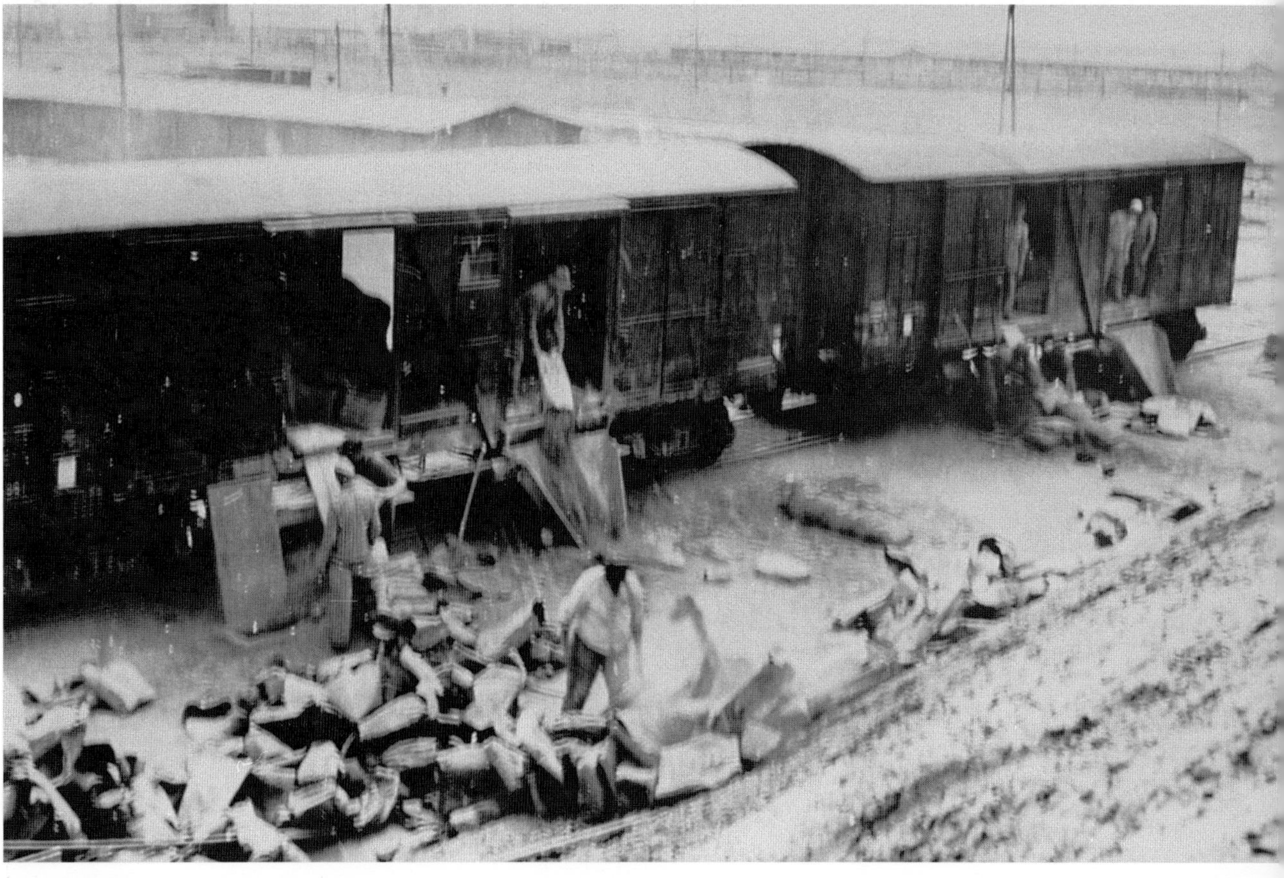

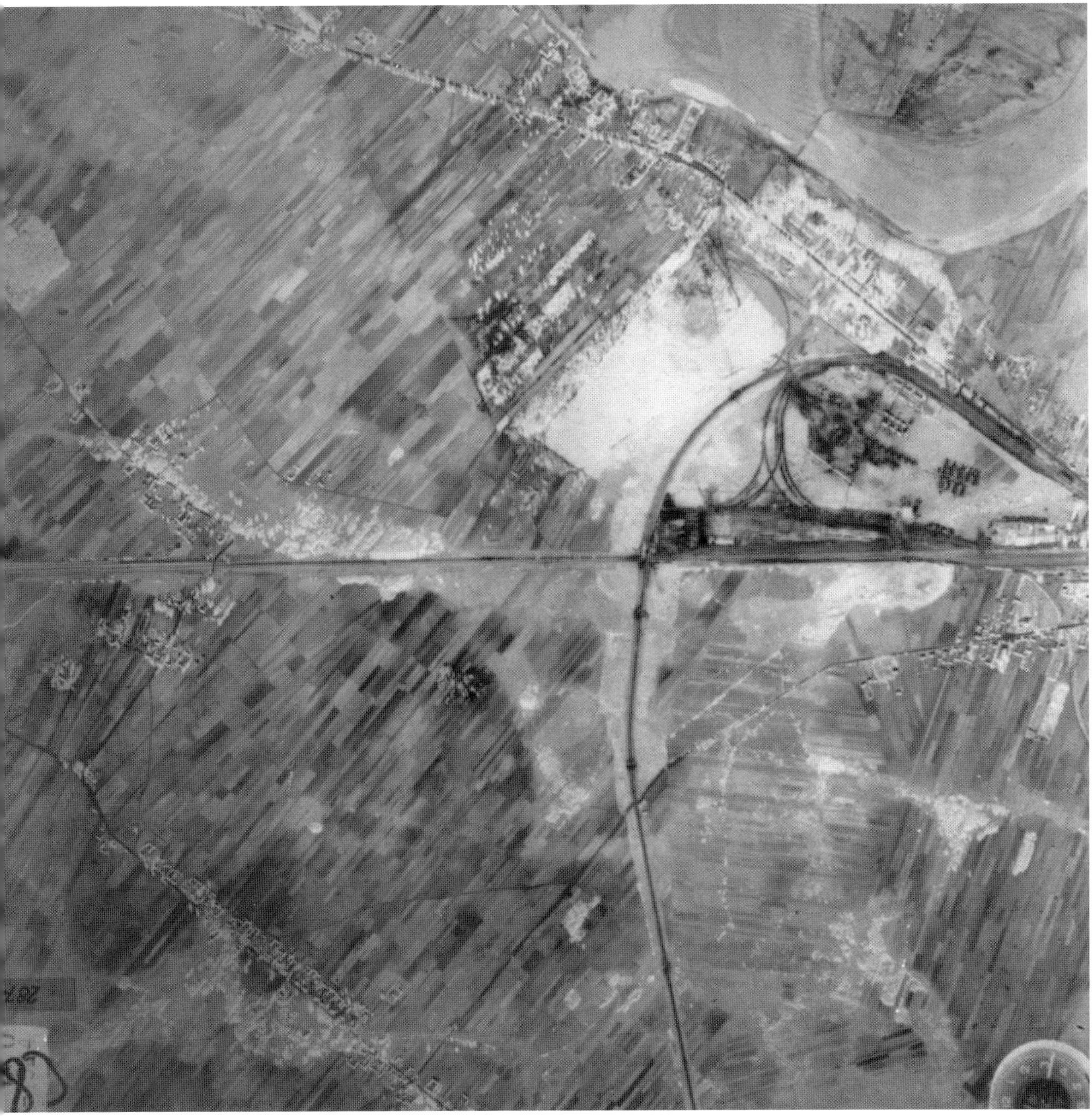

(**Opposite, above**) Jews at a railway station waiting for their train during a deportation action.

(**Opposite, below**) Auschwitz prisoners unloading railcars containing cement at the I.G. Farben factory in Auschwitz-Monowitz.

(**Above**) An aerial photograph taken by the Luftwaffe. The image appears to show the railway line in Małkinia Górna and probably shows where the deportation train transports from Warsaw turned south, then turned and crossed the Bug River towards Treblinka in 1942–43. *(USHMM)*

Chapter Five

Western Deportations

By 1943 German military operations on the Eastern Front had seen a series of major setbacks. During Germany's early victories the Nazis had little to worry about with the logistics of transporting Jews by railway. Their success on the battlefield only fed the lust for more Jewish blood. However, the progression of the war undoubtedly influenced the number of trains and people being transported across Europe. Yet, even as the Wehrmacht struggled to hold their lines against an ever-growing Russian enemy, the Nazis were recklessly determined at all costs to see that Europe was rid of the Jews, even if it meant using railway capacity desperately needed by the army.

The Reinhard camps were still receiving large numbers of transports, and there was no indication that this would stop due to any military setbacks. At the end of March 1943 transports into Treblinka actually increased with shipments of new arrivals from Bulgaria. Following the Bulgarian shipment came a transport from Salonika. During April further transports arrived at the camp including deportees from the last remaining Russian and Polish ghettos. There were further arrivals of Western Jews, this time from Holland, Austria and even Germany. During March and April alone, thousands of Dutch Jews were being successfully transported to Sobibor, where they were immediately put to death. Also at Treblinka the increase in shipments meant that the SS still had moderately safe jobs and did not fear being sent to the front to fight in Russia.

In April and May the majority of some 50,000 residents from the Warsaw ghetto were transported to Treblinka. Clearing of the ghettos in the General Government was almost complete by early summer of 1943, and both Treblinka and Sobibor were receiving their last deliveries. During this period the bulk of the shipments being received were now from Western Europe, including large transports from Holland and even Austria and Germany. In fact, with so many new arrivals and the anticipation of receiving more Western Jews at Christmas 1942, the commandant of Treblinka had ordered the construction of a fake railway station. The commandant wanted to enhance the illusion and deception in order to fool the new arrivals into believing they had arrived at a genuine station for a transit camp. There was a clock painted with numerals and hands that never moved, a ticket-window was constructed and various timetables and arrows indicating train connections to Warsaw, Wolwonoce to Białystok plastered on the walls of the sorting barracks. There were fake doors and windows installed, plus a waiting room, information telegraph office, station manager, rest rooms and there were many trees and beds of flowers.

Dealing with the German and Austrian Jews was the most difficult phase in the transition of Treblinka. While the majority of SS personnel were not emotionally disturbed by these shipments from their country and had created in themselves a capacity for dissociating to some extent from the brutality, there were others that dealt with it quite differently. There were those that felt a kind of pity for the victims, especially German-speaking Jews. Other SS guards standing on the ramps were occasionally confronted by a moral and emotional conflict when they received Western Jews, particularly from the 'Homeland'. They were able to identify them much more easily than those from Poland and Russia for their lives had been very similar to their own. Unlike Eastern Jews whose religious, racial and national feelings were combined in one single identity and had for centuries been ingrained with fear and terror from centuries of pogroms, Western Jews were recognized completely differently as they had not suffered immeasurably from years of pain and anguish. It was for this reason that the SS went to great lengths to mislead the Western Jews when they arrived at the camps. In fact some of the boxcars were made more presentable, convincing the Jews, especially those from Germany and Austria, that they were coming to be resettled. Their naïvety was such that some people from the transport actually arrived and offered tips to those that were unloading them.

When they arrived they were greeted at the ramp that was disguised as a railway station complete with flower beds. There were green fences and normal-looking barracks, and medical orderlies often lined up to 'care' for the 'old and sick'. There were polite voices telling them to disembark at their leisure, but in an orderly fashion. The SS wanted to make it appear as feasible as possible, tricking them into believing that they had reached a resettlement centre where they could rest before returning to their place of work and residence. As they were unloaded off the train, the SS were ordered not to use whips or implement any type of physical abuse.

Normally when German or Austrian Jews arrived by train, they were accompanied by German police. The police officers were quickly ushered to the mess so that they did not witness the unloading. Once the Jews were out of sight and the boxcars cleaned, the police were hurried back onto the train out of Treblinka. As for the Jews, they were led through the camp quietly and kept calm until naked. It was only then that the deception would slowly be unmasked as the SS and the Ukrainian guards escorted them to the gas chambers under the whip, hurling abuse and beating them until they had finally been made physically and mentally incapable of resistance.

Strange as it was – and Treblinka was not an isolated case – the debarkation of the Western Jews was about transition. First they were unloaded onto the ramp and quickly moved away, where they were forced to strip completely naked. It was believed that once they had removed their clothes, they had been dehumanized and their credentials as living beings had been taken away. It was only upon their initial arrival dressed in their fineries and with their luggage were they identified as Western Jews.

However, with the Eastern Jews the SS realized that deceptive precautions were generally unnecessary as they were regarded as a 'subhuman species' that expected terror. All they needed to undertake upon their arrival was to dupe and process them as quickly as possible. The moment the train stopped Ukrainian guards with their whips lining the platform with the SS drawn up behind them deliberately provoked instant dread and foreboding. As soon as the doors to the boxcars were open, the Ukrainians literally whipped them out of the trains, shouting and screaming at them until the moment of their deaths.

The SS displayed acute shrewdness in their understanding of the essential differences between Eastern and Western Jews, and this had become even more apparent during the last phase of transports to the Reinhard camps as more arrivals from the West came to be killed.

Yet, despite the way the SS treated the Eastern and Western Jews, the summer of 1943 had brought about an unusual atmosphere not seen during the history of the camps' operation. This feeling was the direct result of the dire military situation on the Eastern Front. The Wehrmacht had undergone a permanent change. It had lost its courage and will to advance. Hope was now tainted by the growing prospect of being sucked into a long bitter struggle for survival. With nothing but a string of defeats in its wake, the German army was now withdrawing across a bombed and blasted Soviet landscape with little hope of holding back the Red Army. The summer campaign in Russia had been completely disastrous. Against overwhelming superiority the Germans withdrew some 150 miles along a 650-mile front. Slowly and defiantly they retreated but were always outnumbered, constantly low on fuel, ammunition and other desperately-needed supplies. By August the whole German army in the east was faced with a more dangerous and still worsening prospect than ever before. To make matters worse, anti-partisan conflict added yet another dimension to the war in Russia. With word of the advancing Soviet army, Ukrainian nationalist partisans, Communist partisans and Polish underground groups began raiding German outposts, barracks, police stations, supply dumps, rail depots and trains.

Yet despite the dire military situation, the Nazis' vision of disposing of the Jews meant that they would speed up the deportation programme before the murder camps were dismantled. On 18 August came transports from the Białystok Ghetto to Treblinka comprising some thirty-seven cars. Some 25,000 Jews from the ghetto were destined for the camp. The following day came another transport from Białystok, this time with thirty-nine cars. The other three transports, two of which had been originally earmarked for Treblinka, were redirected. One was destined for Auschwitz, another to Majdanek and one to Theresienstadt which contained a consignment of children.

Białystok transport had not run smoothly due to logistical problems, and as a result many of the Jews remained locked in the boxcars for hours waiting to die. Conditions in the cars quickly deteriorated. Many victims, especially children, became filthy and their clothes were soiled. The old and the sick died of dehydration. Those that remained alive stood crammed with others, all gasping for air through the slats of the car.

When they were eventually unloaded there was widespread relief, but this was short-lived as the selection process separated men from women, husbands from wives and resulted in many emotional disturbances. Particular efforts were made to reassure the Jews as it was in the interests of the SS to keep them as calm as possible for they knew they lacked sufficient numbers of personnel and workers to deal with the transports.

The following day saw another transport from Białystok arrive, this time in thirty-nine wagons. This was known as 'Transport PJ-204' and would be the last shipment of Jews to Treblinka. All the remaining trains bypassed the camp, bound for Majdanek and Sobibor.

Throughout the remainder of October and the rest of November, the liquidation within the camp continued. On 20 November transport wagons Nos 22757, 22536, 70136 and 139789 were shipped out to Sobibor. During this period more than a hundred wagons of equipment left Treblinka.

(**Opposite**) The first of seven photographs taken in sequence showing Jewish deportees carrying a few personal belongings in bundles and suitcases marching through the town from the assembly centre at the Platzscher Garten to the railway station during a 'transportation action'. The Jews of Würzburg including other communities comprising Mainfranken, Schweinfurt, Kitzingen and Bad Kissingen were rounded up and deported to ghettos and concentration camps in the east in six transports beginning in November 1941 and completed by June 1943. Before their departure the deportees endured a succession of humiliating identity card checks, and luggage and body searches at assembly centres. Many of the Jews had all their personal property confiscated and then were escorted and marched through the town to the railway station with many local residents ridiculing them as they trudged along the road. A total of 2,063 Jews were deported in six transports, among them the Jews of Würzburg. (USHMM)

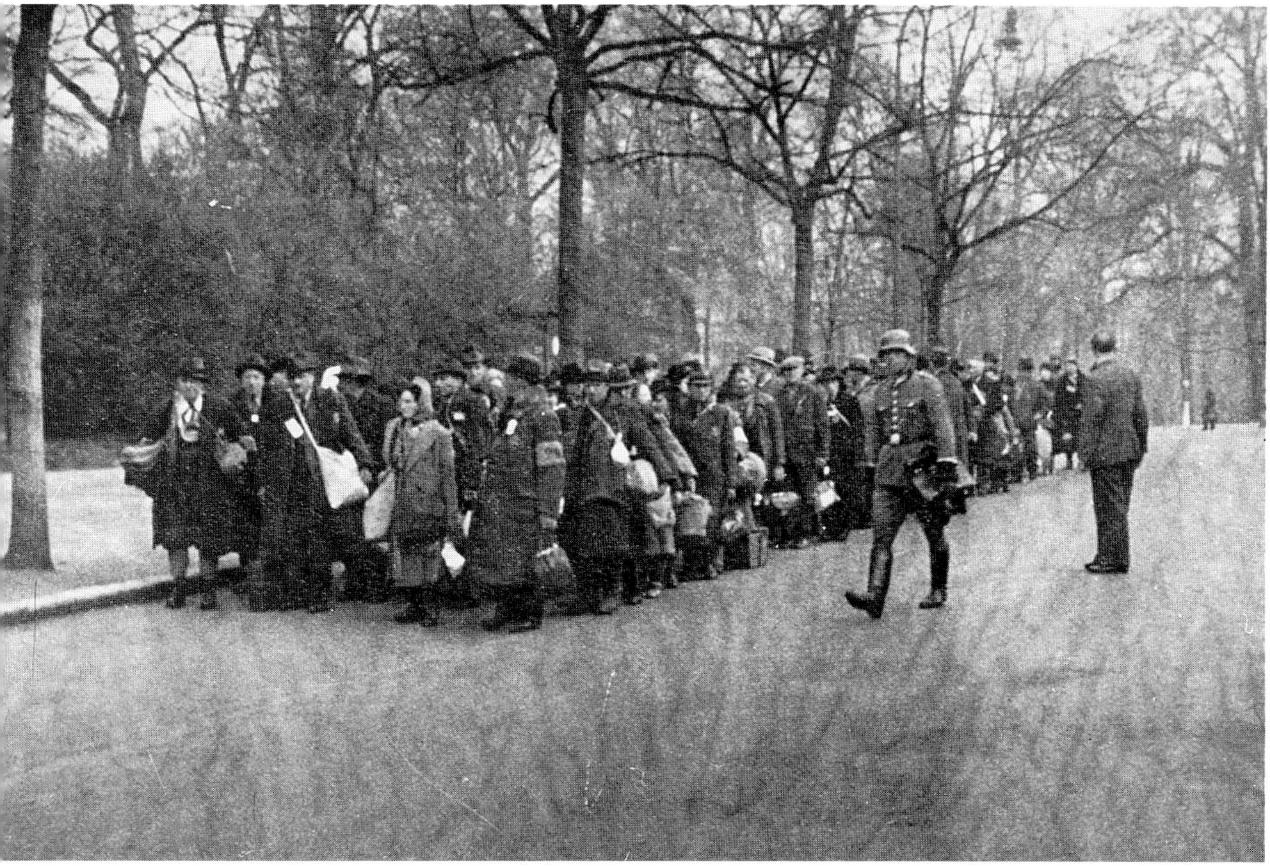

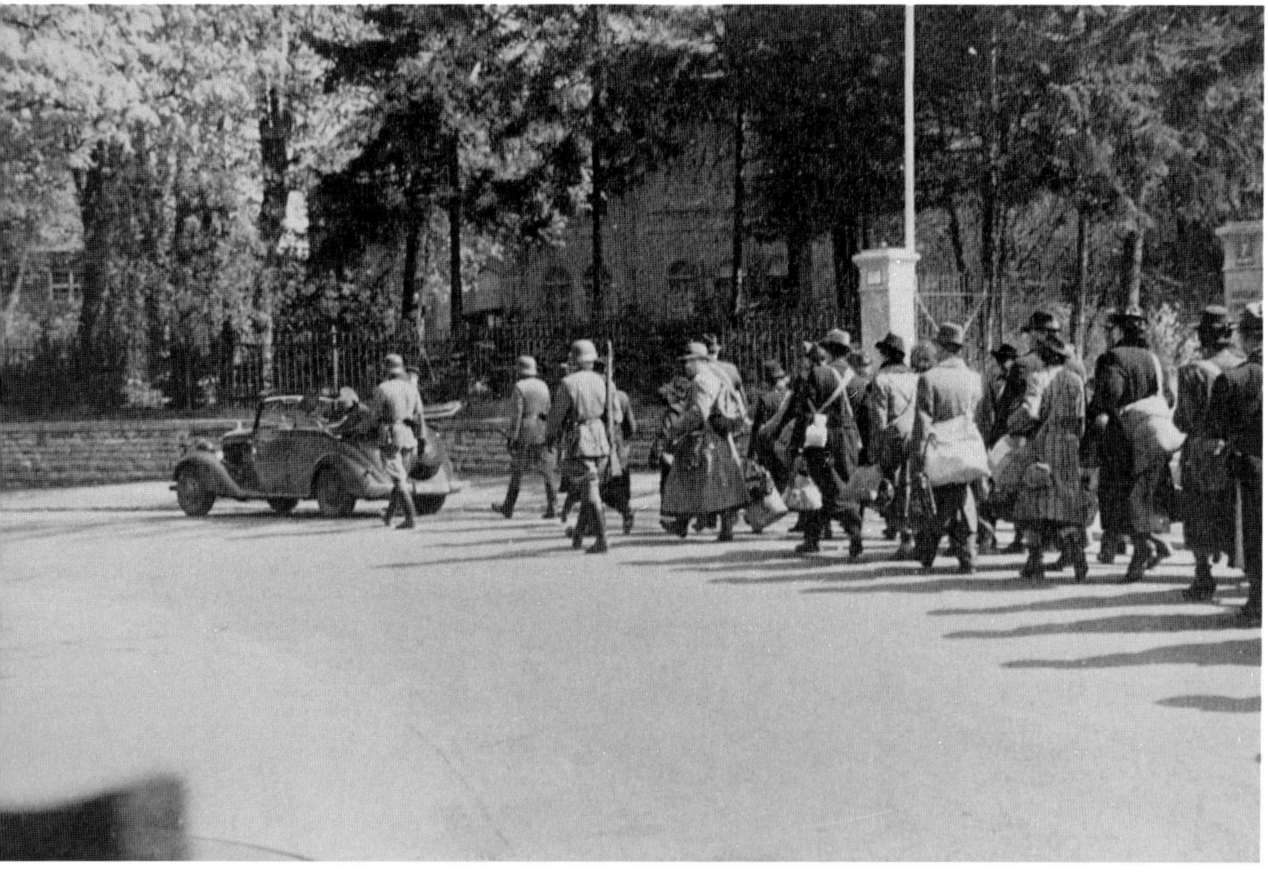

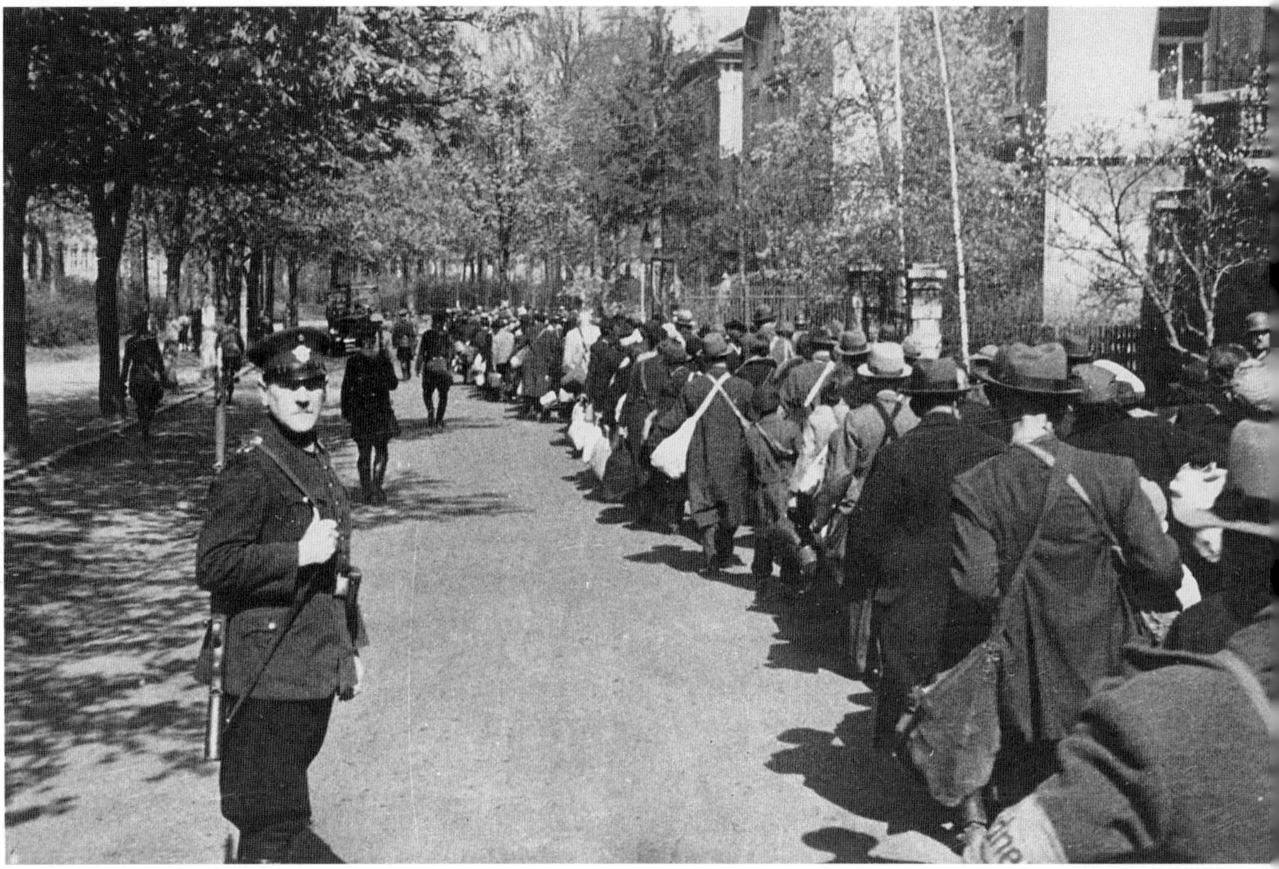

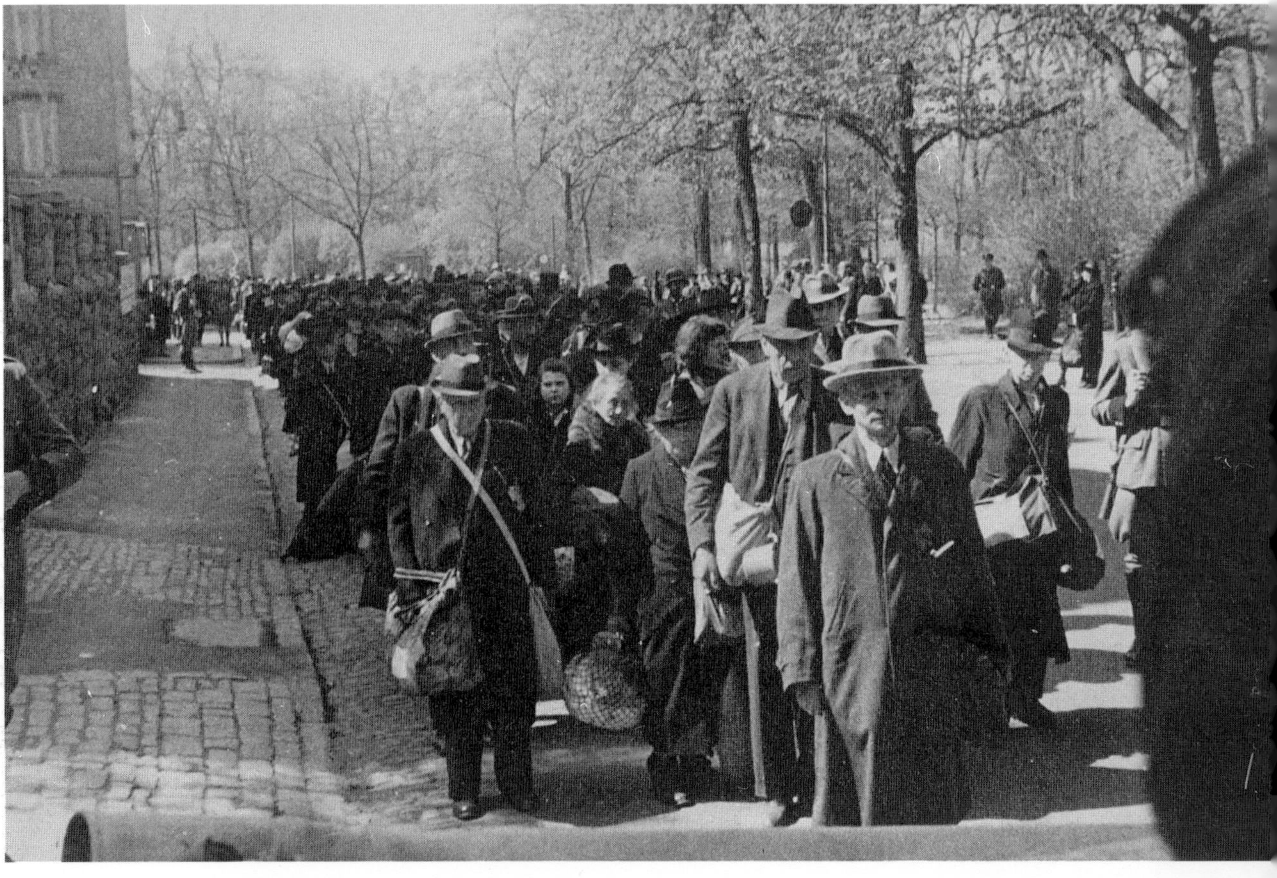

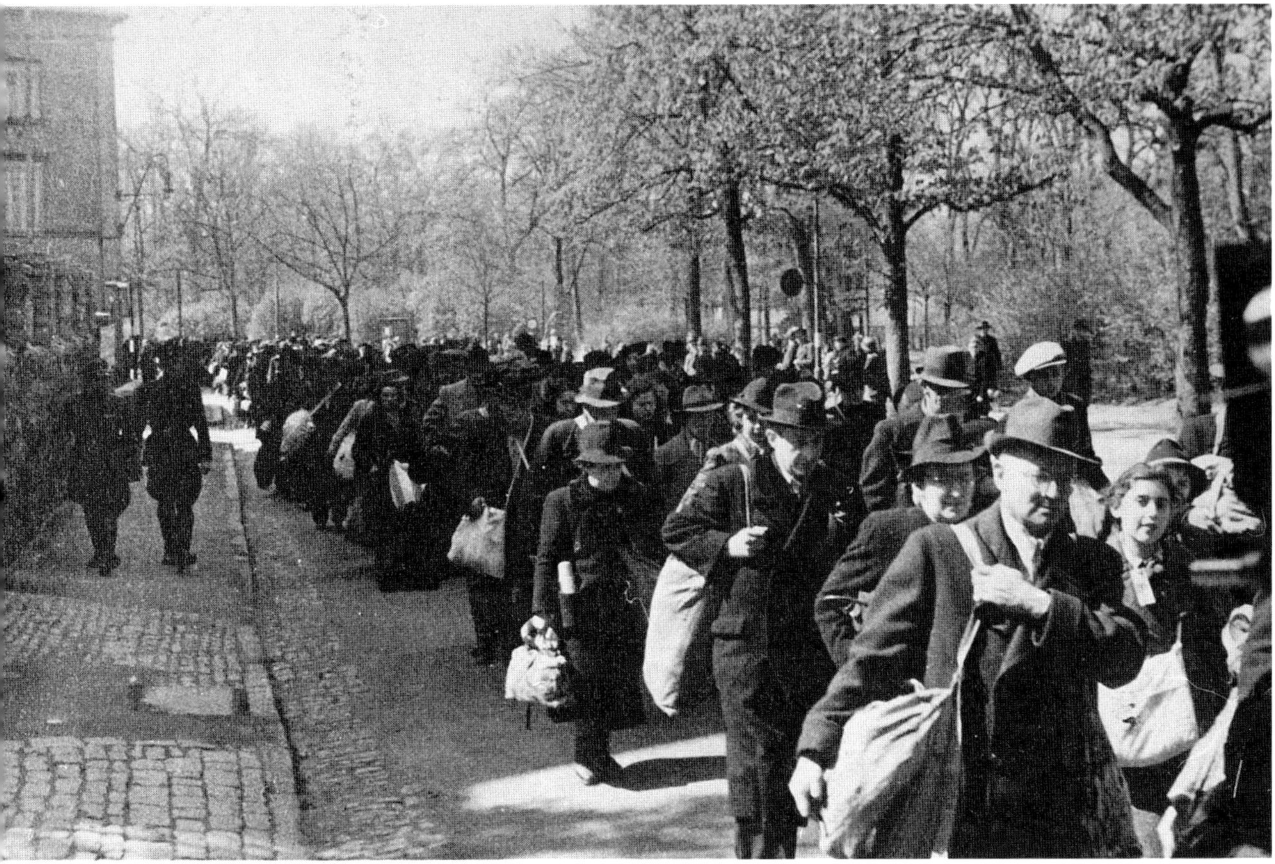

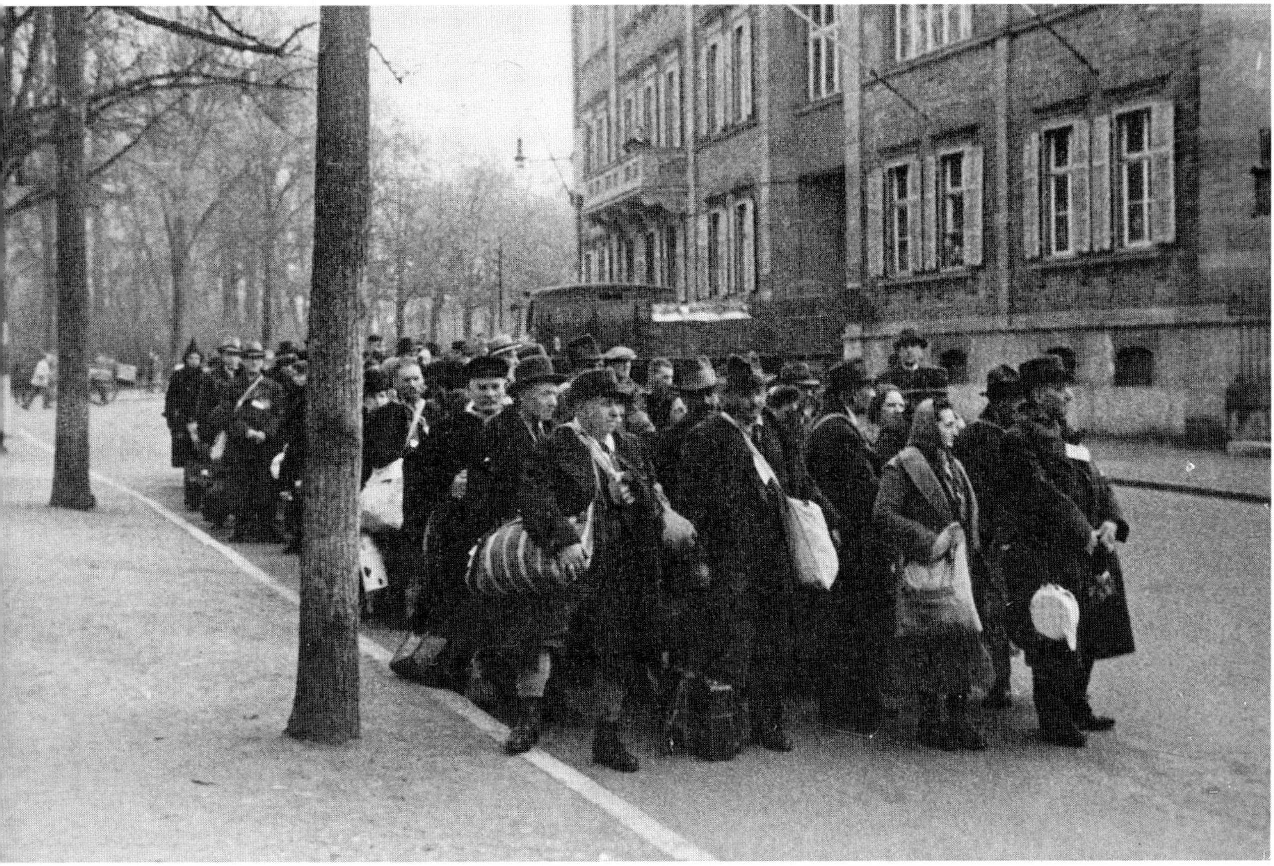

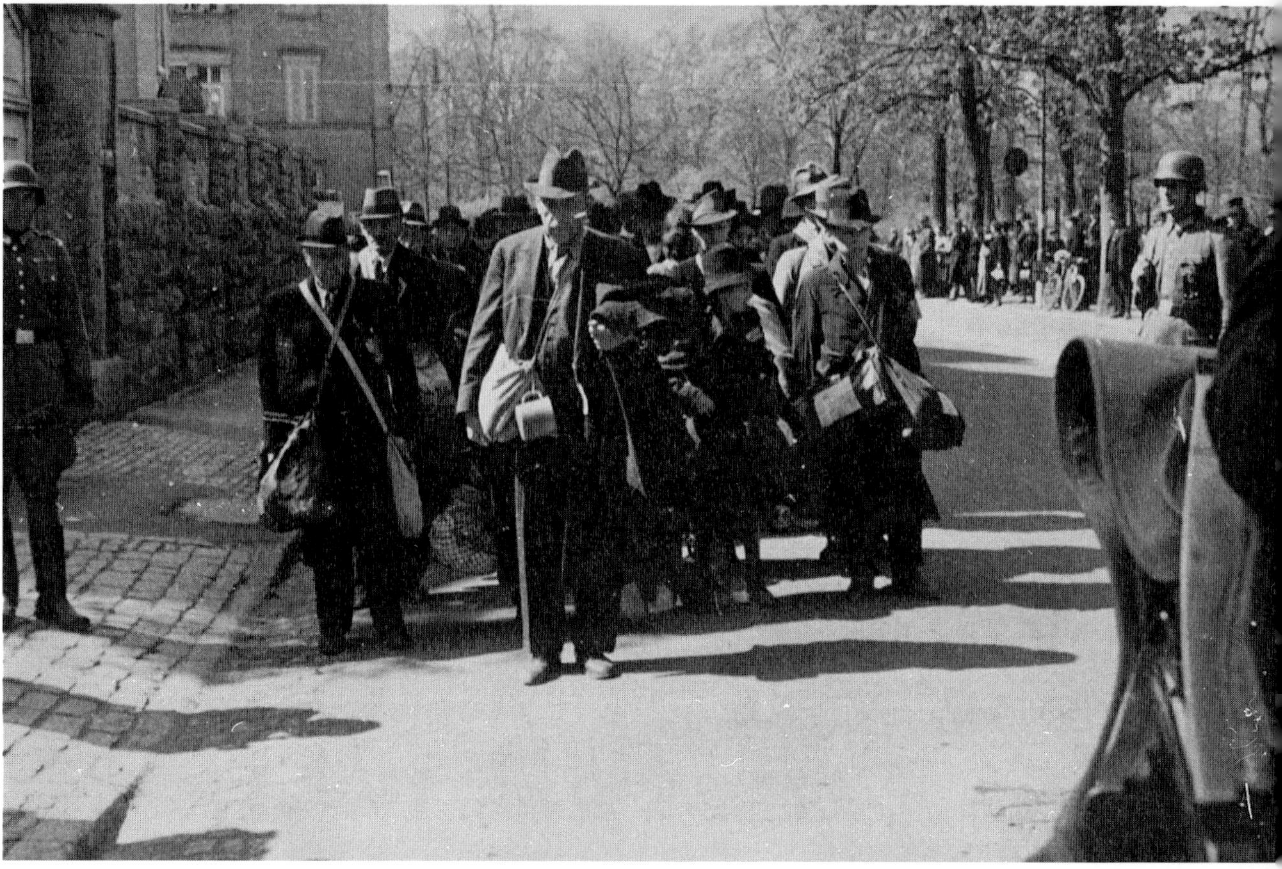

The children of captured Yugoslavian partisans from Celje, who were forcibly separated from their parents, arriving in Frohnleiten, Austria on their way to the Reich. *(USHMM)*

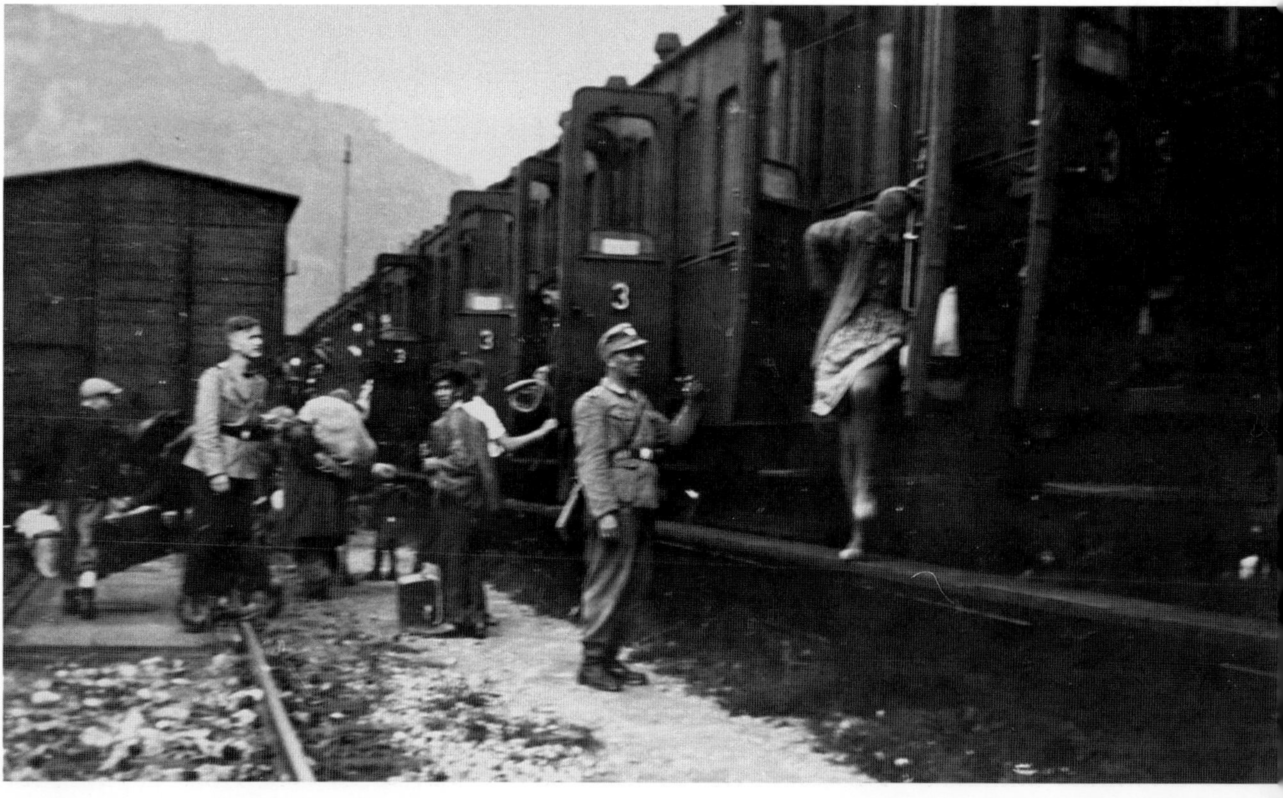

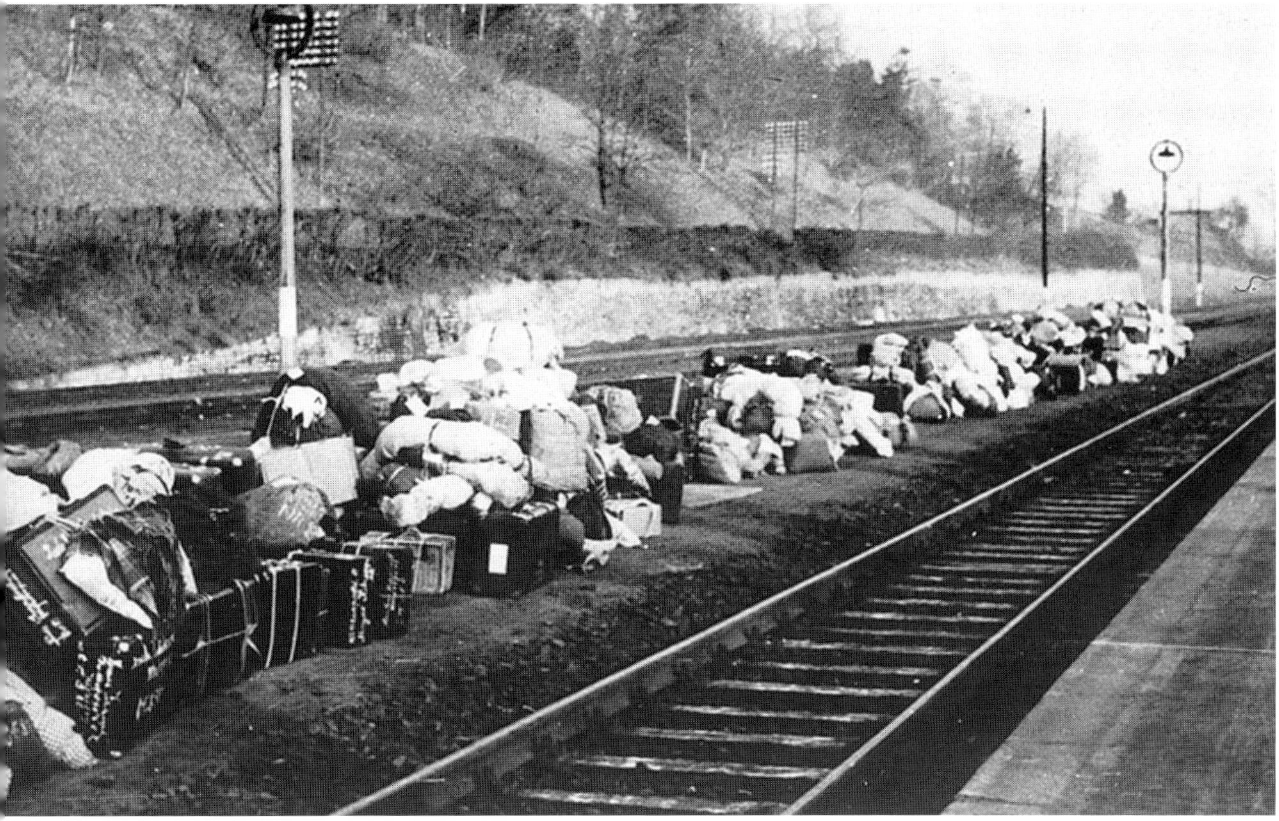

Two photographs taken on 24 March 1942. Note the bundles of possessions left behind at the Kitzingen railway station from the Würzburg deportation action. These images are part of a photograph album of the Jews of Mainfranken (part of Lower Franconia). *(USHMM)*

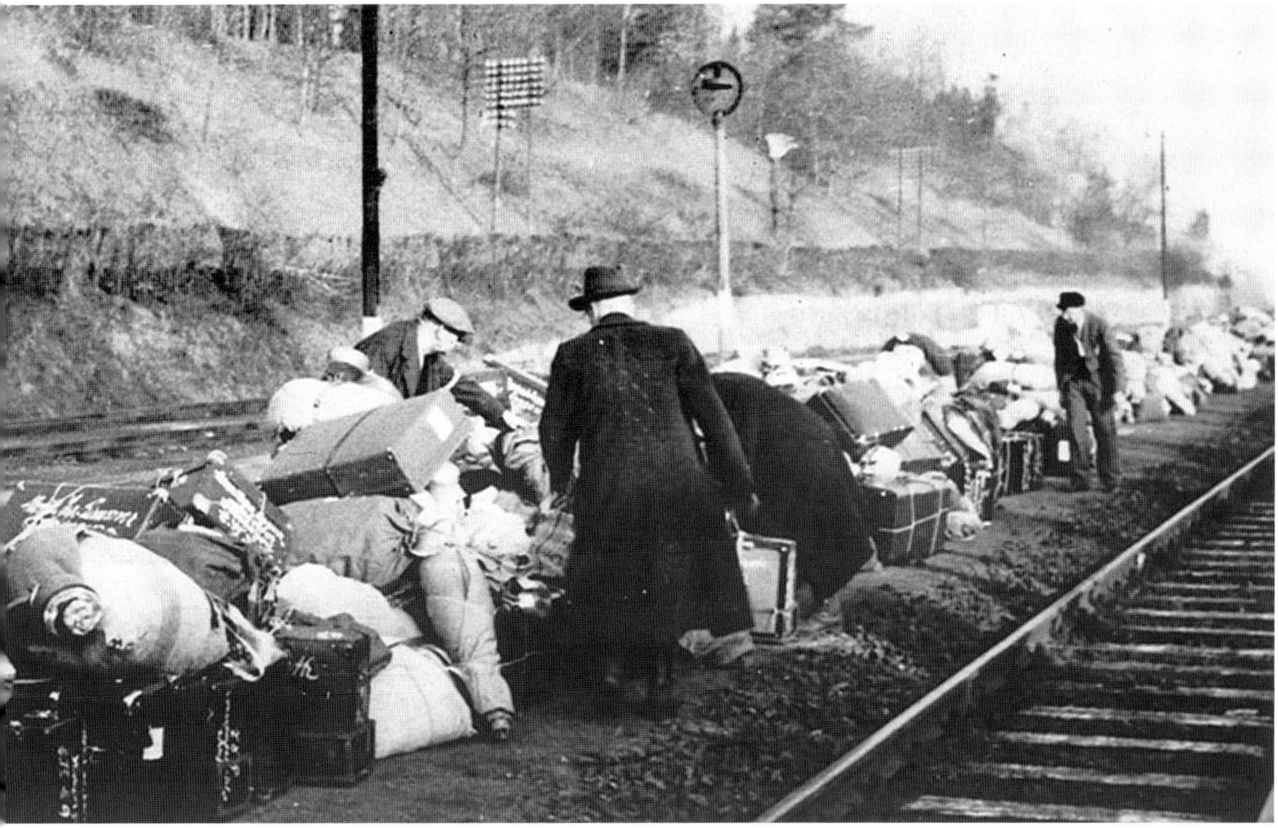

(**Above**) Jews carrying suitcases and baskets are rounded up for deportation from Zrenjanin, Serbia. In the summer of 1941 German authorities in Serbia began a mass deportation action of Jewish men in Serbia. Those from northern Serbia were sent to the Topovske Šupe concentration camp in Belgrade. From there they were removed in groups and executed. Late that year, Jewish women and children of Serbia were rounded up and transported to the Sajmište camp in Belgrade, where most were killed in mobile gas vans between March and May 1942. (*USHMM*)

(**Opposite, above**) An image showing the deportation of Jews from Marseilles during the early-morning hours of 24 January 1943 at the Gare d'Arenc railway station. The deportation of French Jews began in 1942, lasted until July 1944 and was conducted by German and French policemen. Of the 340,000 Jews living in metropolitan/continental France in 1940, more than 75,000 were deported to death camps where about 72,500 were murdered. The first deportation action began on 27 March 1942, when the first convoy by train left Paris for Auschwitz. Four months later 13,000 Jews were arrested by French police, which was known as the 'Vel' d'Hiv Round-Up', and sent by train to internment camps. (*USHMM*)

(**Opposite, below**) Dutch Jews board the train that will take them to Auschwitz. The first deportations from to Auschwitz-Birkenau, which was still in its infancy of evolving into a mass killing centre, began on 15 July 1942 when 1,135 Dutch Jews were transported east. By the end of July, more than 6,000 had been transported to the camp. However, in order to process such large numbers efficiently and quickly, a main railway line was constructed that ran directly into Westerbork to assist deportations to Auschwitz-Birkenau, Bergen-Belsen, Theresienstadt, Vittel and Sobibor. More than 103,000 Jews were deported to Auschwitz-Birkenau from Holland and only 5,000 survived.

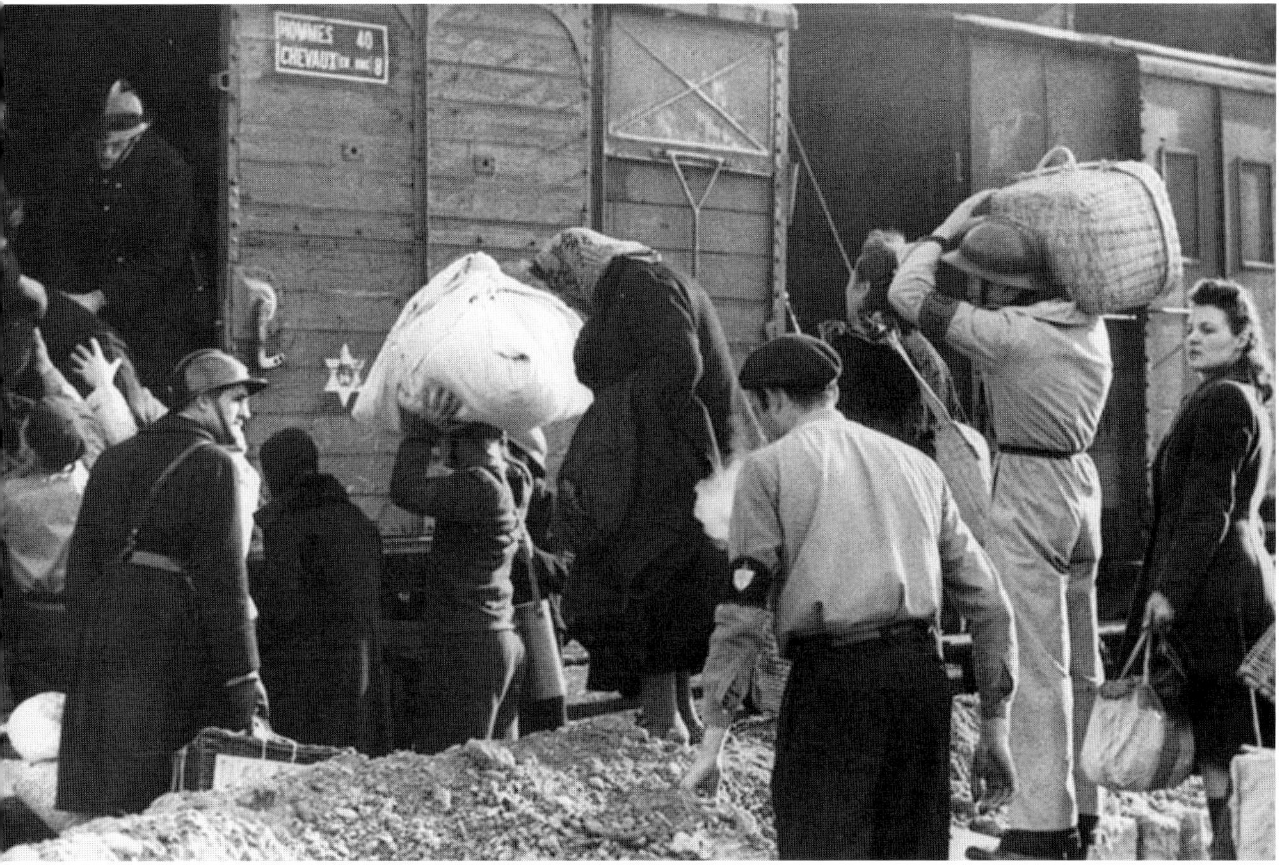
HOMMES 40
CHEVAUX 8

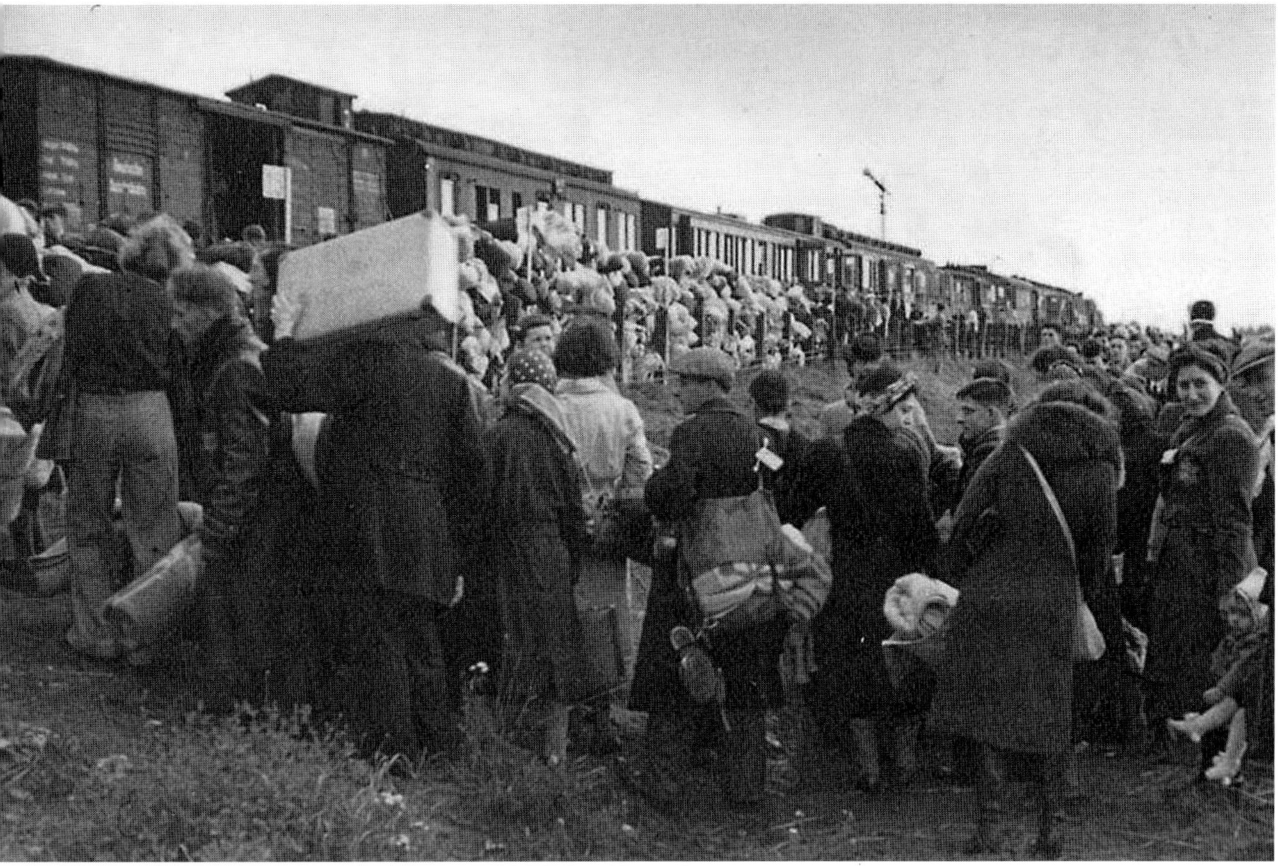

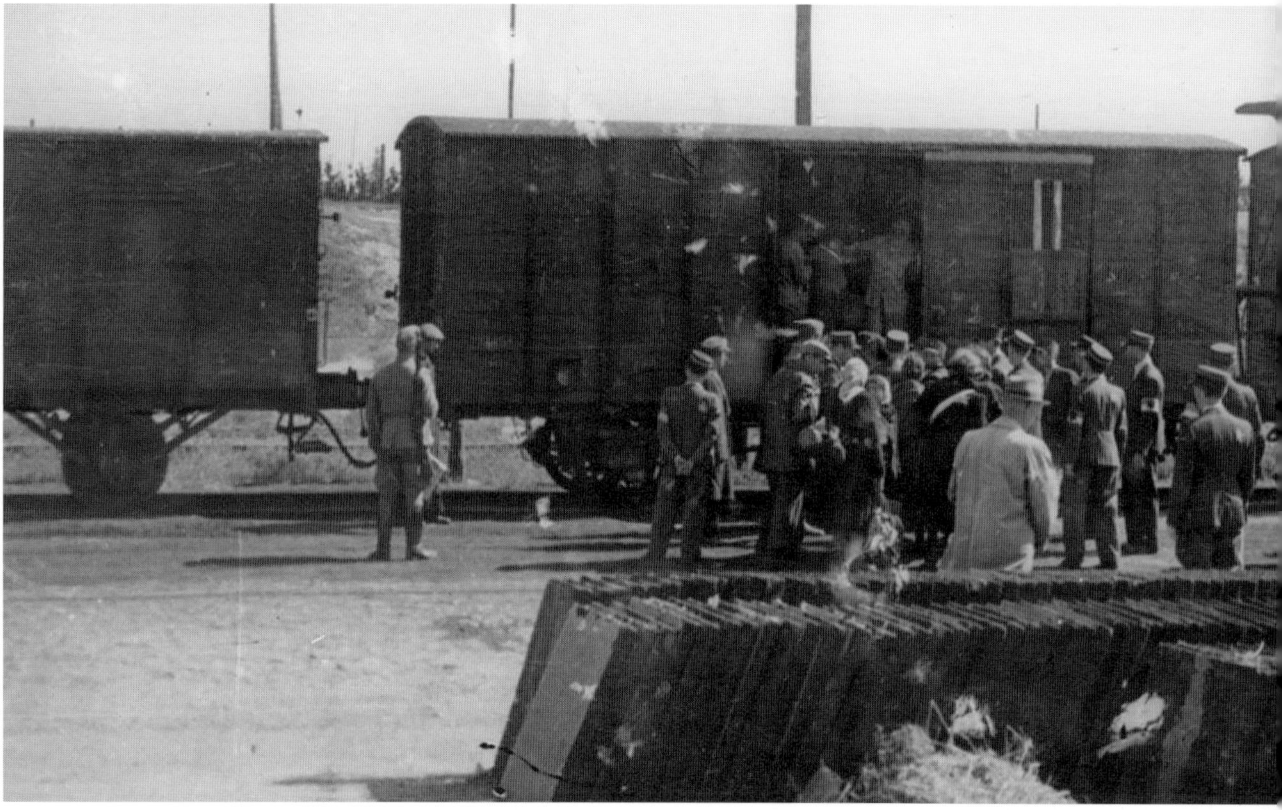

The deportation by train of Jews from the Lodz Ghetto in August 1944. From January to May 1942, 55,000 out of 160,000 Jews from Lodz were sent to their deaths in Chelmno death camp. *(Yad Vashem Photo Archives, 35BO3)*

An SS officer overseeing supplies being removed from a boxcar in 1943. Across Europe while Jews were being transported by train to the various camps, maintaining army supply lines with food, armaments, ammunitions, vehicles, spare parts and the transportation of troops themselves were of the utmost importance. Often rail timetables for the shipment of Jews had to be planned around military transport, which was often a logistical nightmare. *(NARA)*

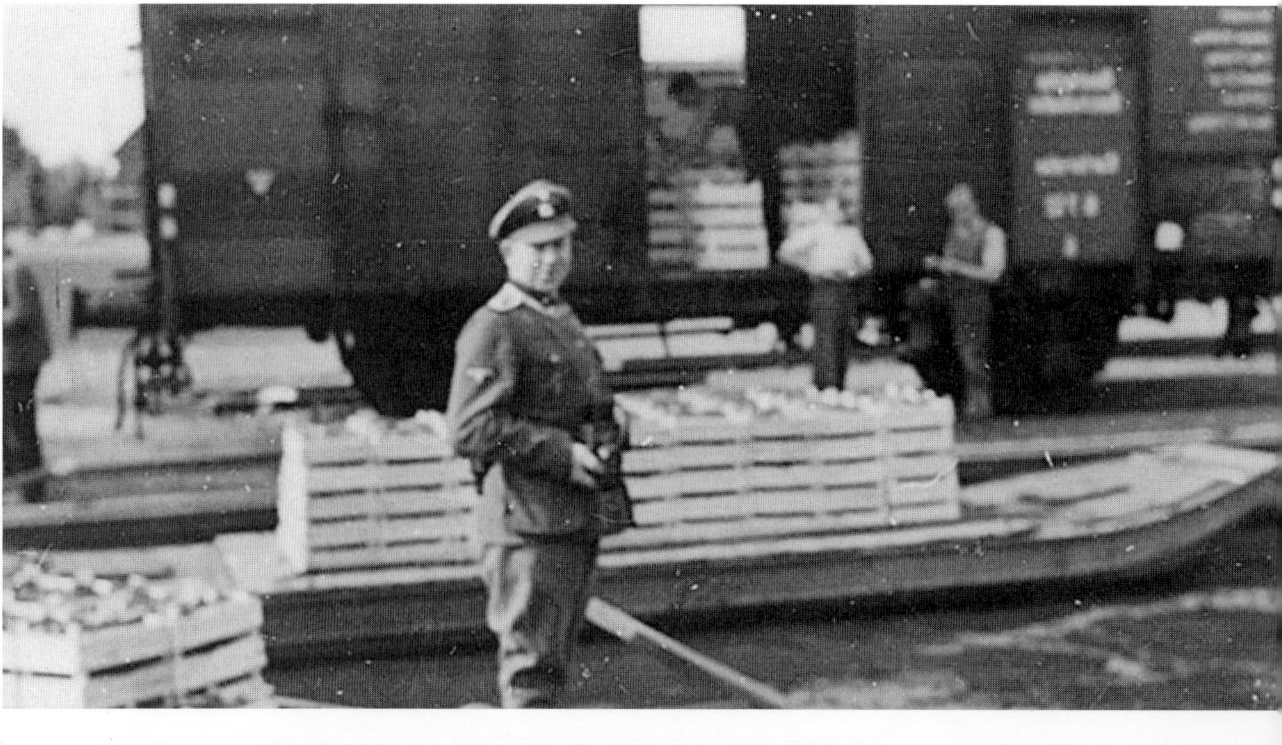

Chapter Six

Hungarian Transports

With death camps like Chełmno, Sobibor, Belzec and Treblinka now closed down, it was up to the other camps, in particular Auschwitz-Birkenau, to take responsibility for the remnants of the Jewish communities of Poland, France, the Netherlands, Italy and the rest of occupied Europe. Over the coming weeks and months hundreds of trains made various journeys across Europe to Auschwitz-Birkenau, but there was one country in particular with a large contingent of Jews wanted by the Nazis: Hungary.

For some time the German Foreign Office had been badgering the Hungarian government to toughen its anti-Jewish laws. According to reports from Eichmann's office there were almost 725,000 Jews on Hungarian territory, and for the German government that figure was too great an opportunity to resist. When the German occupation forces rolled across into Hungary on 19 March 1944 they were followed by an advance party of the *Sonder Einsatzkommando* [Special Forces Command] and Eichmann with 140 trucks and command vehicles. On 21 March Eichmann was assigned temporary living quarters in the Hotel Majestic in the Schwabenberg district of Budapest. It would be from here that Eichmann would direct the fate of thousands of Hungarian Jews.

Himmler now wanted the Hungarian Jews transported to Auschwitz where they would be selected for slave labour and shipped out again through the various concentration camps that served the German industry. Those that were selected for labour would be held in quarantine until transport was made readily available to them. In effect, the *Reichsführer* was planning to turn Auschwitz into a huge labour exchange, just as he had done with the main camp in 1940, but now it was on a greater scale than ever before. The Auschwitz authorities were informed that they were to prepare for a huge assignment of Hungarian Jews. They were also told that more of an effort was to be made to separate those Jews who could serve the German war effort through work, but were to continue to use 'special treatment' on those that served absolutely no purpose for the Reich. Eichmann, who was in charge of transporting the Hungarian Jews directly to Auschwitz, began negotiating with the Hungarian police and helped organize the so-called ghettoization of the Jewish population in Hungary. In a meeting held with Höss, Eichmann boastfully said that his job had been made much easier because of the Hungarian government's willingness to cast out their Jewish compatriots so easily, but despite the readiness of the Hungarian government to remove the Jews from their country, the operation was by no means an easy feat to achieve. It would take some considerable time to organize, so it was very important to reassure the Jewish community that nothing too bad was going to happen to them.

Eichmann confirmed that deportation plans had been made and the trains carrying more than 3,000 Jews each day would start arriving in Auschwitz sometime in May 1944. The task, he said, was on an immense scale and because of the huge amount of rolling stock required, every effort had been made to ensure that it would avoid disrupting the war effort. For this reason no Jews from Budapest would be transported to Auschwitz in the first wave. He hoped to deliver more than 760,000 Jews, almost 5 per cent of the population, to Auschwitz during the summer but realistically expected slightly less than that exaggerated figure. The operation would be undertaken with the full co-operation of Hungarian railway officials who ran the Hungarian State Railway.

For the operation Höss was officially charged with preparing the massive influx of Hungarian Jews to Auschwitz. During late April and early May Höss made a number of visits to Budapest where he consulted with Eichmann in preparation for the shipments to Auschwitz. Höss and Eichmann also met Hungarian railway officials. They agreed that on alternate days two trains of deportees, then three trains, should be dispatched. The agreement with railway officials in Budapest provided a total of 111 trains for the Hungarian operation. It was discussed and planned that for the first transports of deported Hungarian Jews, Eichmann would travel back to Birkenau for an inspection of the extermination facilities to ensure they would be run properly. To conceal the vast number of prisoners that arrived at the camp's ramps and were selected from the transports to be sent directly to the gas chambers, two new series of numerals for Jewish prisoners beginning with A-1 – one each for men and women, and later a series beginning with B-1 for men only – would be adopted. It was agreed that from the mass transports of Hungarian Jews, only the young, healthy and strong of both sexes were to be selected for work detail. Due to the workload process of selection, the prisoners used for labour could not be recorded in the camp registers.

The first transport of Hungarian Jews consisting of 1,800 people arrived in Birkenau on 2 May 1944. The first selection recorded that two transports had arrived from Hungary: the first sent from Budapest on 29 April and comprising approximately 1,800 able-bodied Jewish men and women between the ages of 16 and 50; the second sent on 30 April from Topolya and containing 2,000 able-bodied prisoners. The Jews were ordered to unload their luggage and told to stand in rows of five. They were selected and those unfit for work were led in the direction of the crematoria. After the first selection, 486 men given Nos 186645 to 187130 and 616 women given Nos 76385 to 76459 and 80000 to 80540 were admitted to the camp. The remaining 2,698 men and women were killed in the gas chambers.

In order to assist in the smooth arrival of the Hungarian Jews and to provide a direct link between the Auschwitz station and the crematoria the train lines were extended through the main entrance of Birkenau with plans to run them right up to Crematoria II and III. Night and day hundreds of prisoners had been busy laying the three-way railway track through the camp and constructing the loading and unloading ramps. By the second week of May the railway line was completed and the finishing touches were made to the ramps. From these ramps Höss would then coordinate the destruction of the Hungarian Jews, code-named *Aktion Höss*. Once they arrived, the train pulled over the new spur through the gate into Birkenau and halted at the ramps. Here at the ramps *Aktion Höss* was put into operation; first the unloading of the Jews from the boxcars. Once the Jews were unloaded, they were immediately separated into two columns for selection.

By 28 May, it had been reported that some 184,049 Jews had arrived in Auschwitz in fifty-eight trains. Two weeks later on 13 June the German Foreign Ministry was notified that the deportation of Jews from the areas of Carpathia and Siebenbürgen, known as Zones I and II, had been completed. A total of 289,357 Jews had been deported in ninety-two trains, each of which consisted of forty-five cars. The concentration of Jews from the area north of Budapest, known as Zone III, was completed on 10 June. More transports were being prepared between 11 and 16 June in twenty-one trains. Some 67,000 deportees would be shipped directly to Auschwitz. In Zone IV, east of the Danube River, plans were put together for the deportation of almost 45,000 Jews between 25 and 28 June.

Between 16 May and 13 June more than 300,000 Hungarian Jews were delivered to the camp on 113 trains. However, due to logistical problems from 13 June there was a pause of several days in the transports of Hungarian Jews to Auschwitz. When the shipments resumed, in addition there was a transport of 2,500 French Jews, 1,500 Italian Jews and two transports of 50 Czech Jews. There were also 100 English and American citizens of Jewish descent delivered. During this period of mass shipments via rail 4,500 prisoners – among them 2,900 Poles and 1,600 Russians from the Auschwitz main camp – were transported and killed.

Over a period of 56 days, some 437,402 Jews were deported from Hungary in 147 trains. The majority of the transports were handed over by the Hungarian authorities to the Germans at Kassa. The head of the Kassa railway station collected a list of the trains that passed through the station. According to the Kassa list, the Germans transported more than 400,426 Jews in 137 trains from the Hungarian gendarmes at Kassa.

There were also transport lists compiled by the German rail officials detailing the transports between May and August 1944. The trains listed show that they arrived at

Auschwitz every day except for two periods: one of these was from 16 to 25 June when the Strasshof trains started, and the other interruption to the transports arriving was from 11 to 22 July when the Hungarian action was almost completed.

Following the deportation of some 438,000 Hungarian Jews to Auschwitz-Birkenau in the summer of 1944, it is reported that only 10 per cent were used for slave labour, while the remainder were all murdered in the gas chambers. By the end of July Eichmann confirmed to government officials in Budapest that the deportations to Auschwitz-Birkenau were to be suspended and the operation was to end. Yet there were still Hungarian Jews that had not been deported to Poland. Following a number of meetings with a delegation in Budapest, Eichmann, obsessed by the removal of the Hungarian Jews, made preparations in late September to transport the remaining Jews to Auschwitz. Even as the Soviet army approached Hungary and plans were being made to fortify the city against a Russian attack, Eichmann was determined to complete his operation. The new Hungarian government under the control of Ferenc Szálasi, the leader of the fascist and radically anti-Semitic Arrow Cross Party, was more than willing to assist Eichmann. However, in October Russian forces entered Hungary and the 35,000 Jews rounded up for Auschwitz were used for slave labour instead. The remaining 160,000 Jews in Budapest suffered at the hands of the Arrow Cross, with some 20,000 dying during the winter from cold, hunger, disease and the heavy Russian bombardment.

(**Opposite, above**) The deportation of Jews from Hungary being sent to Auschwitz during the summer of 1944. More than 6,300 Hungarian Jews had boarded the first two transports from the ghettos of Nyiregyhaza and Munkács. This first major transport steamed its way through to Auschwitz on 15 May 1944, arriving the next day ahead of schedule because the journey had been unhindered by local partisans or by enemy aircraft. The deportation schedule was for three or four trains each day. The victims were loaded at seventy to ninety per boxcar with two buckets – one filled with water and the other empty – for excrement. Each train was accompanied and guarded by Hungarian gendarmes until their arrival in Kassa, where they were replaced by SS personnel.

(**Opposite, below**) A photograph of a boxcar destined for Auschwitz-Birkenau.

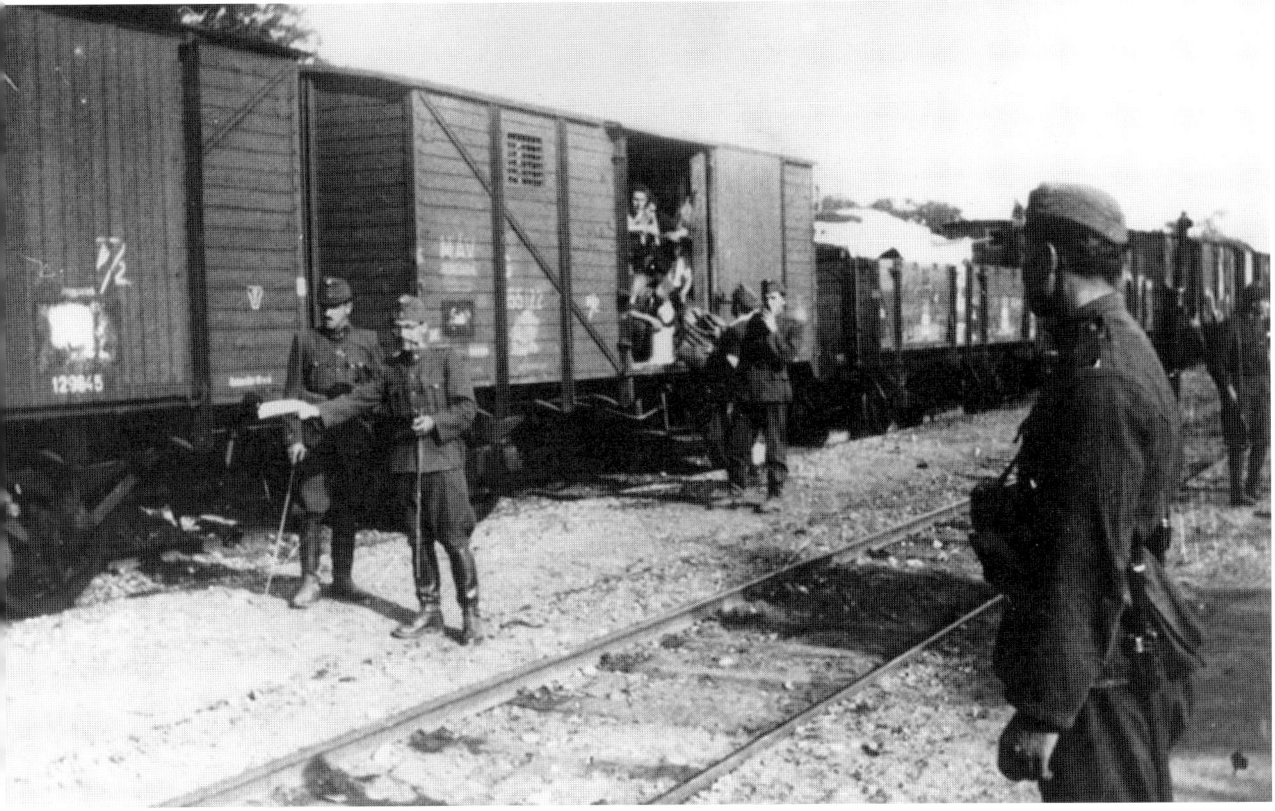

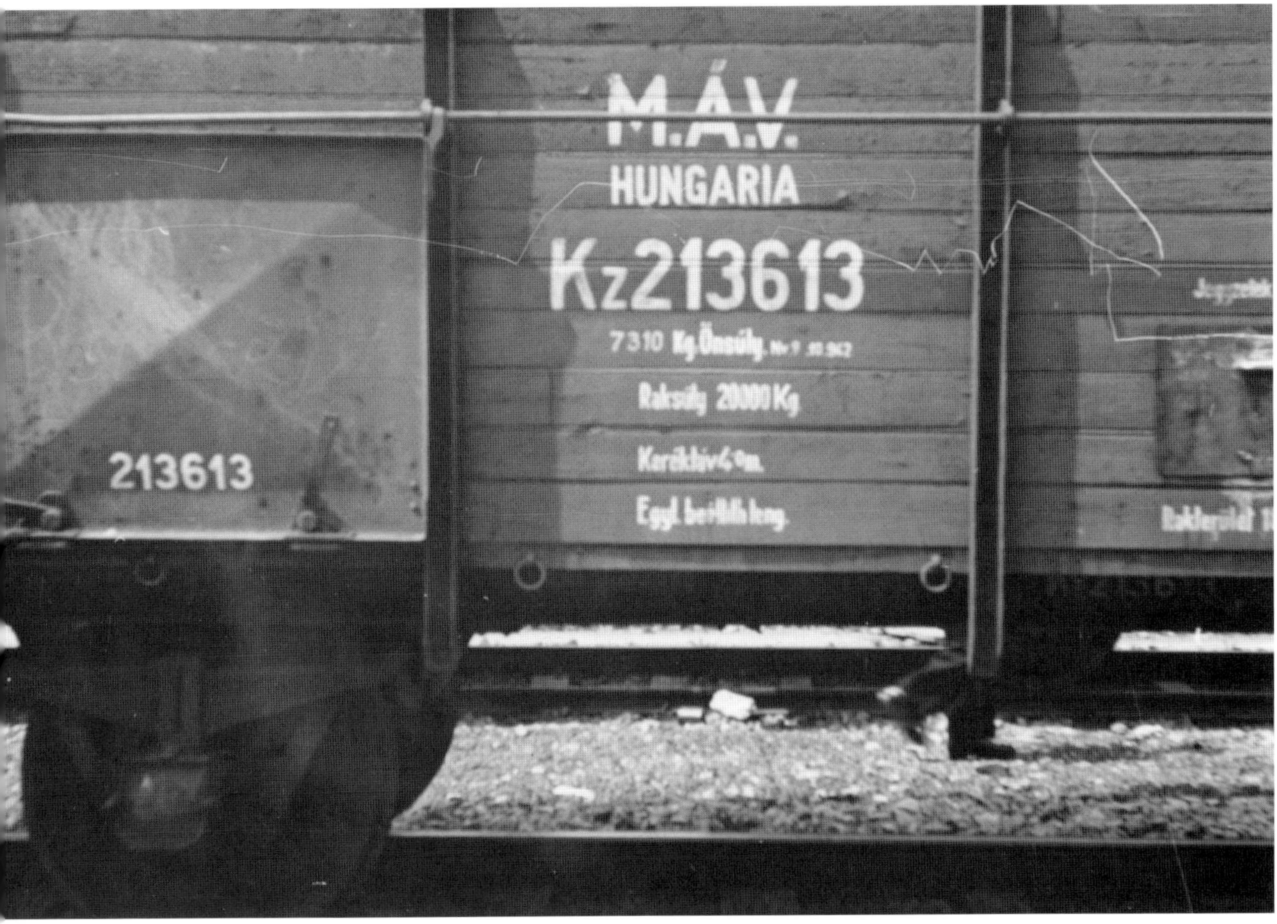
M.Á.V.
HUNGARIA
Kz213613
Raksúly 20000 Kg
213613

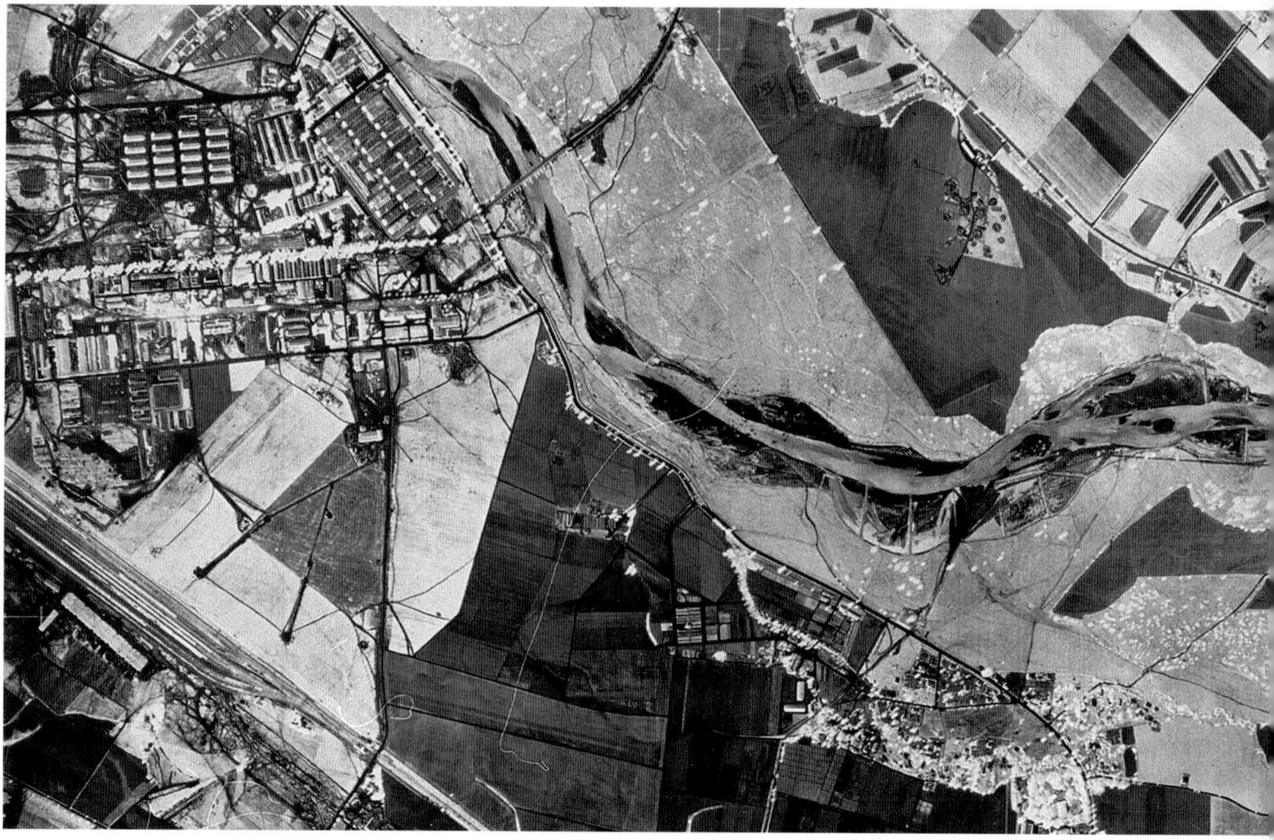

Two photographs showing an aerial reconnaissance photograph of the Auschwitz I camp showing the barracks, administration buildings and main railway yard. *(USHMM)*

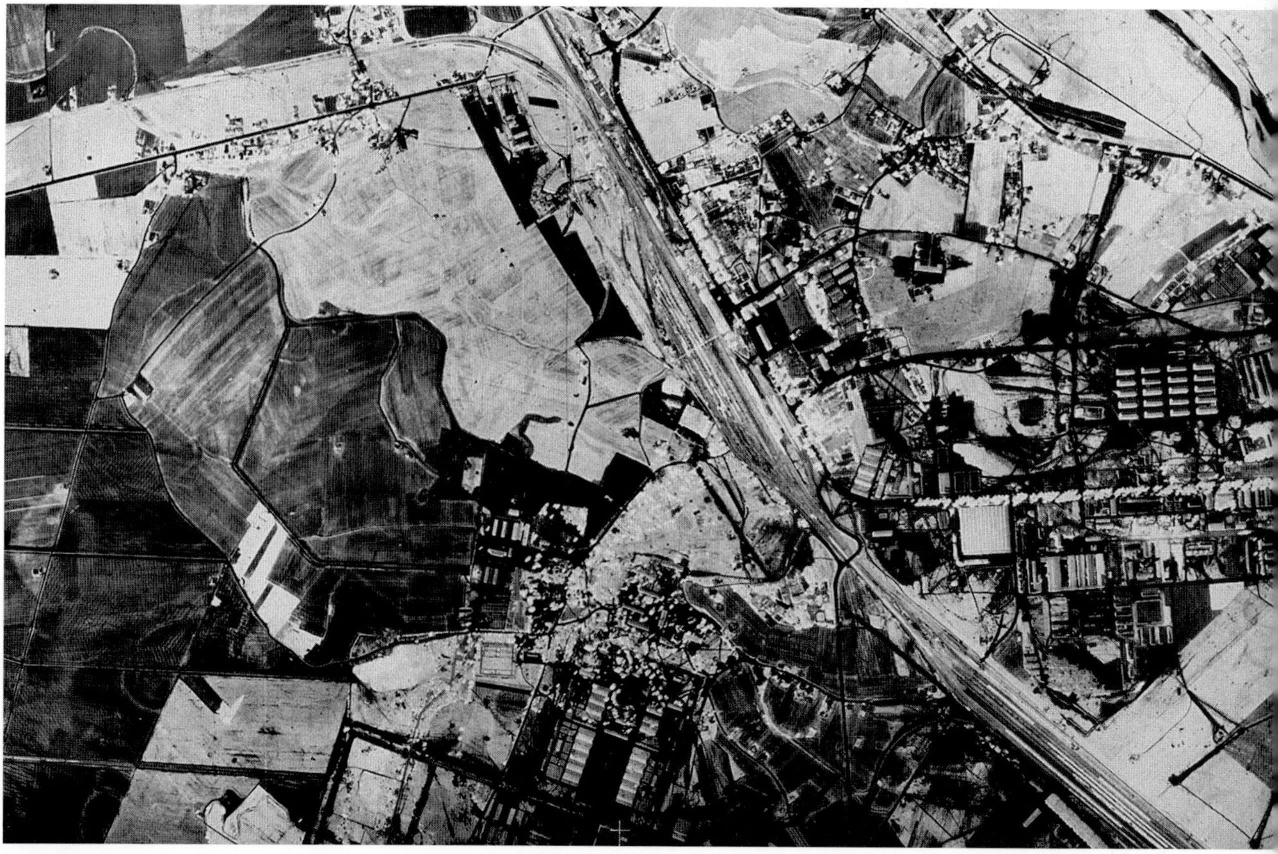

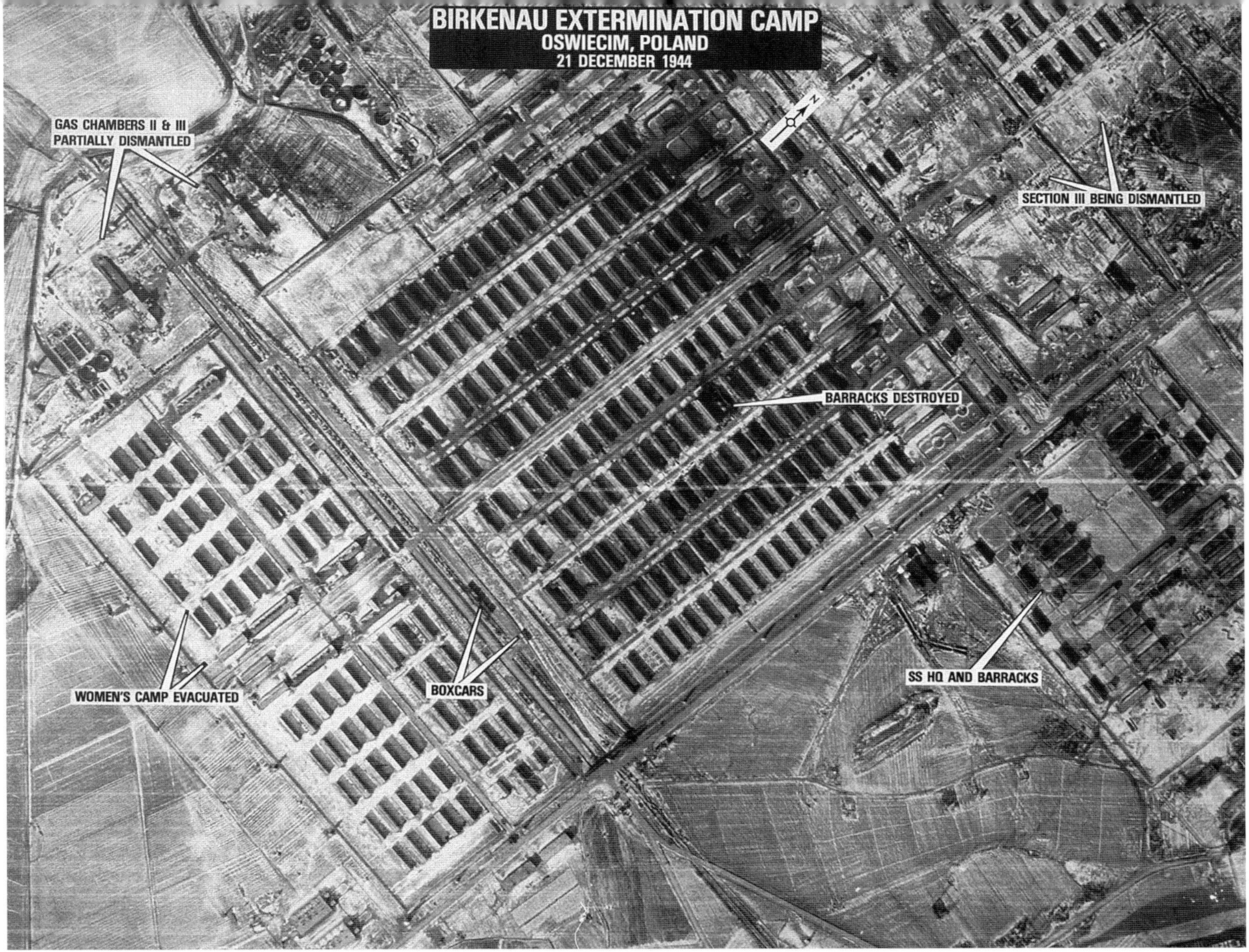
BIRKENAU EXTERMINATION CAMP
OSWIECIM, POLAND
21 DECEMBER 1944
N
GAS CHAMBERS II & III
PARTIALLY DISMANTLED
SECTION III BEING DISMANTLED
BARRACKS DESTROYED
SS HQ AND BARRACKS
BOXCARS
WOMEN'S CAMP EVACUATED

An aerial reconnaissance photograph of the Auschwitz-Birkenau concentration camp. Note the railway line into the camp and the boxcars. (*USHMM*)

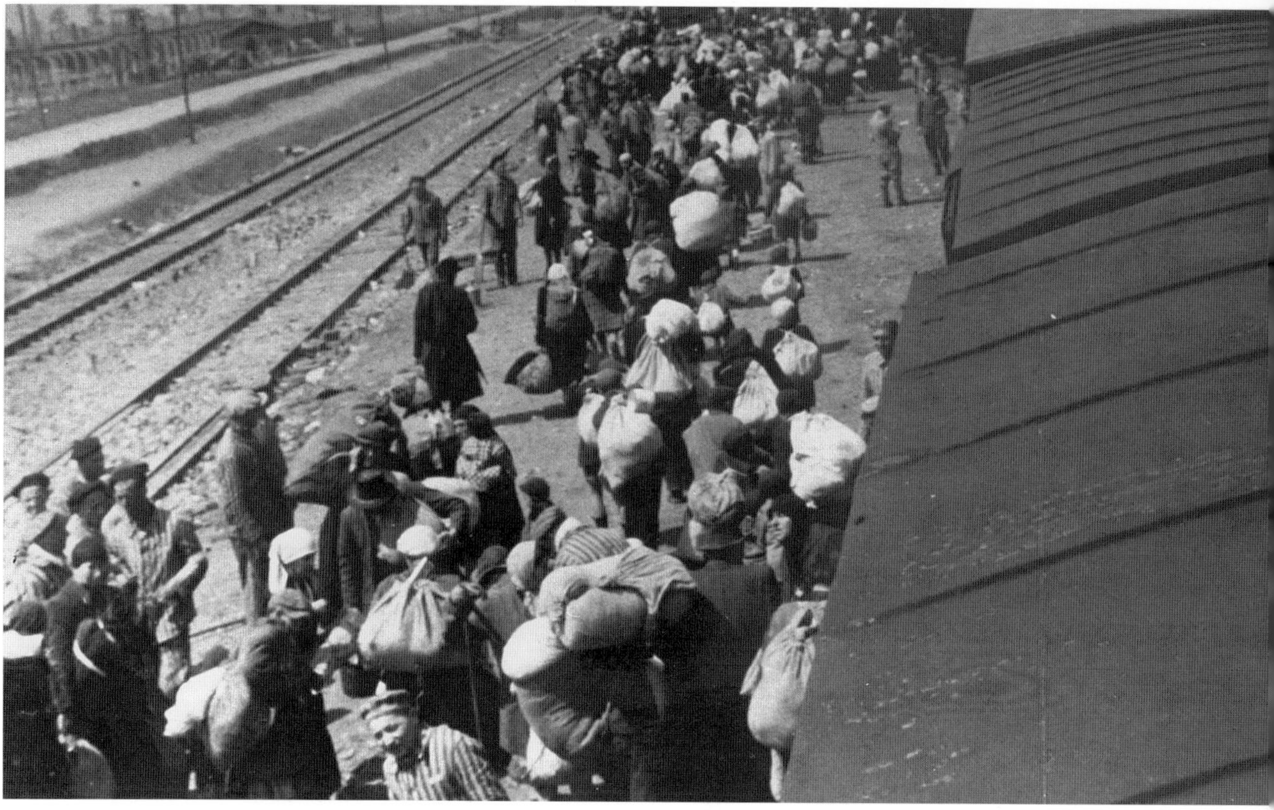

Two photographs taken in sequence showing the mass debarkation of Jewish men women and children, all holding onto their bundles of belongings. The journey to the camp could often last for days with appalling sanitary conditions. Although there was widespread relief on arrival, the stress and fear of what would happen to them can only be imagined. Note in the distance from left to right are Crematoria II and III. *(Yad Vashem/Auschwitz-Birkenau Museum)*

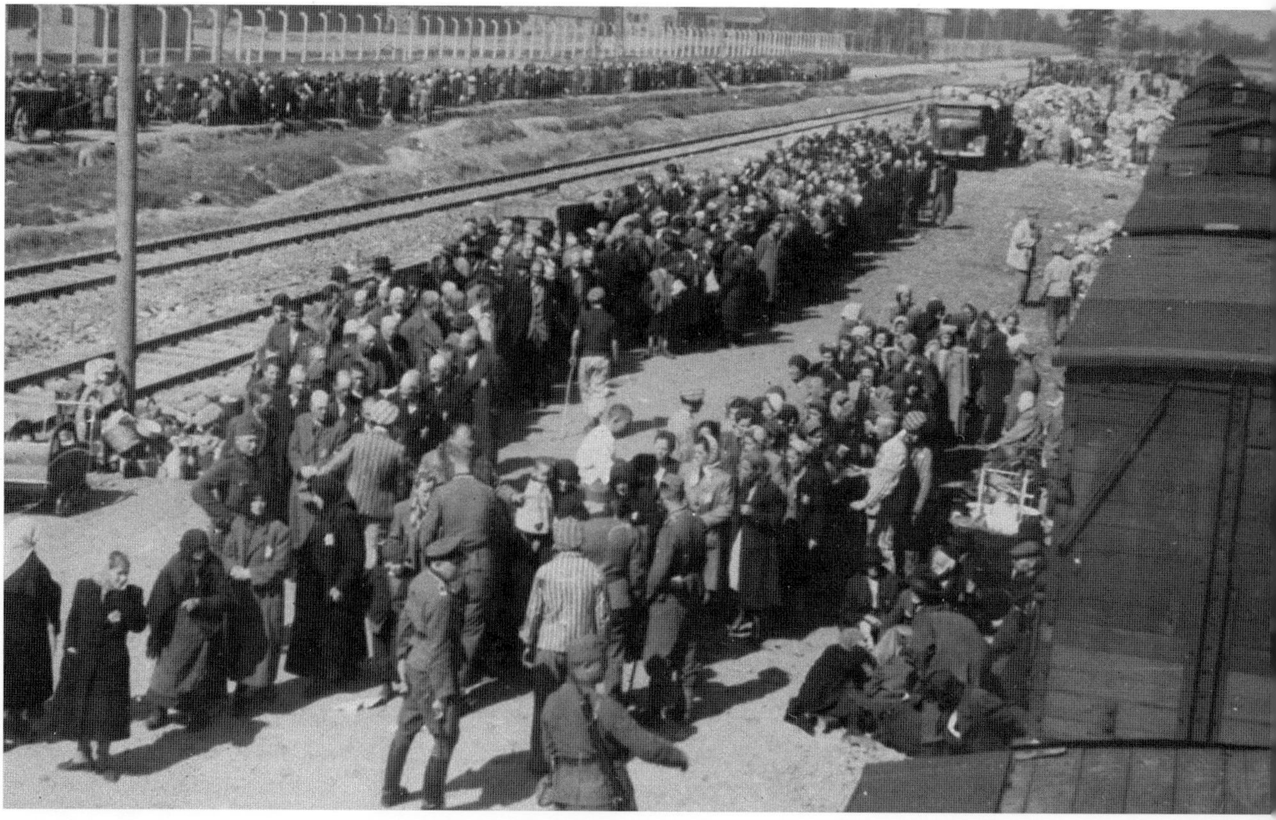

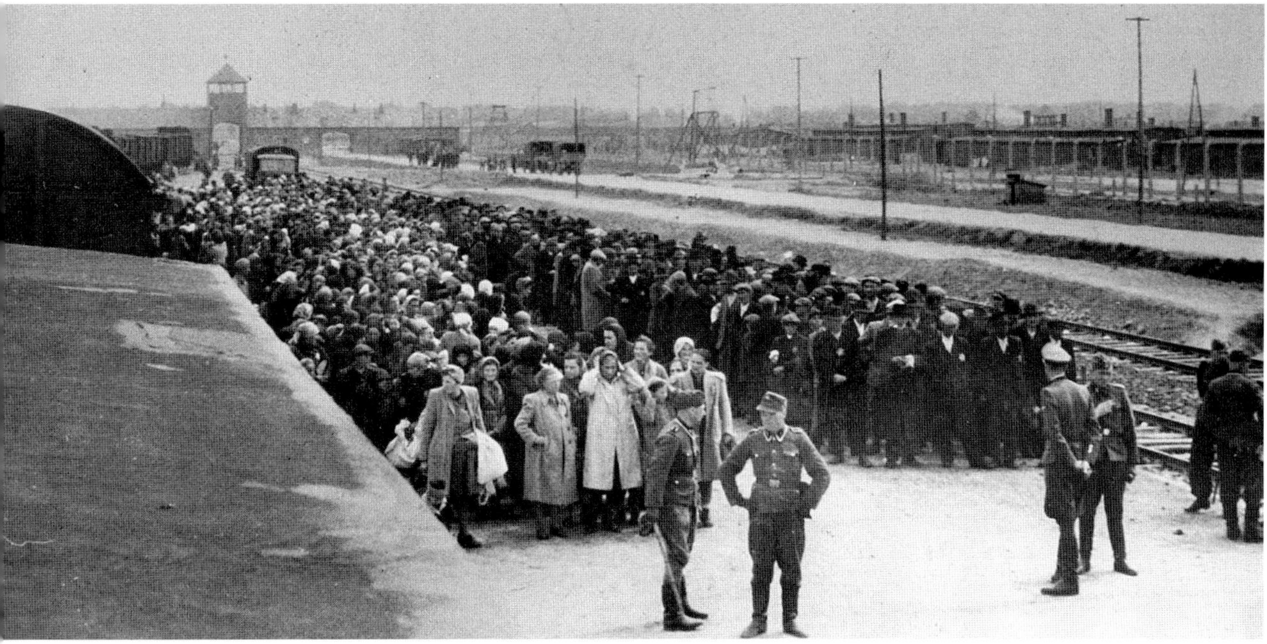

A photograph showing Jews separating into columns following their arrival. Once they were unloaded onto the ramps they were immediately separated into two columns: one of women and children; the other of men. A selection was then carried out by one or two SS doctors and the two columns were divided into four columns: two of women and children, and two of men. Those unfit for labour were sent straight ahead towards the crematoria, while all able-bodied workers were interned in Auschwitz or were retained, ready at a moment's notice to be transferred to other camps in the Reich. The selection for labour in each transport varied; sometimes it was as low as 10 per cent or as high as 50 per cent, but the majority of Jews that arrived through the gates of Birkenau were immediately sent to their deaths. There were around 3,300 people per day arriving, and sometimes that figure rose to 4,300. *(USHMM)*

Following the selection of the new arrivals camp personnel walk along the ramp before the last of the belongings are cleared and taken to the Canada Stores. Note in the distance Crematoria II on the left and Crematoria III on the right.

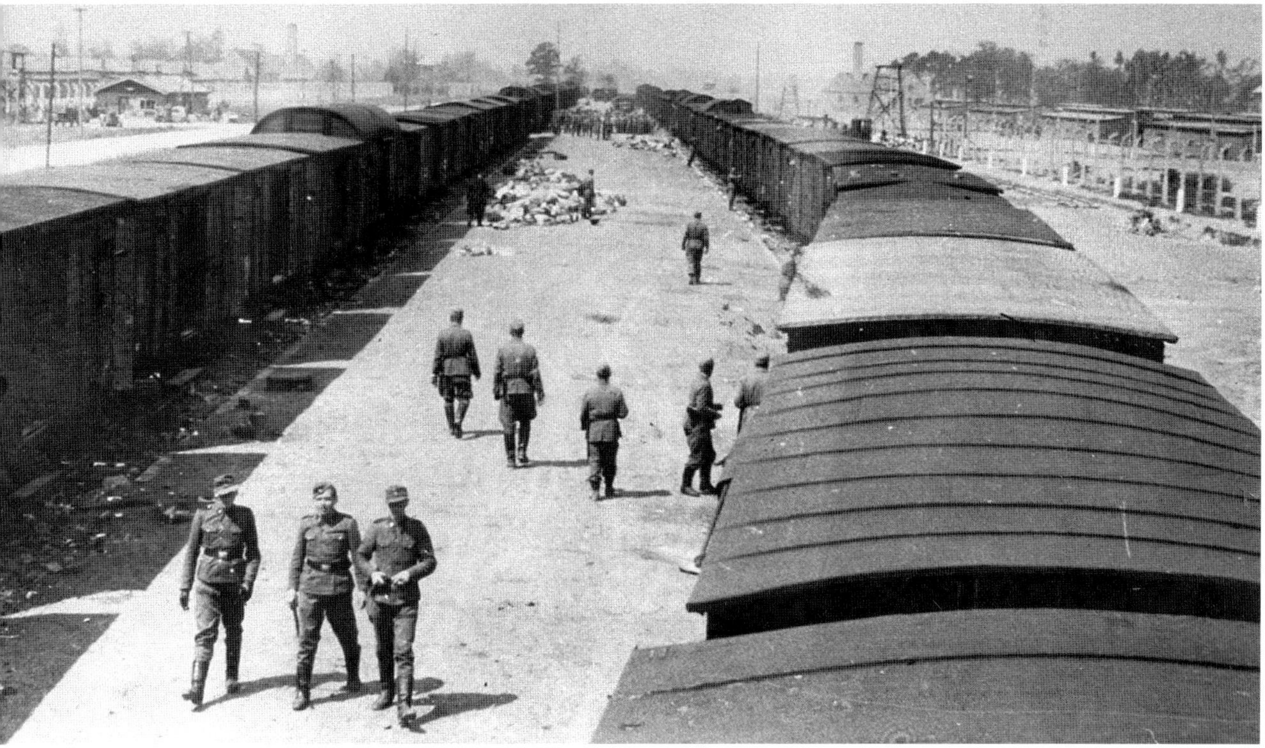

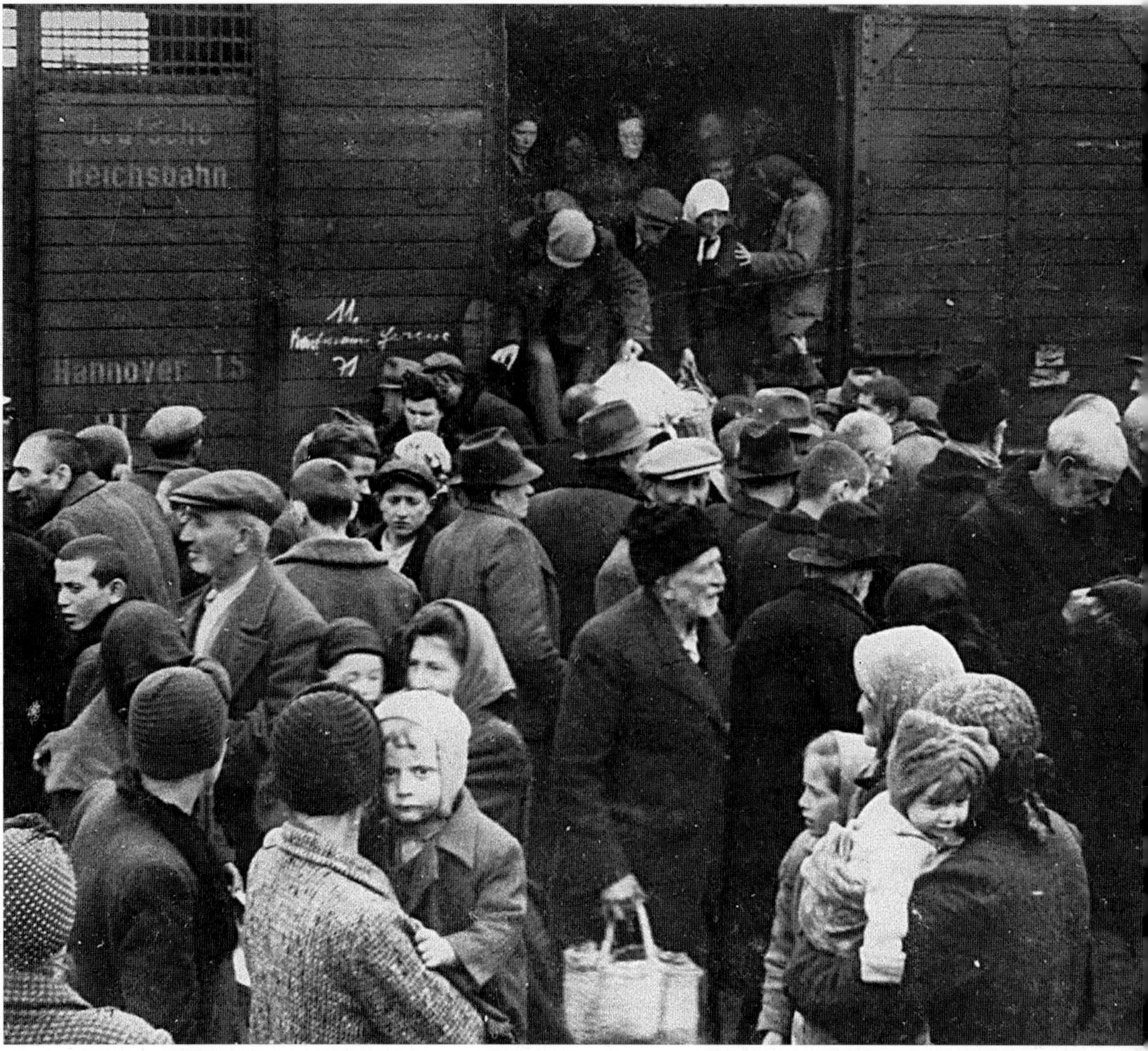
Reichsbahn
Hannover 15

(**Above**) A transport of Jews from Subcarpathian Rus are taken off the trains and assembled on the ramp at Auschwitz-Birkenau. *(USHMM)*

(**Opposite, above**) A throng of men, women and children are seen here after disembarking from their transport. *(USHMM)*

(**Opposite, below**) Jewish people can be seen here disembarking from the cattle cars at Birkenau. Mothers are seen with their children walking along the ramp for selection. This was known as the 'third ramp', was built inside Birkenau and went into operation in May 1944. It was built purely in connection with the anticipated arrival of transports of Hungarian Jews. *(USHMM)*

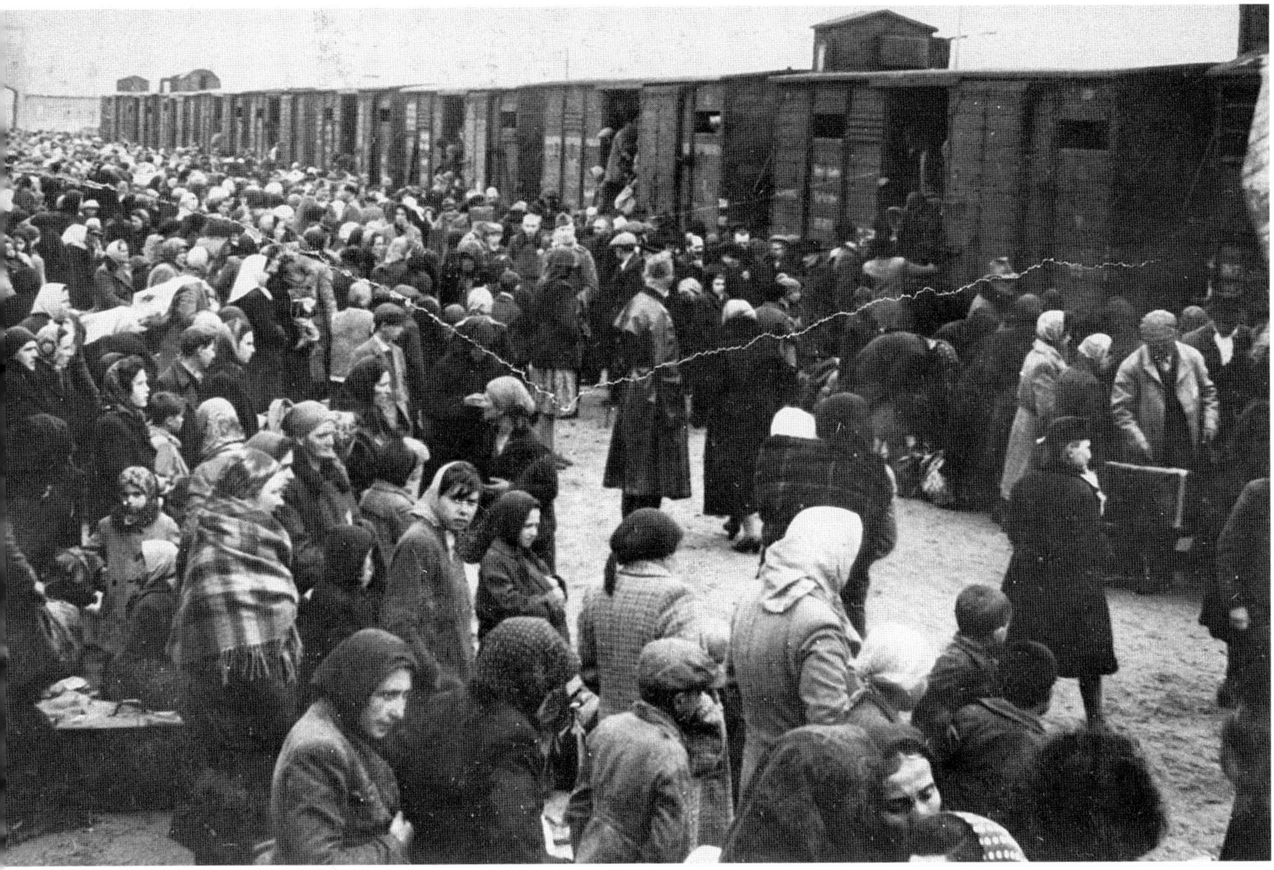

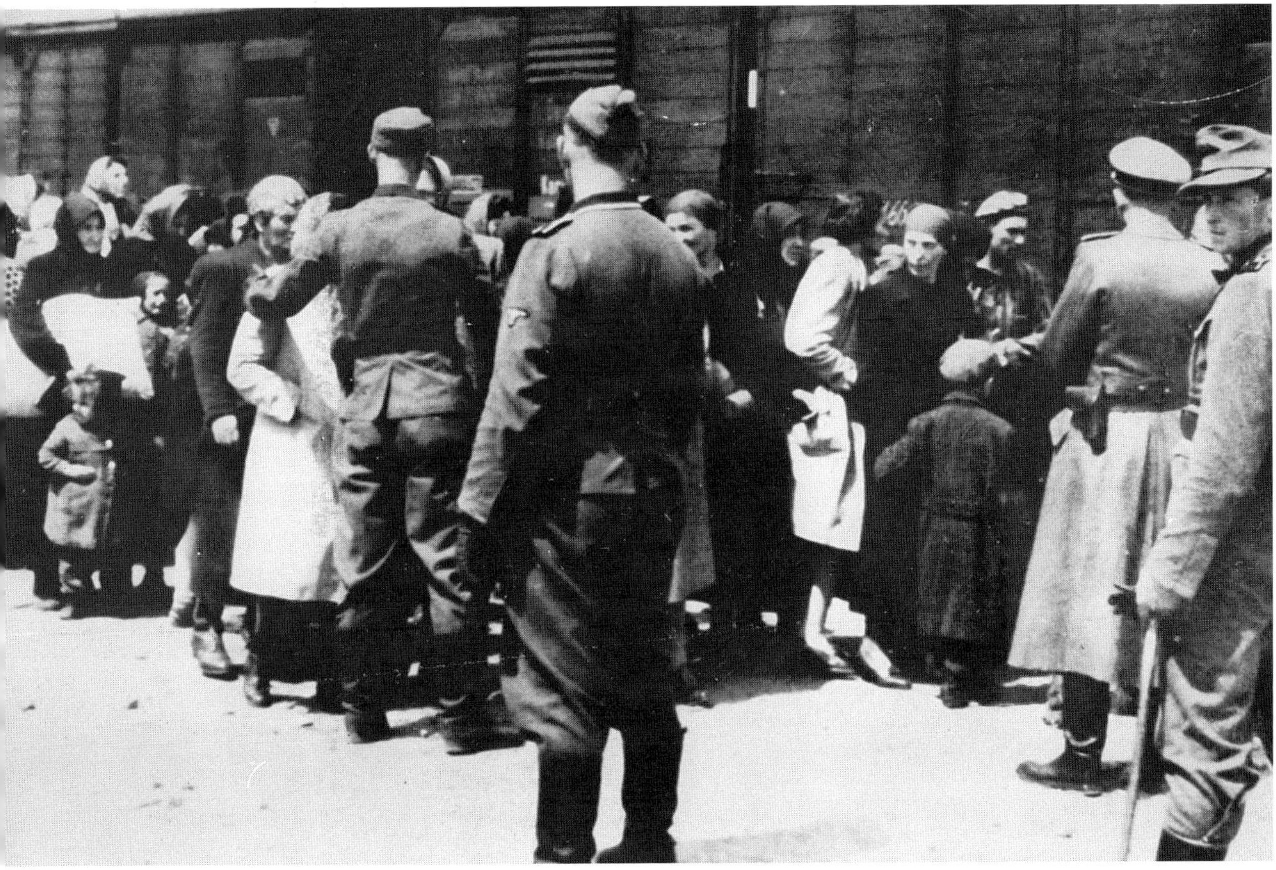

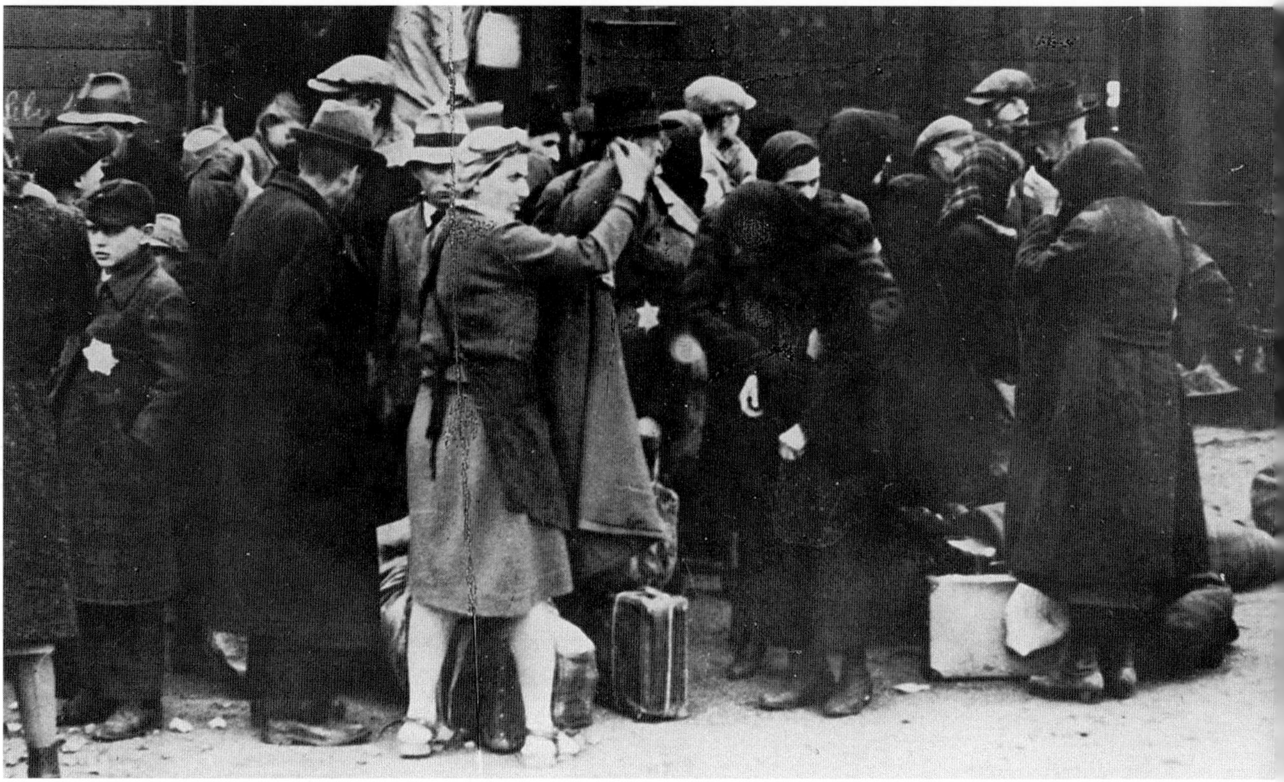

Hungarian Jews are seen here arriving at Birkenau and disembarking from the cattle cars to await selection. While the fear of arriving at the camp was widespread, their journey by train was long and arduous and the conditions were appalling. Even in 1944, the Nazis' 'Final Solution' was disguised as the mass 'resettlement to the east'. *(USHMM)*

Jews from Subcarpathian Rus getting off the deportation train and assembling on the ramp at Auschwitz-Birkenau.

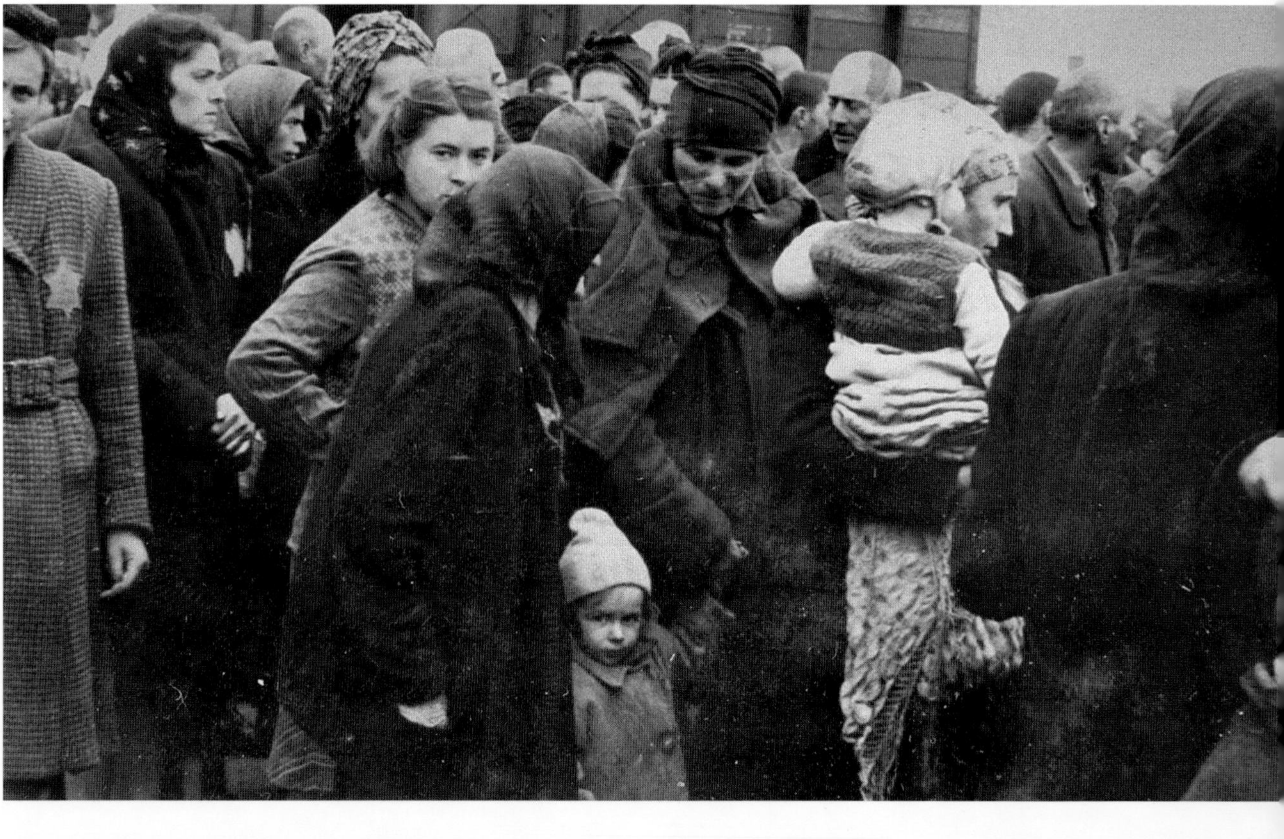

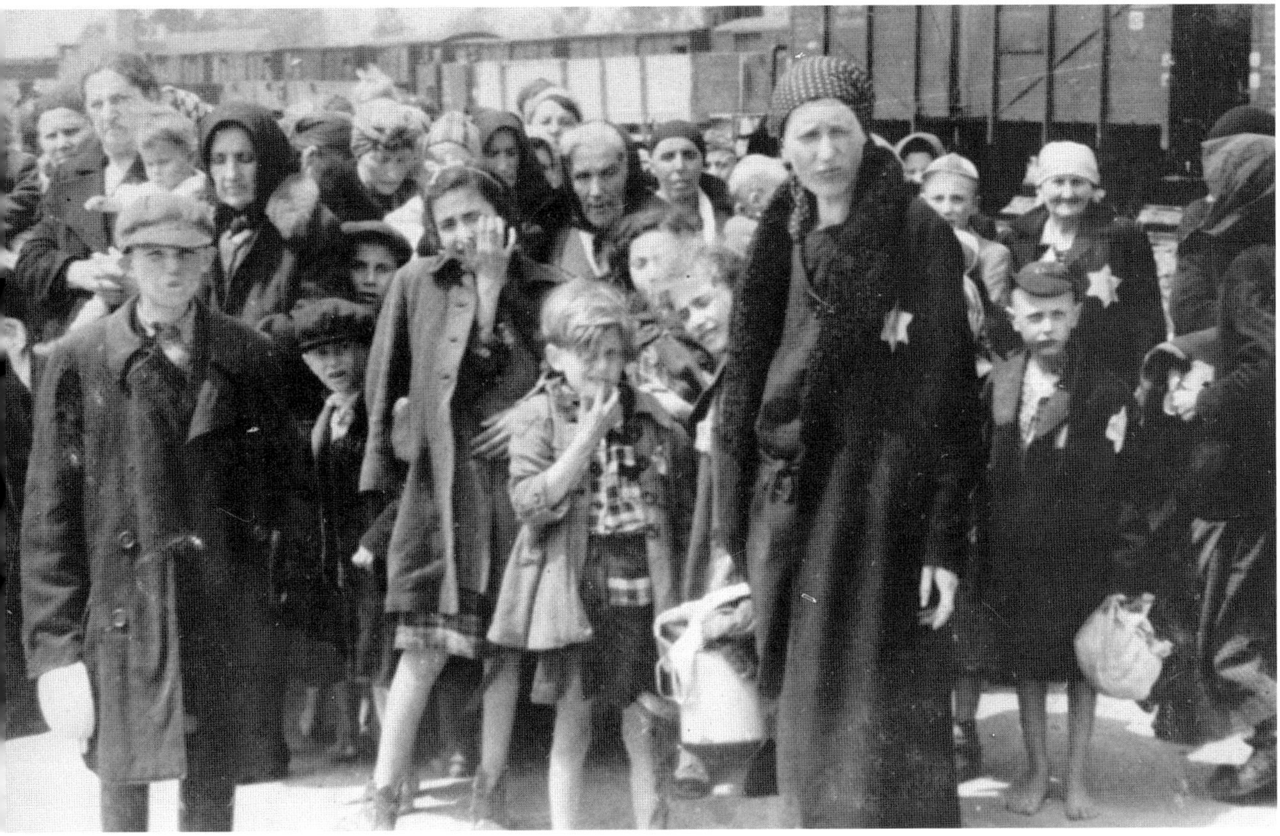

Two photographs showing Jewish women and children from Subcarpathian Rus who have been selected for death walking towards the gas chambers. *(USHMM/Yad Vashem)*

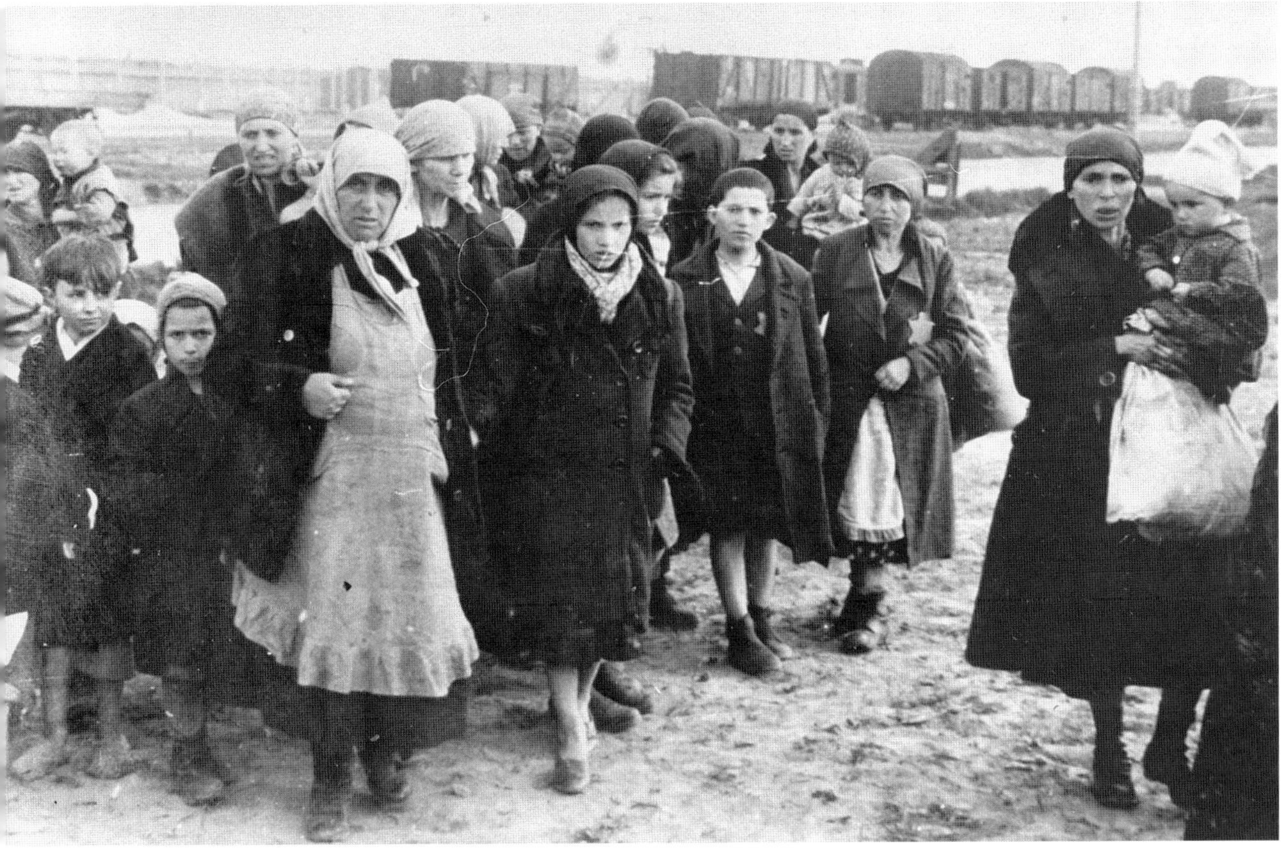

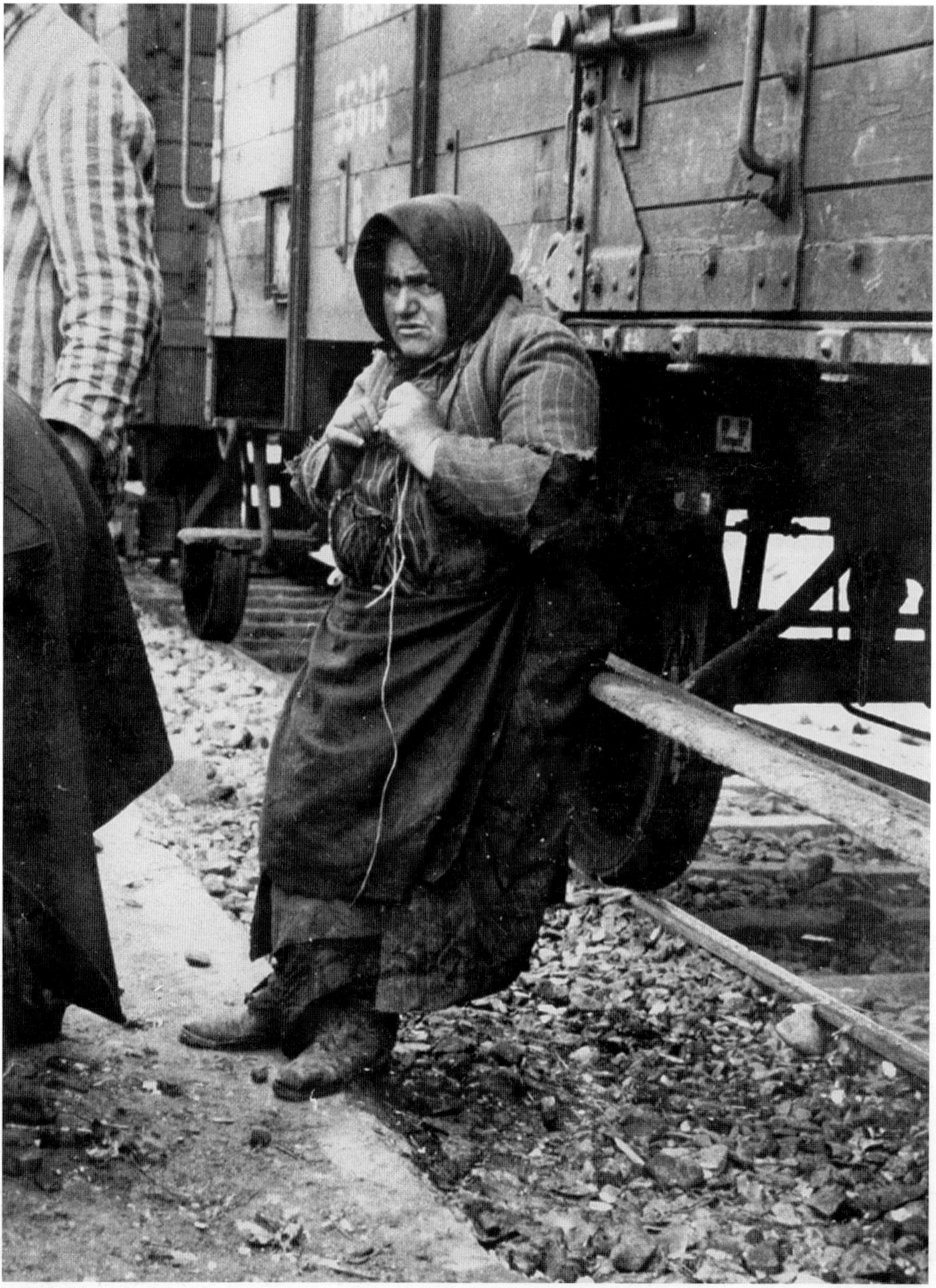

Babo Batren, an elderly Jewish woman from Tecso, leans against the deportation train in Auschwitz-Birkenau while waiting to be taken to the gas chambers. *(USHMM)*

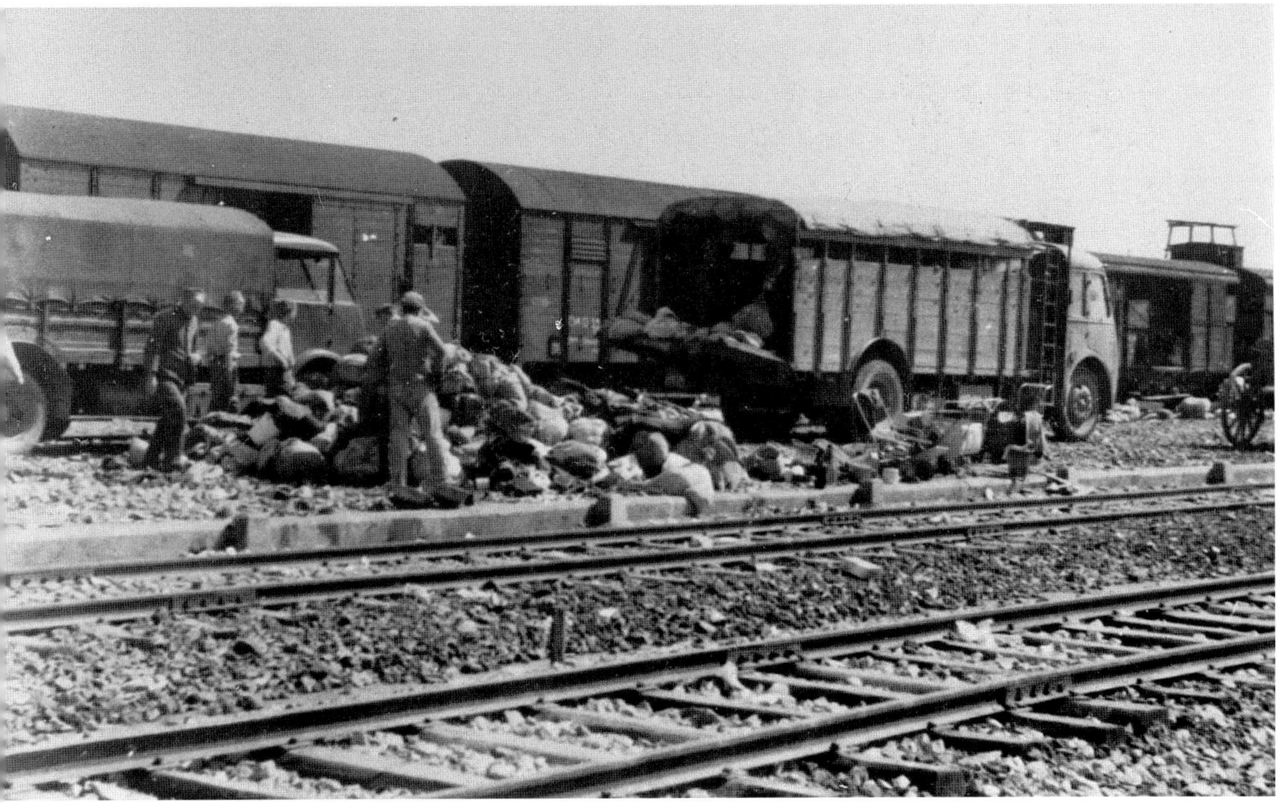

Two photographs showing prisoners in the *Aufräumungskommando* ('clearing-up commando') sort through a mound of personal belongings confiscated from the arriving transport of Jews from Subcarpathian Rus. (*USHMM*)

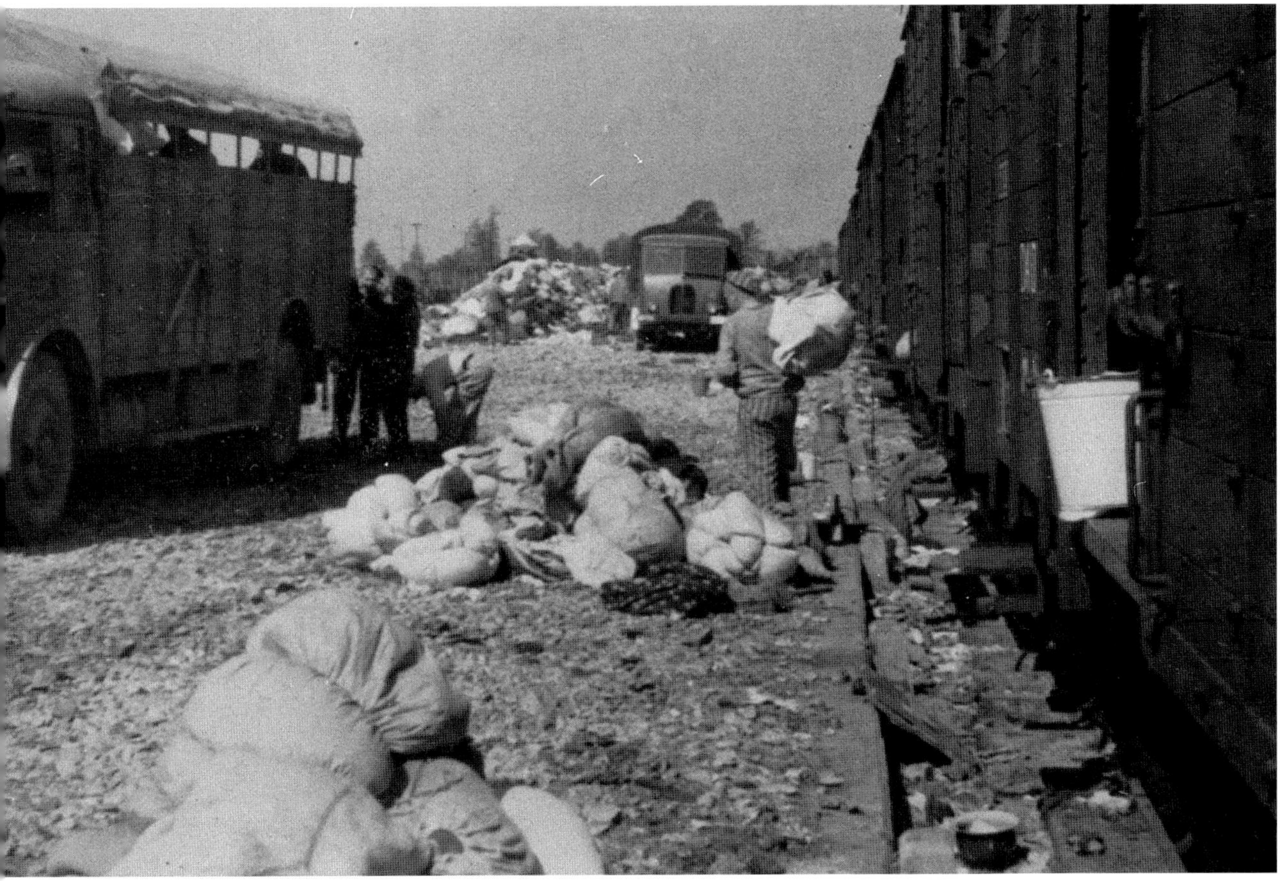

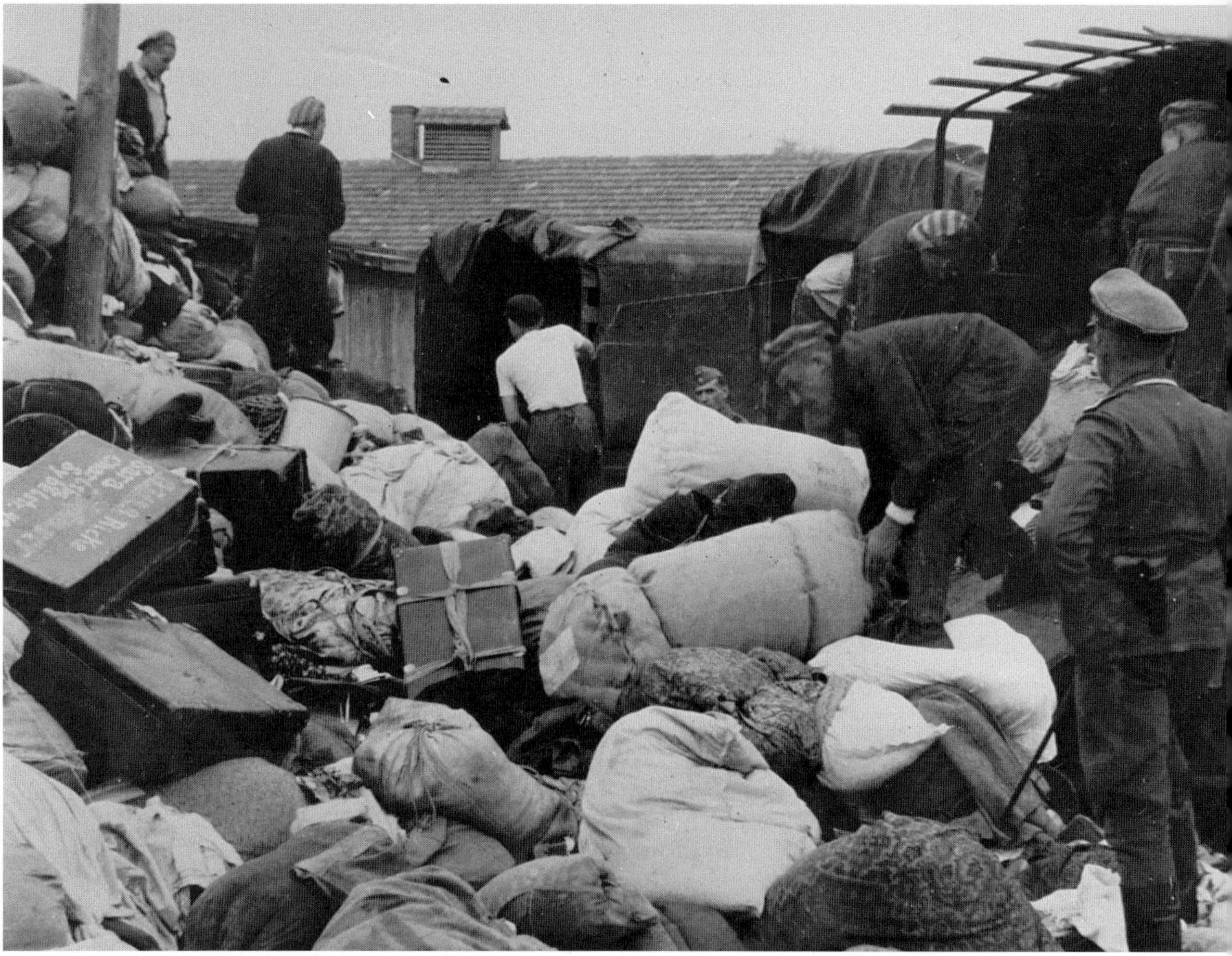

Prisoners in the *Aufräumungskommando* unload the confiscated property of a transport of Jews from Subcarpathian Rus at a warehouse in Auschwitz-Birkenau. *(USHMM)*

Aftermath

By November 1944 transports via rail gradually ceased into Auschwitz-Birkenau as the Red Army advanced through southern Poland. As for the other camps across Europe, the rail lines that had so effectively sent millions of people to their deaths now began suffering widespread destruction. More than half the main lines and a quarter of the branch lines were inoperable by the end of 1944. Many of the rail bridges were destroyed, including many buildings being ruined or inoperable. The rolling stock was either destroyed or distributed to other lines that still remained and were rolling the last connections to the camps. Hundreds of locomotives also began running out fuel and were often pulled up in rail sidings with boxcars still crammed full of dead deportees. Red Army troops including American and British soldiers regularly came across boxcars that had simply been abandoned on the rail lines as the camps were closed down and the trains had nowhere to go. Guards accompanying the trains including engine drivers often deserted their cargo, fearing harsh reprisals. In fact, on some routes where trains had halted and were awaiting further orders as to where to go next, engineers had received orders to blow up the trains or drive the locomotives into rivers off damaged bridges in order to kill or drown their human cargo.

Whatever the outcome of the last trains that were left at the end of the war, no one could hide the fact of how important the rail system had been in the implementation of the Holocaust. The massive deportation action involving the use of freight trains across Europe had ultimately assisted in the total murder of 6 million Jews. The *Deutsche Reichsbahn* had played a crucial and effective part in the action that finally sent Jews and other victims from thousands of towns and cities throughout Europe to meet their deaths in the Nazi concentration camp system.

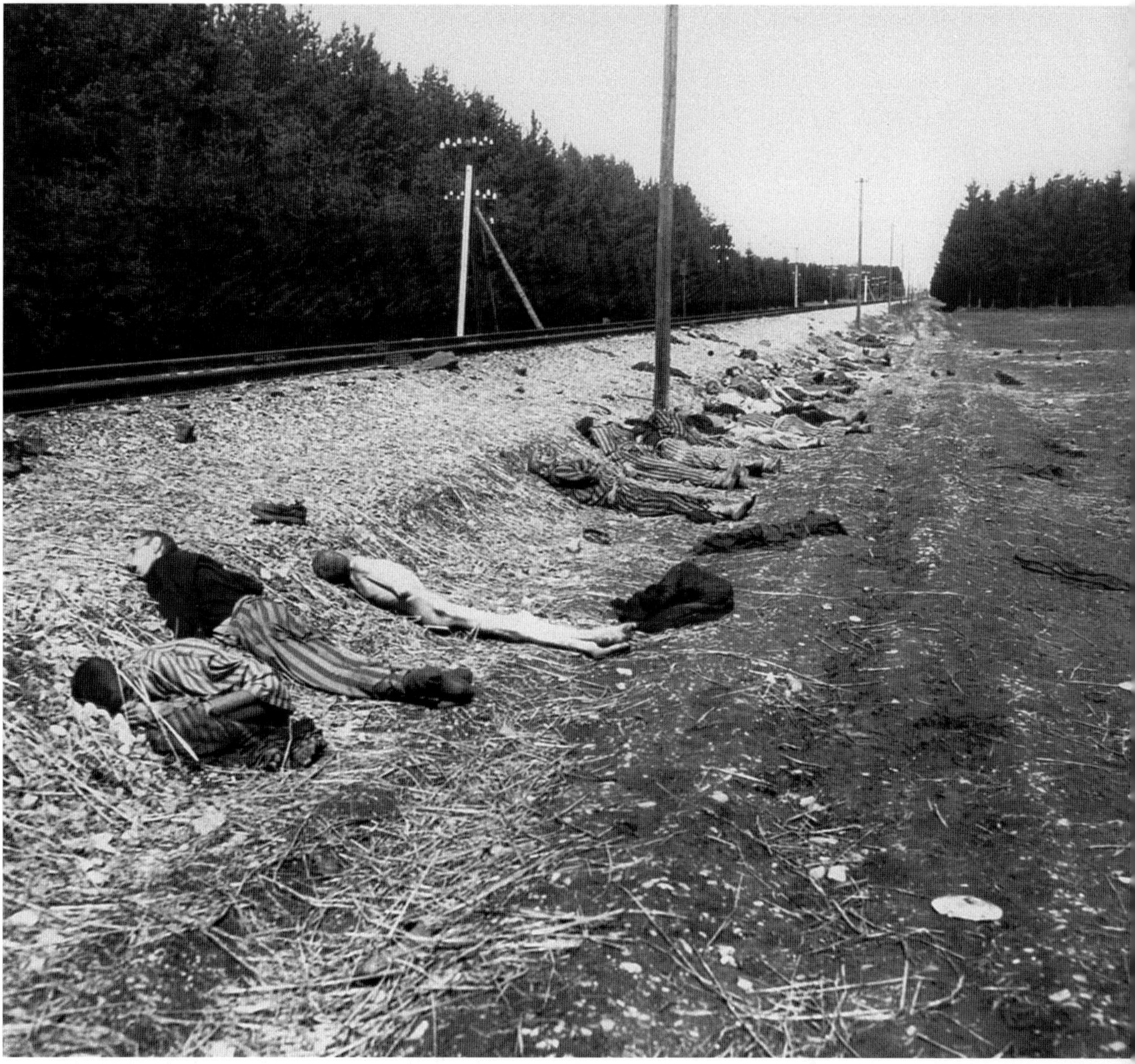

(**Above**) A photograph taken in April 1945 showing corpses lying beside the rail spur that served the Kaufering IV concentration camp. Kaufering was the name of a system of eleven sub-camps of Dachau concentration camp which operated between 18 June 1944 and 27 April 1945. *(USHMM)*

(**Opposite**) Seven photographs showing abandoned boxcars with dead prisoners inside. As Allied forces advanced into Germany, the SS tried to evacuate prisoners at Buchenwald concentration camp. The prisoners had been loaded into both open and closed boxcars three weeks prior to their arrival at Dachau concentration camp. Most died during the journey; others survived it. The photographs were probably taken on or around 29 April 1945 following the liberation of the camp by elements of the US 42rd and 45th infantry divisions. *(USHMM)*

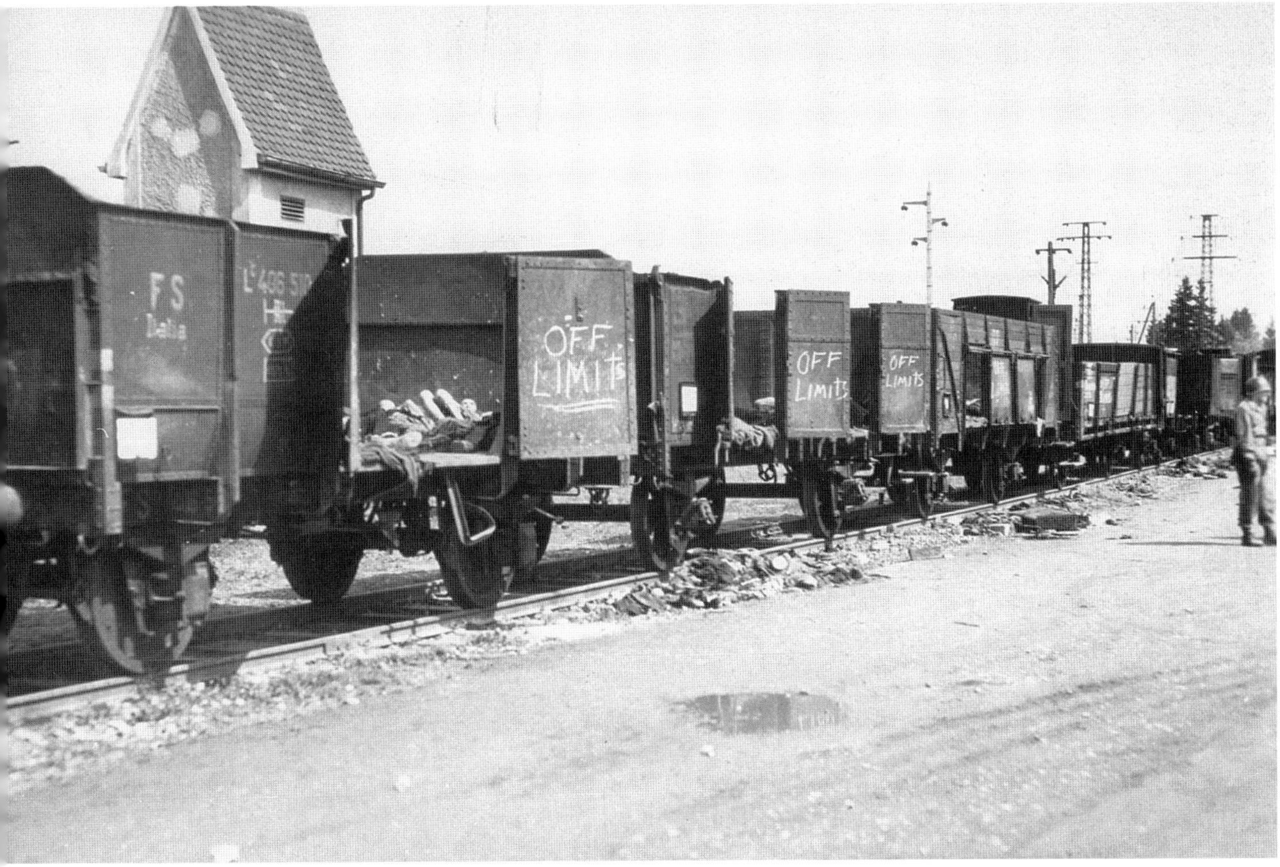
FS
OFF LIMITS
OFF Limits
OFF Limits

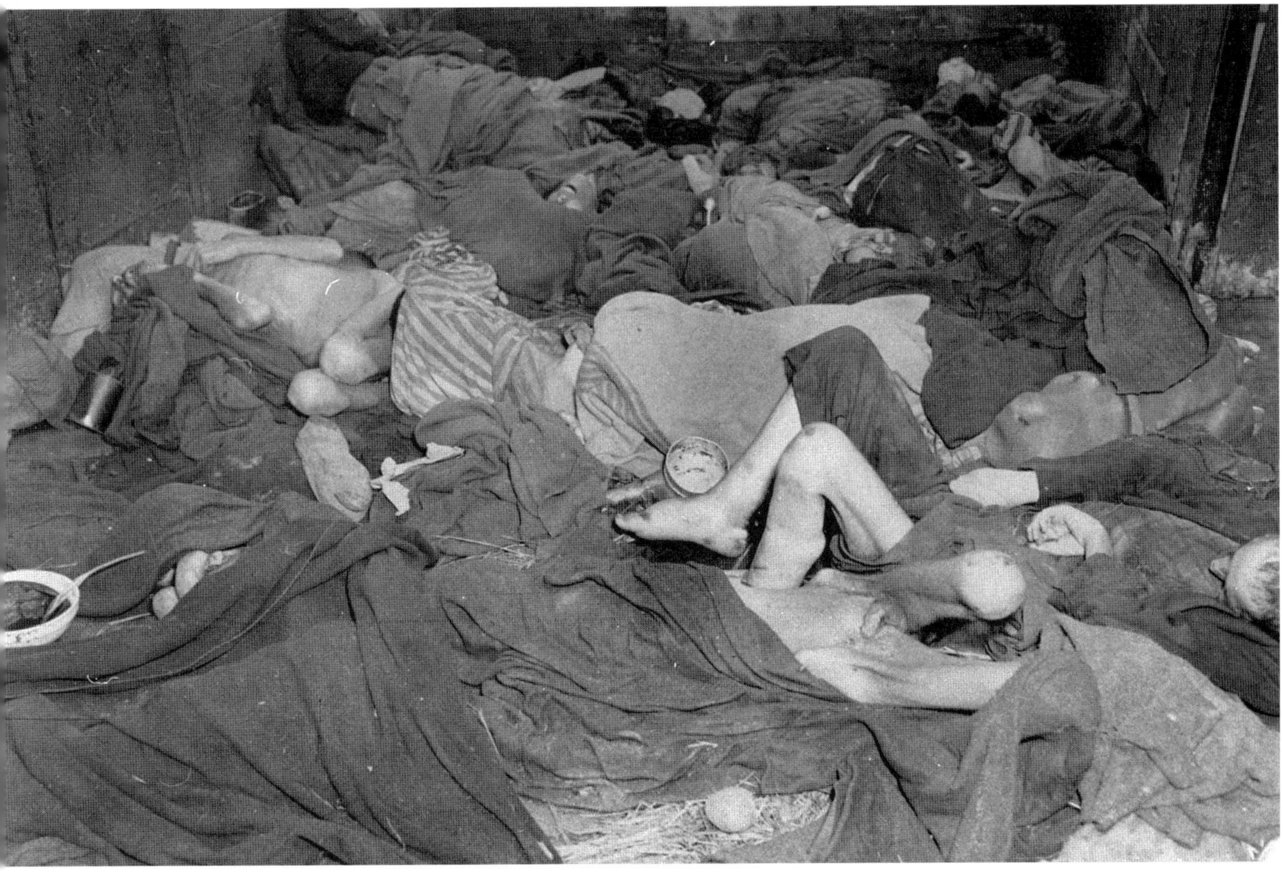

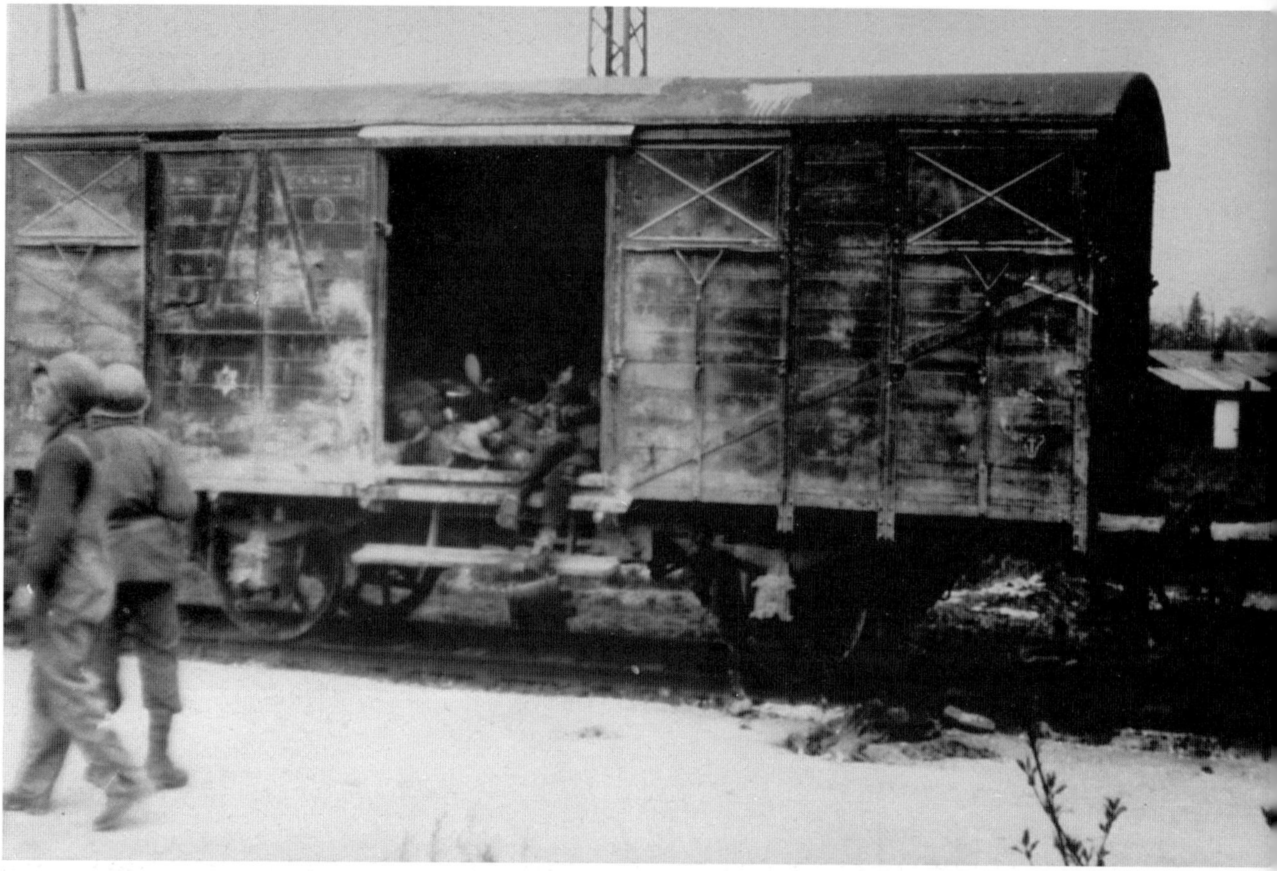

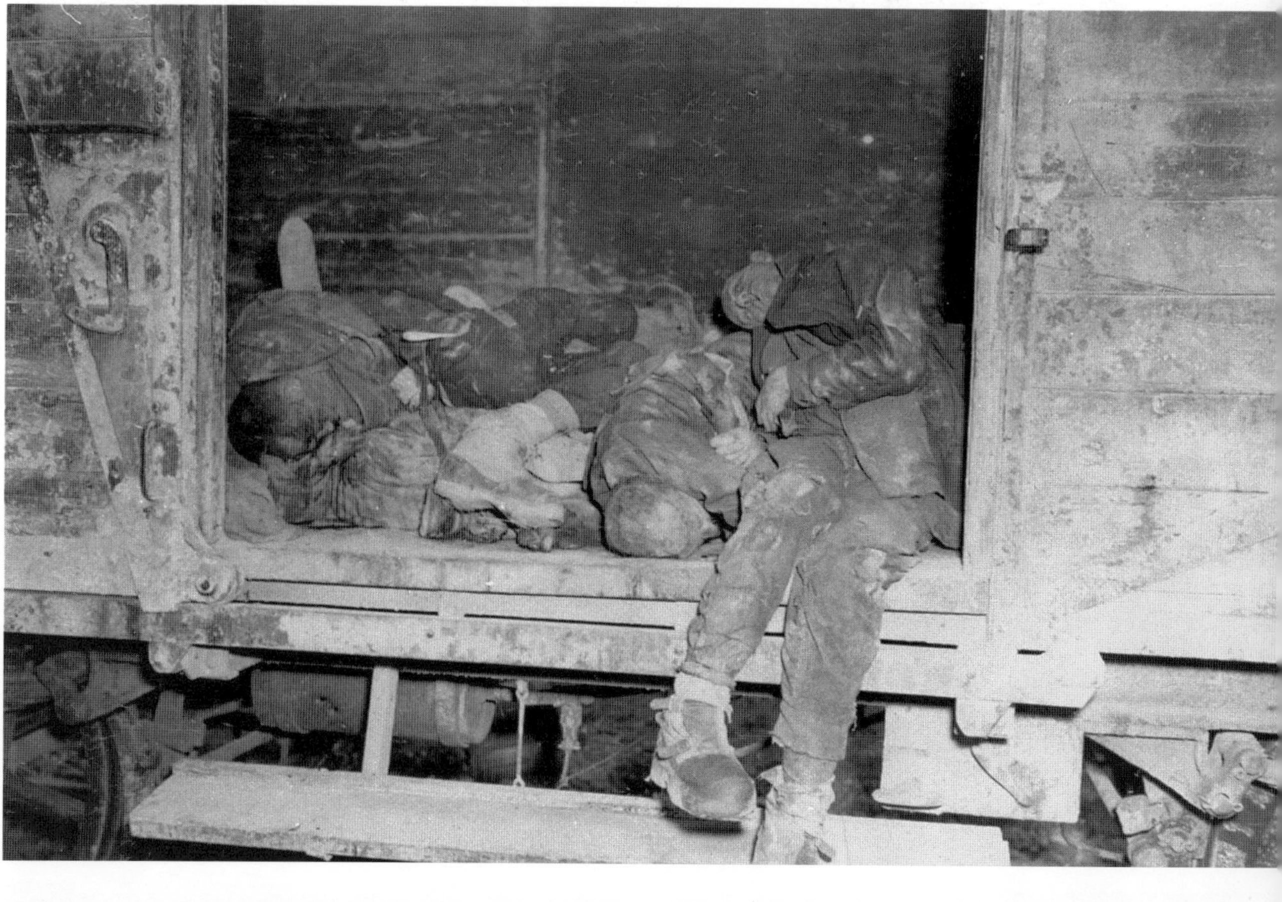

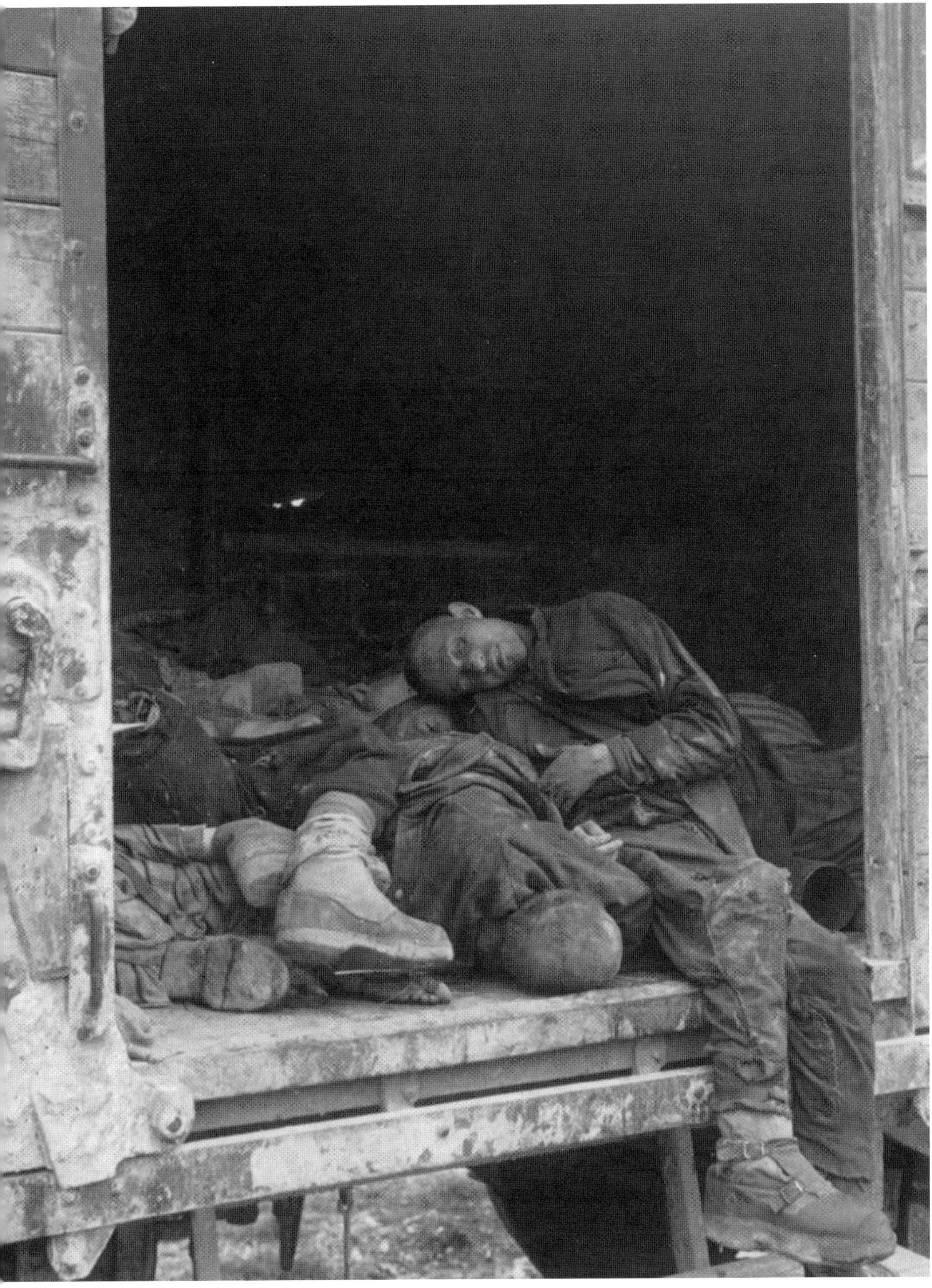

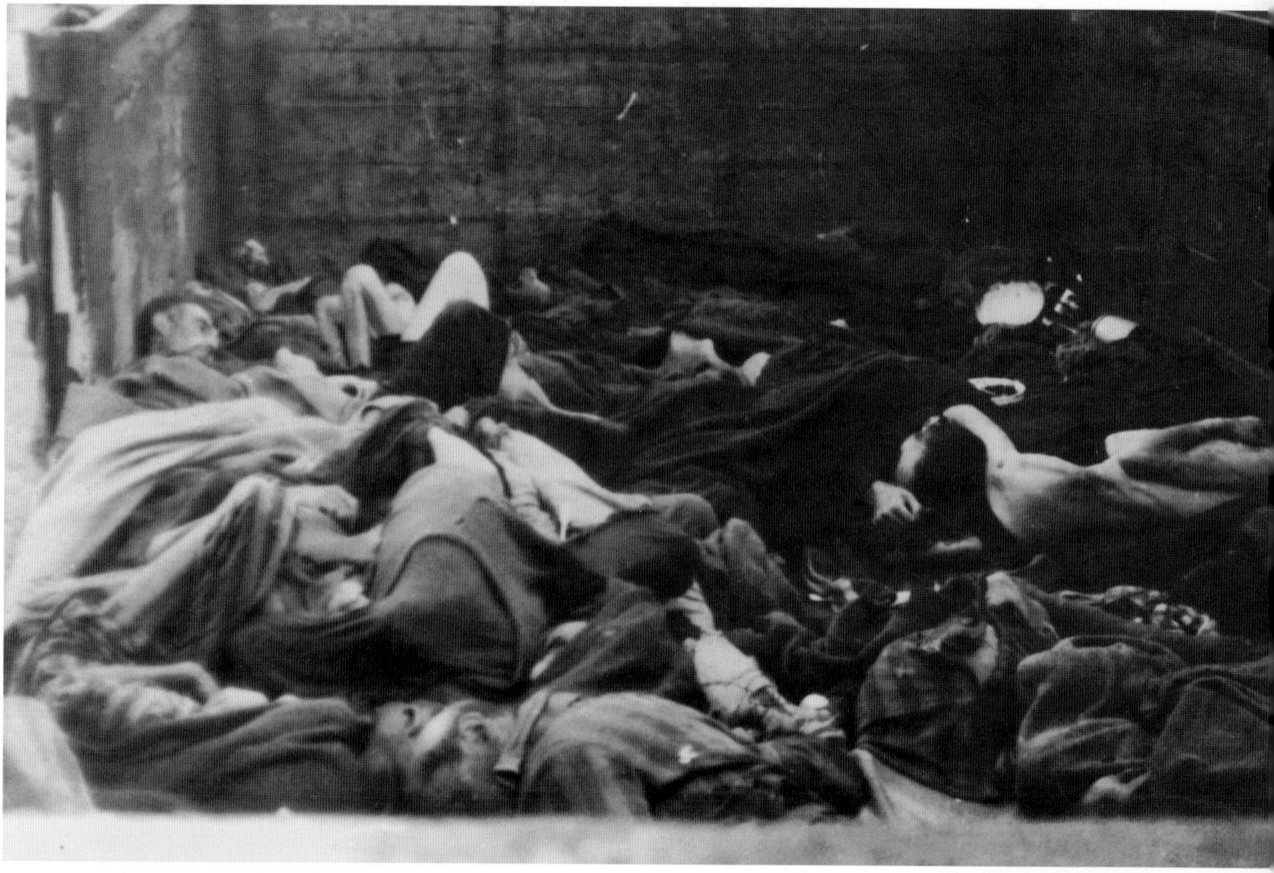

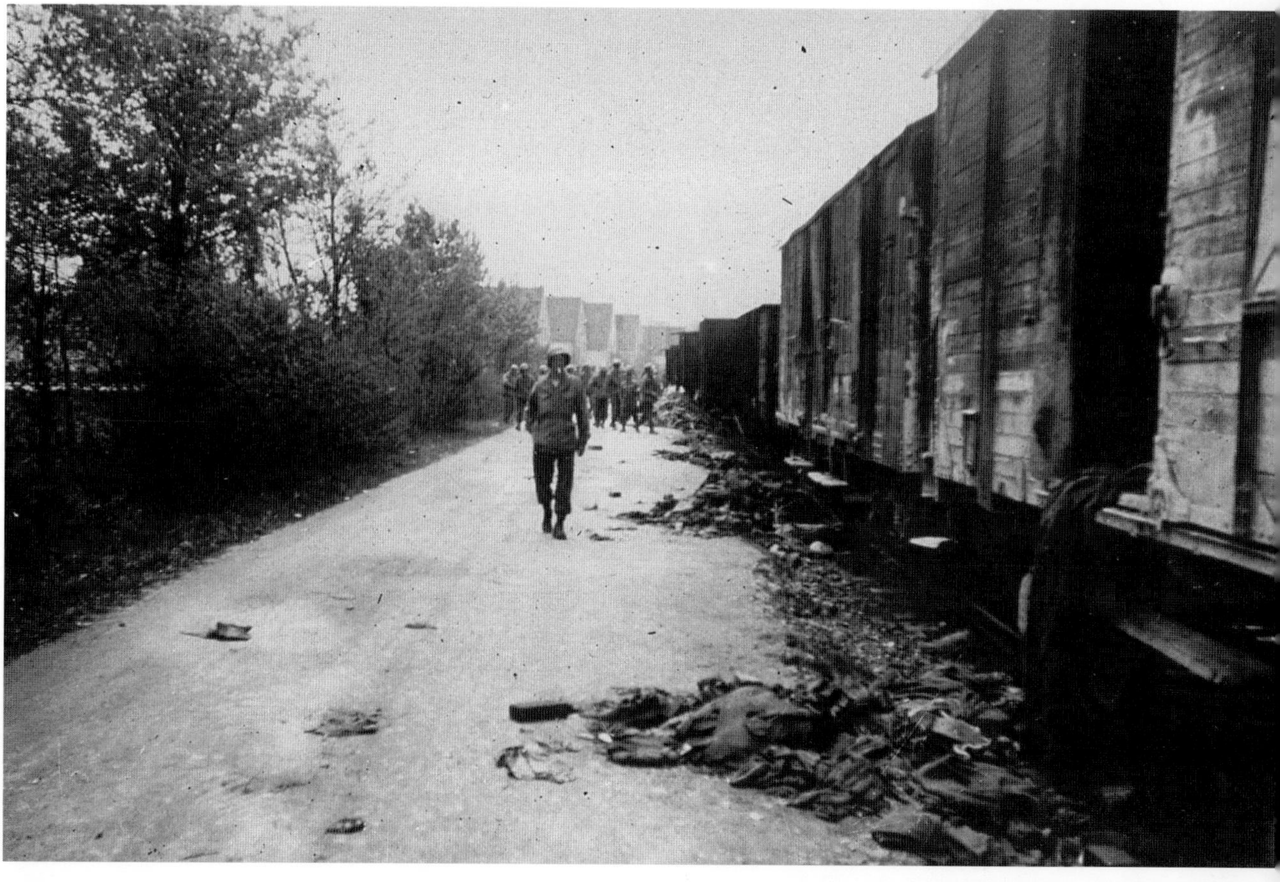

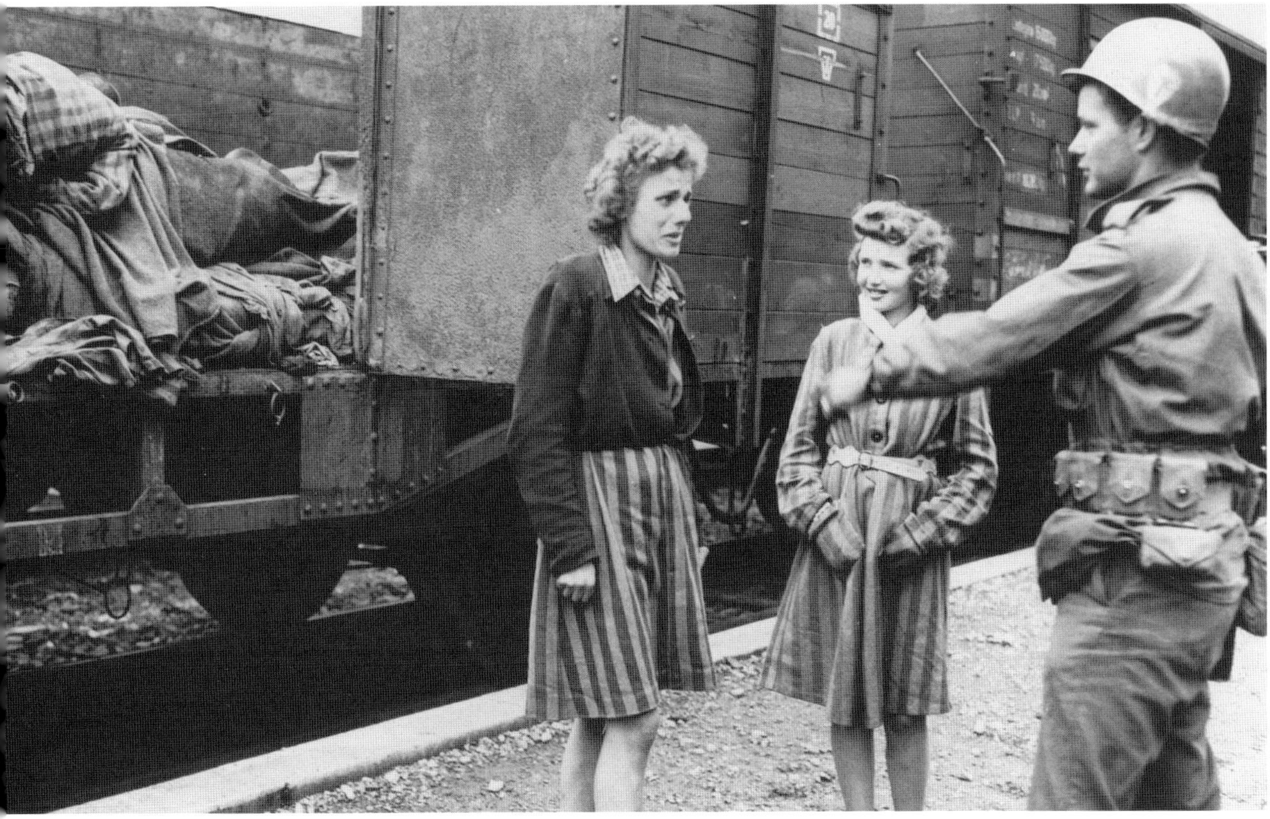

Private First Class Andrew E. Dubill speaks with two Jewish girls who were held prisoner by the SS. They can be seen standing next to open boxcars full of dead prisoners who died while on an evacuation transport presumably heading for Dachau concentration camp. *(USHMM/NARA)*

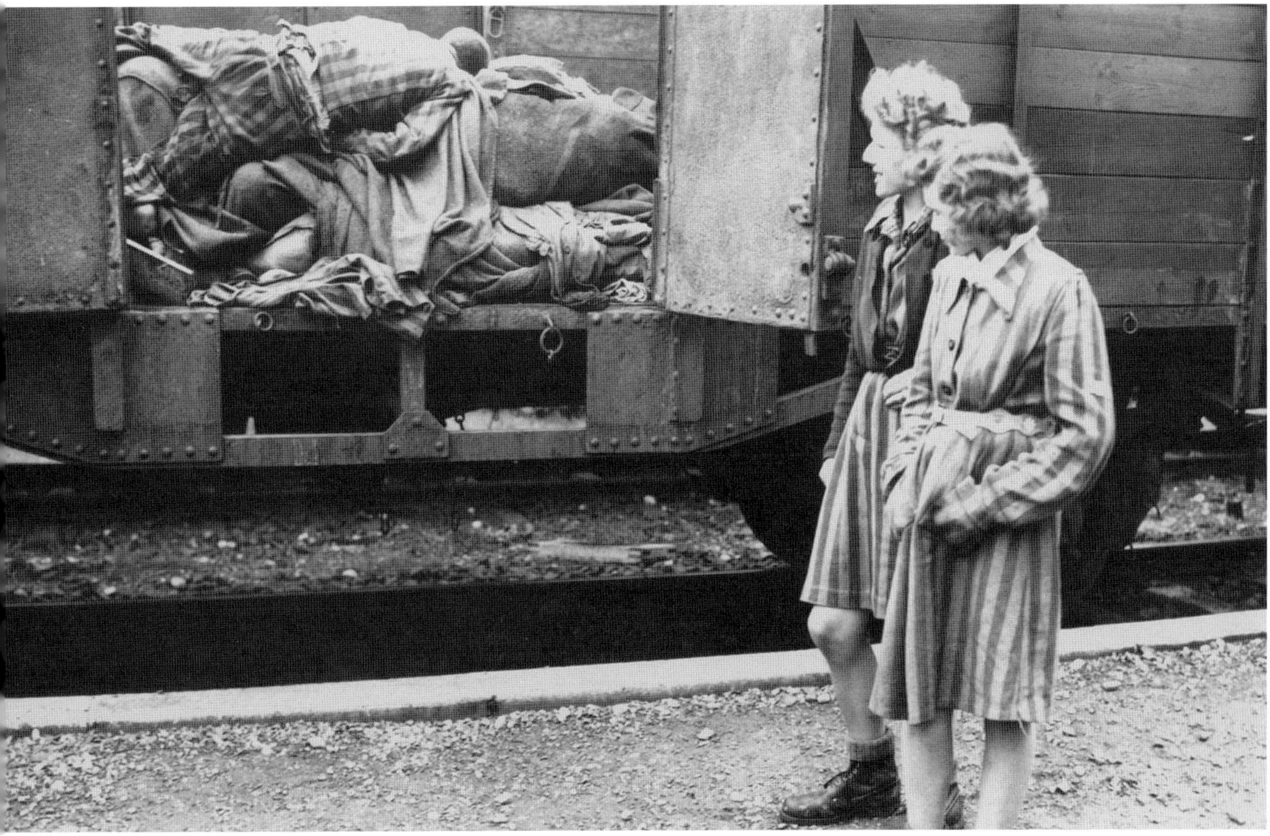

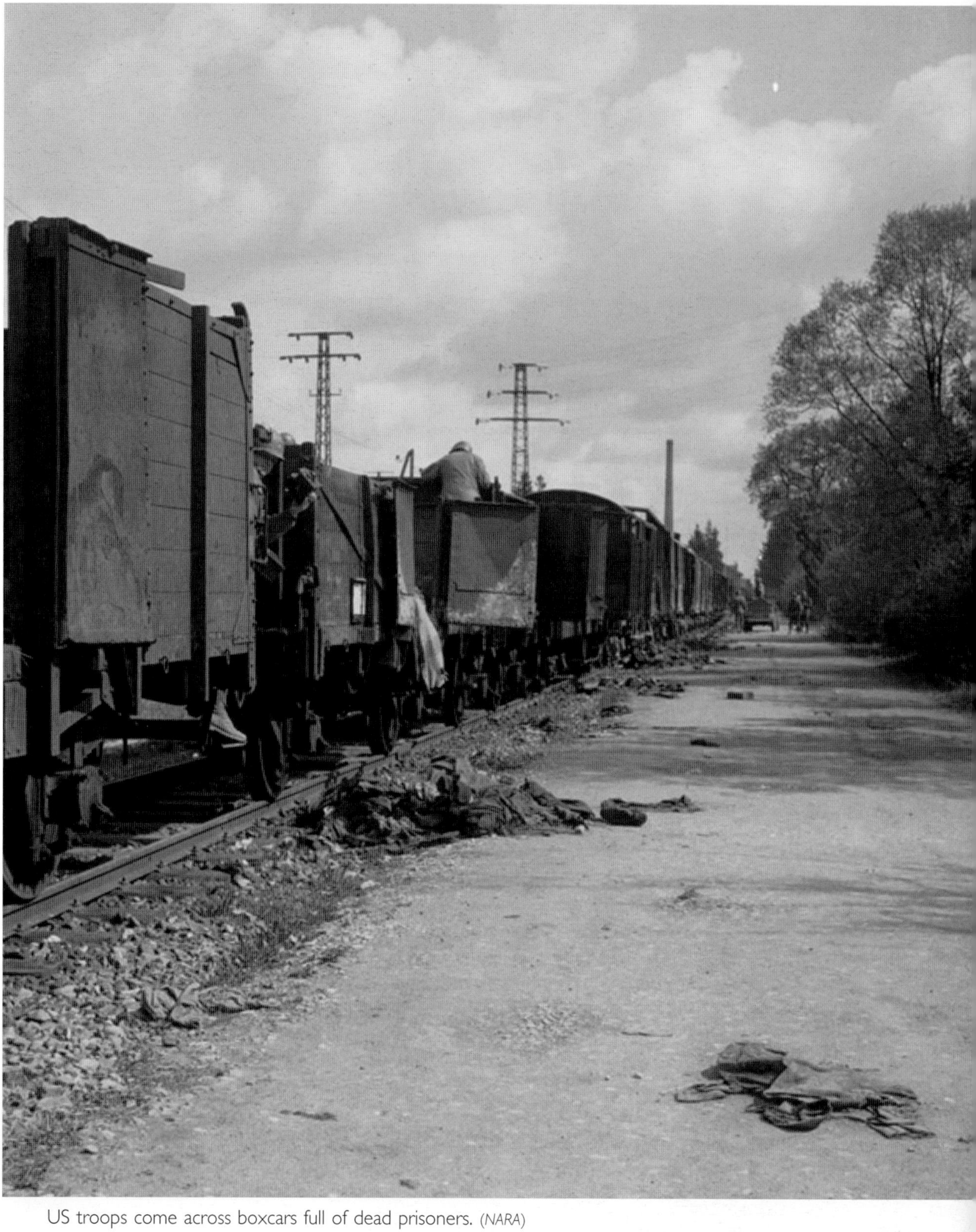

US troops come across boxcars full of dead prisoners. *(NARA)*

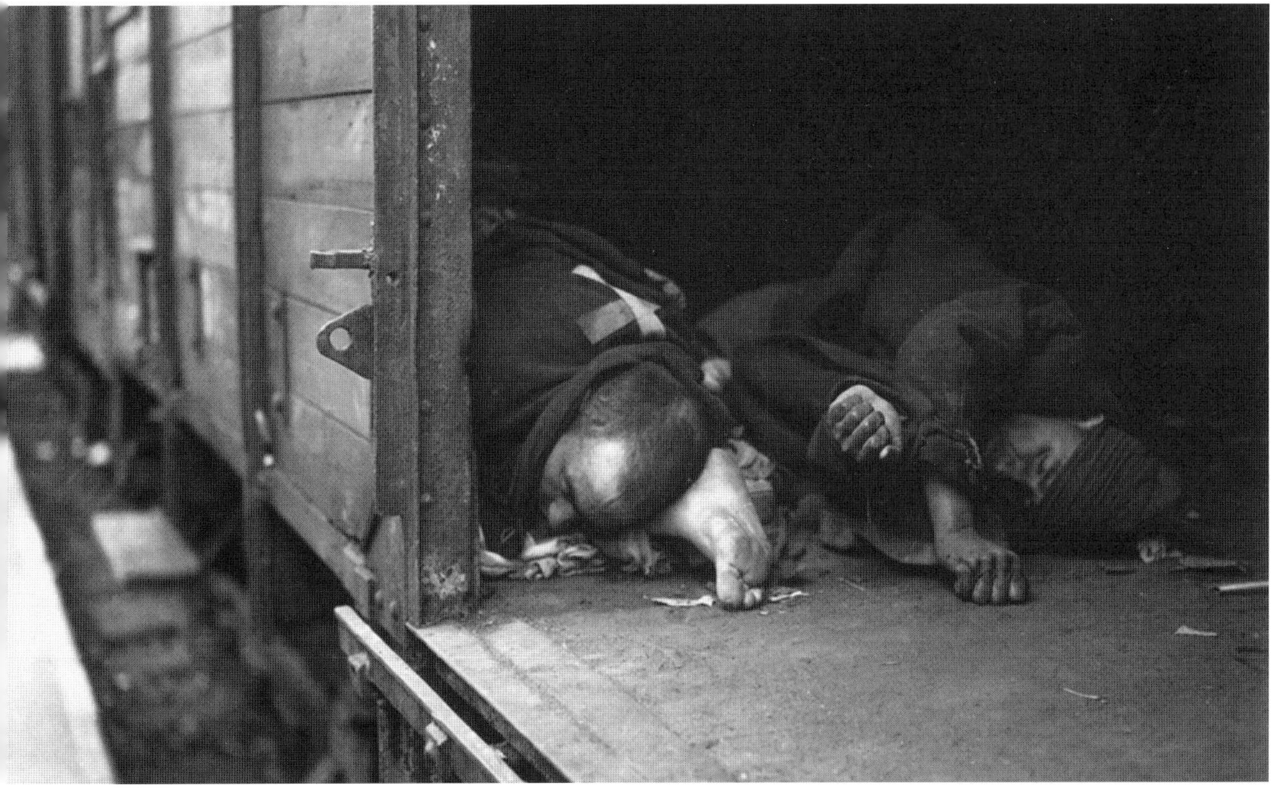

At the doorway of this box car are the dead bodies of three political prisoners. All prisoners on the train were killed by machine guns at the hands of SS troops. *(NARA)*

Survivors rest on an embankment next to a halted train. Red Army troops including American and British soldiers regularly came across boxcars that had simply been abandoned on the rail lines as the camps were closed down and the trains had nowhere to go. *(USHMM)*

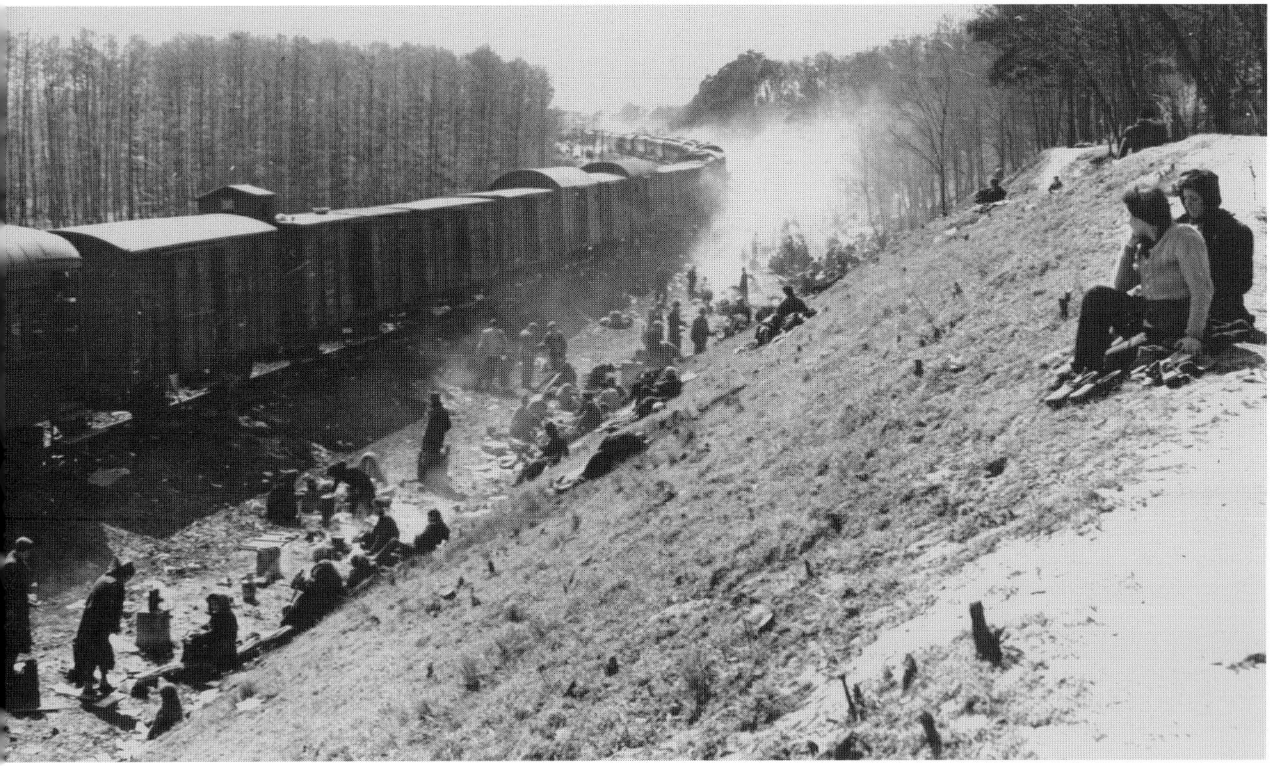

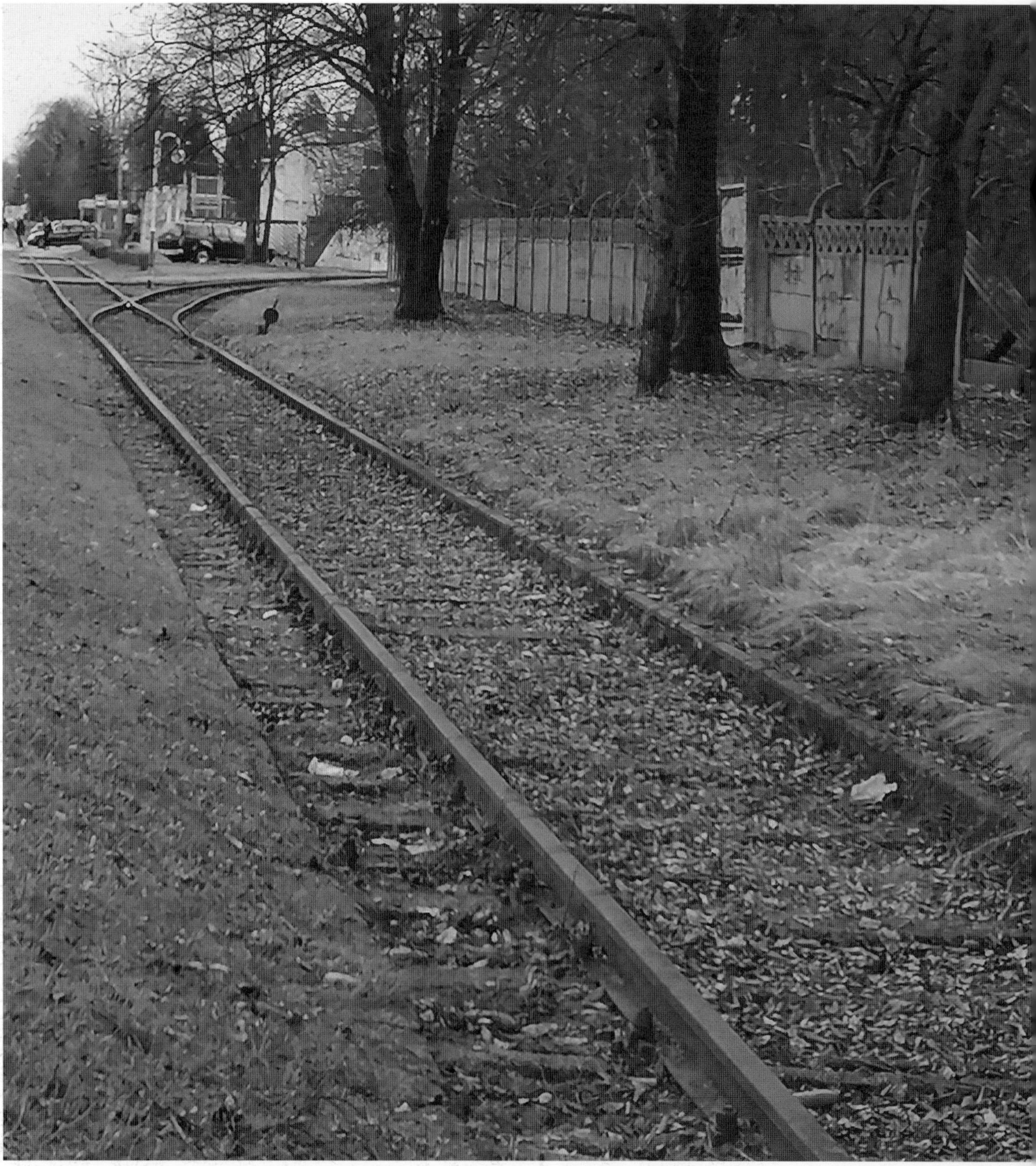

Two photographs taken in the town of Auschwitz by the author's niece during a visit in February 2022. The images show the old rail spur to the main line which was used to mainly transport material and forced labour to the sub-camps and various factories that were constructed throughout the Upper Silesian Industrial Region. The Auschwitz prisoners were forced to work in local coal mines, mills, armaments plants and at large building sites for new industrial facilities of importance to the German war economy. *(Lilly Comer)*

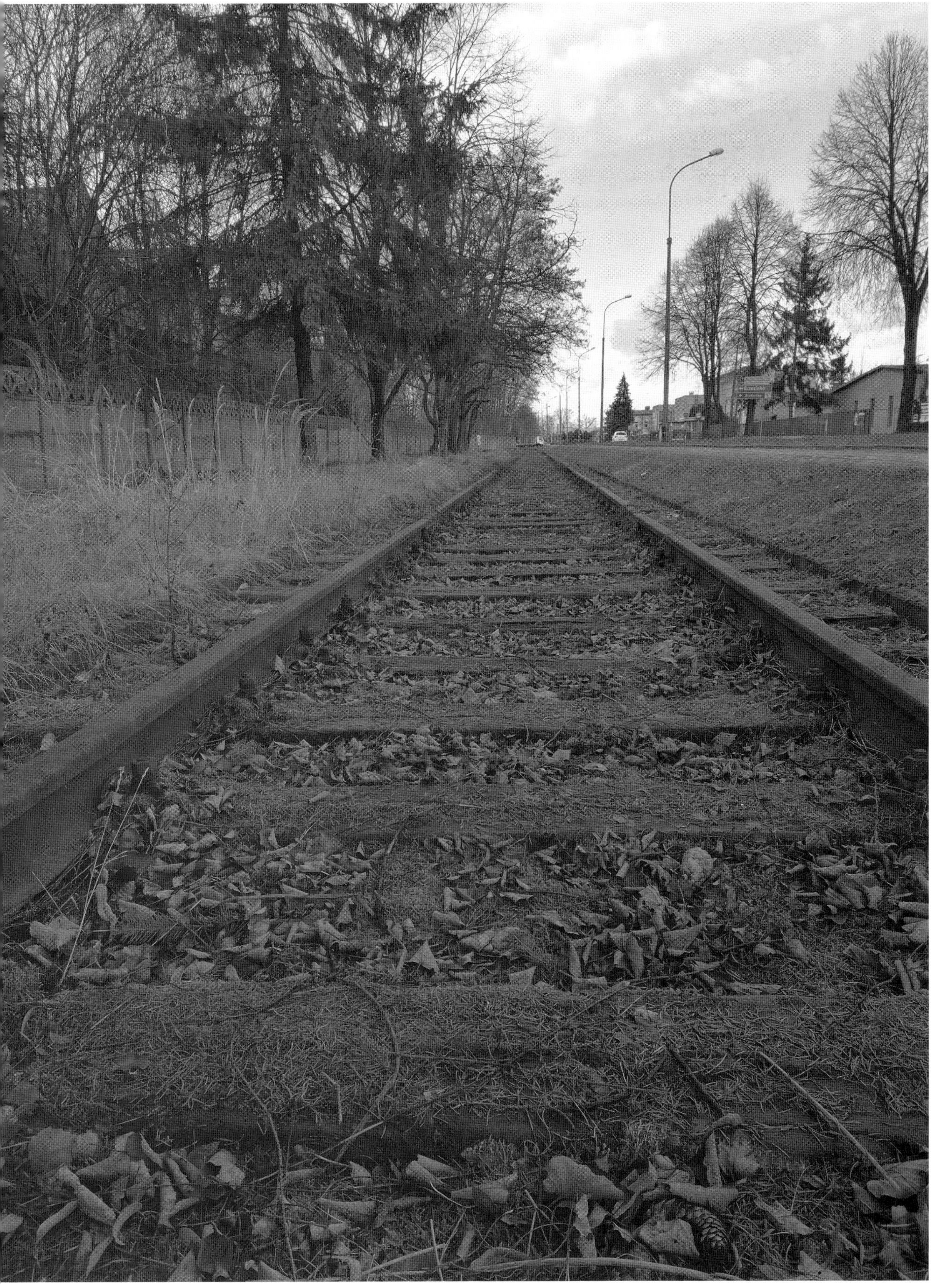

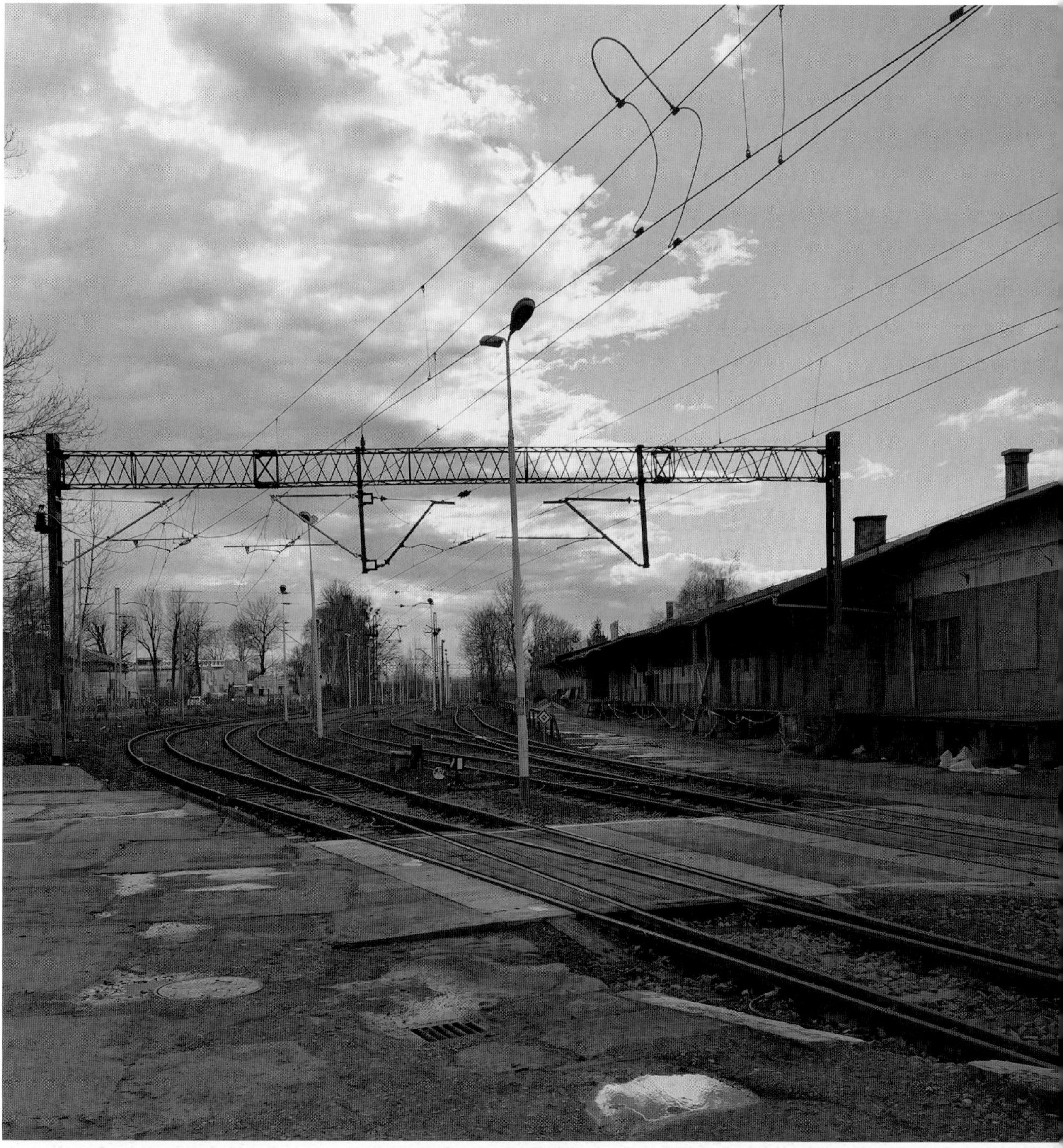

Two photographs showing Auschwitz station and a railway siding taken by the author's niece during a visit in February 2022. The railway line looks south-west towards the towns of Brzeszcze and Czechowice. This railway line was key to the success of transporting hundreds of thousands of Jews to Auschwitz and later Auschwitz-Birkenau. The line also served for transporting labour and materials for the Auschwitz sub-camps including the Buna I.G. Farben company at Monowitz. There were more than forty Auschwitz sub-camps in the area. *(Lilly Corner)*

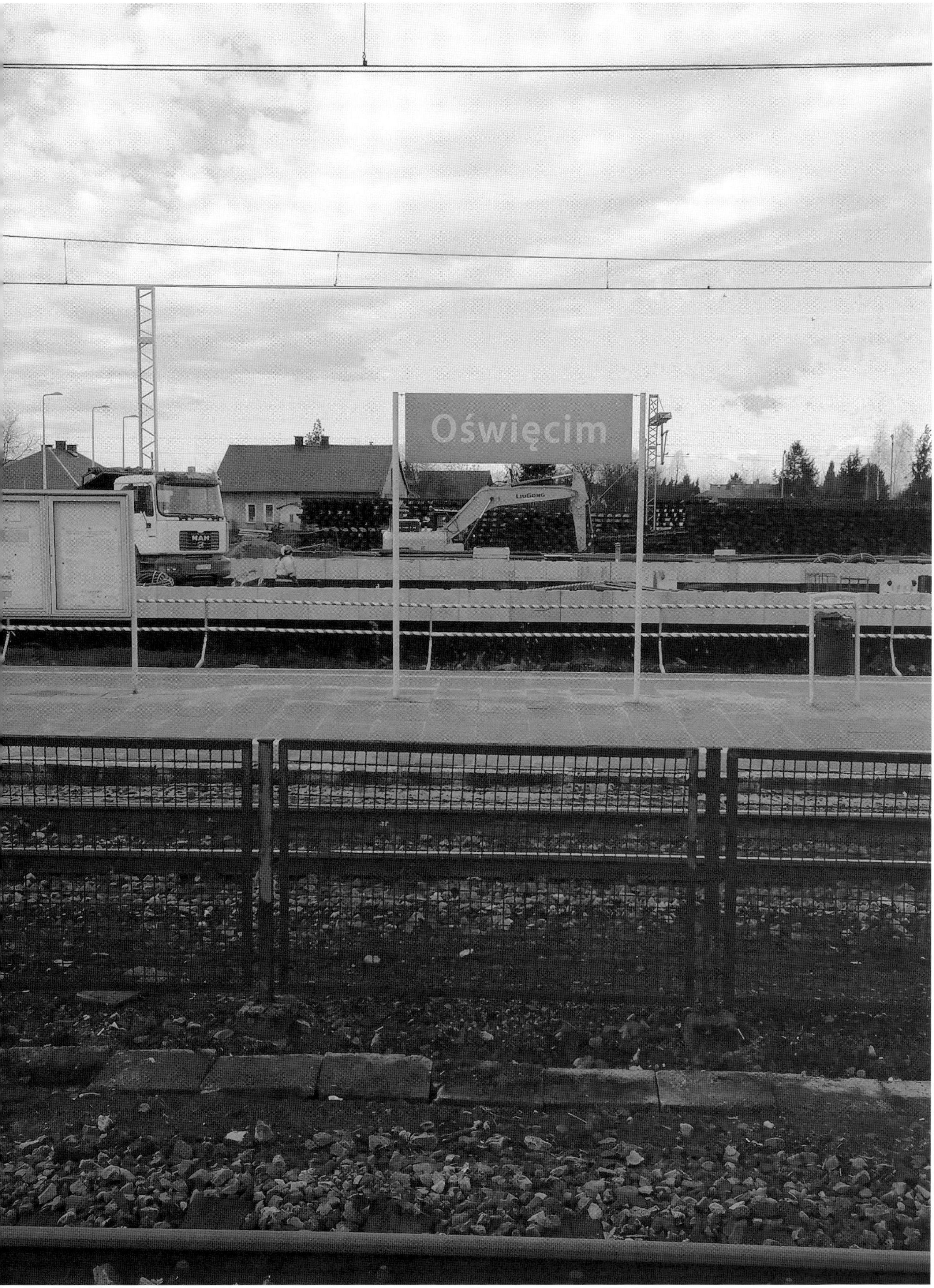
Oświęcim

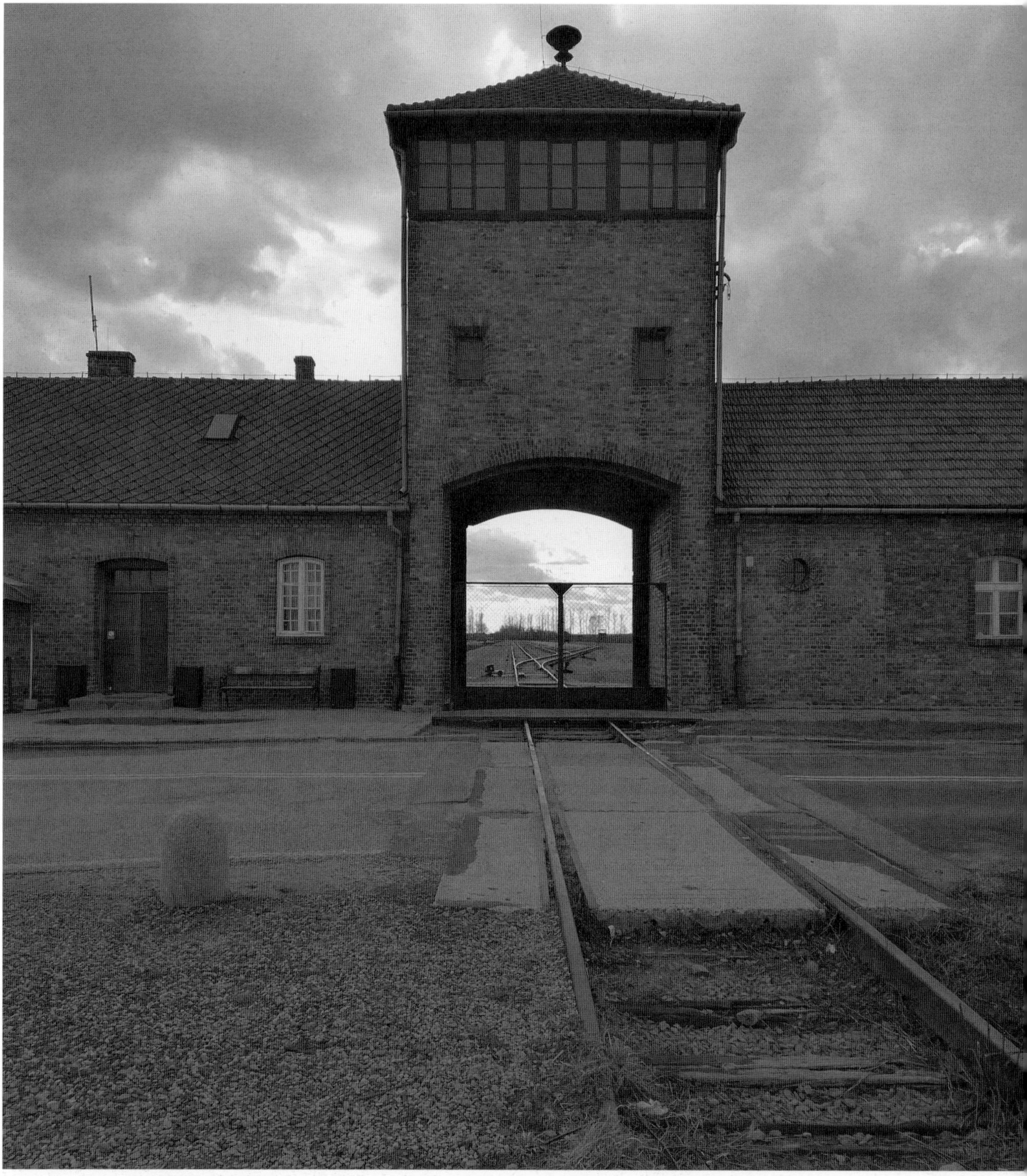

Four photographs showing the Auschwitz-Birkenau railway line taken by the author's niece during a visit to Auschwitz in February 2022. The railway line and what was known as the third ramp were built from 1943 inside the Birkenau camp and went into operation in May 1944 to coincide with the anticipated arrival of transports of Hungarian Jews. The railway spur along this ramp ran as far as the gas chambers and Crematoria II and III. *(Lilly Corner)*

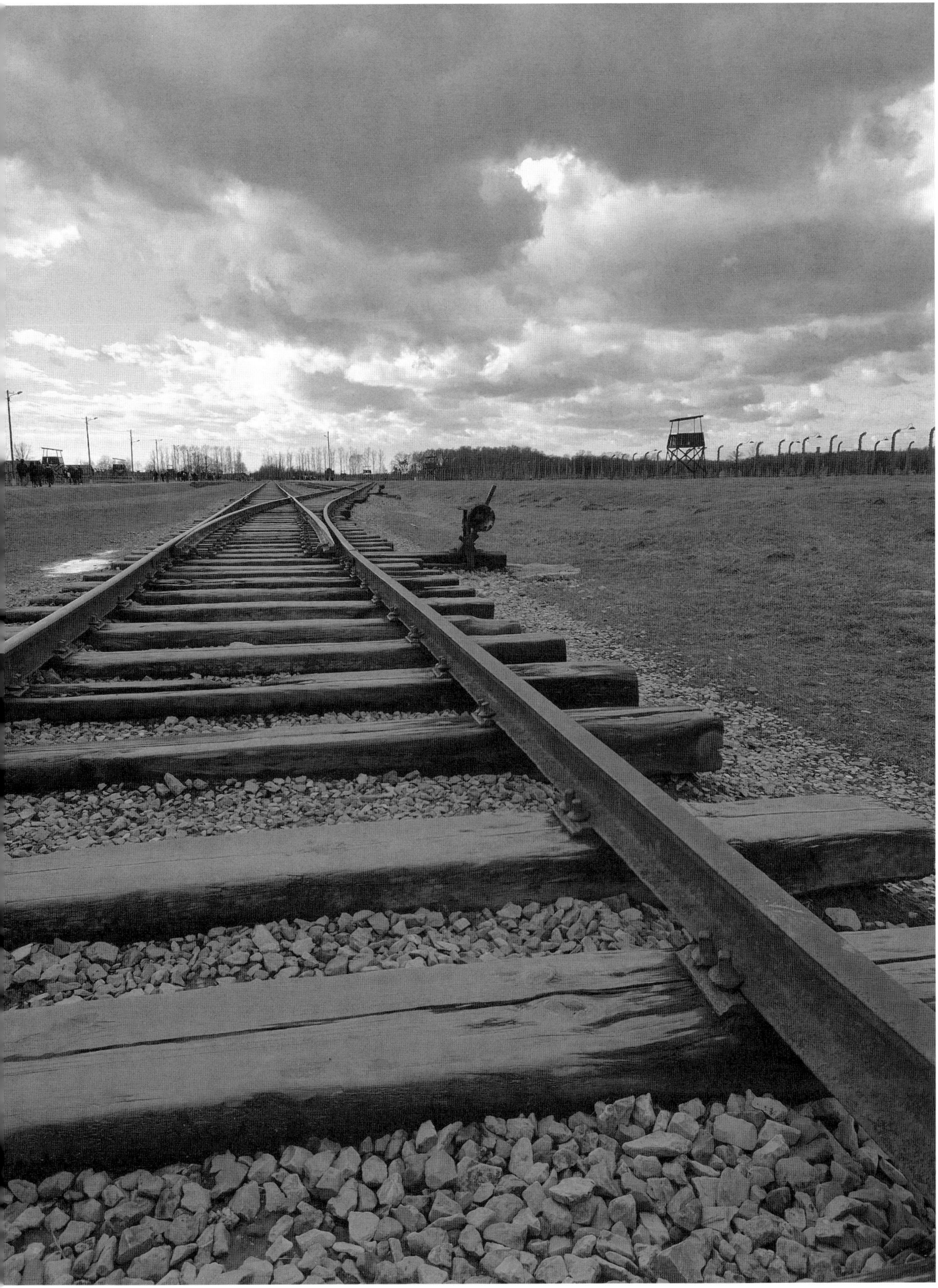

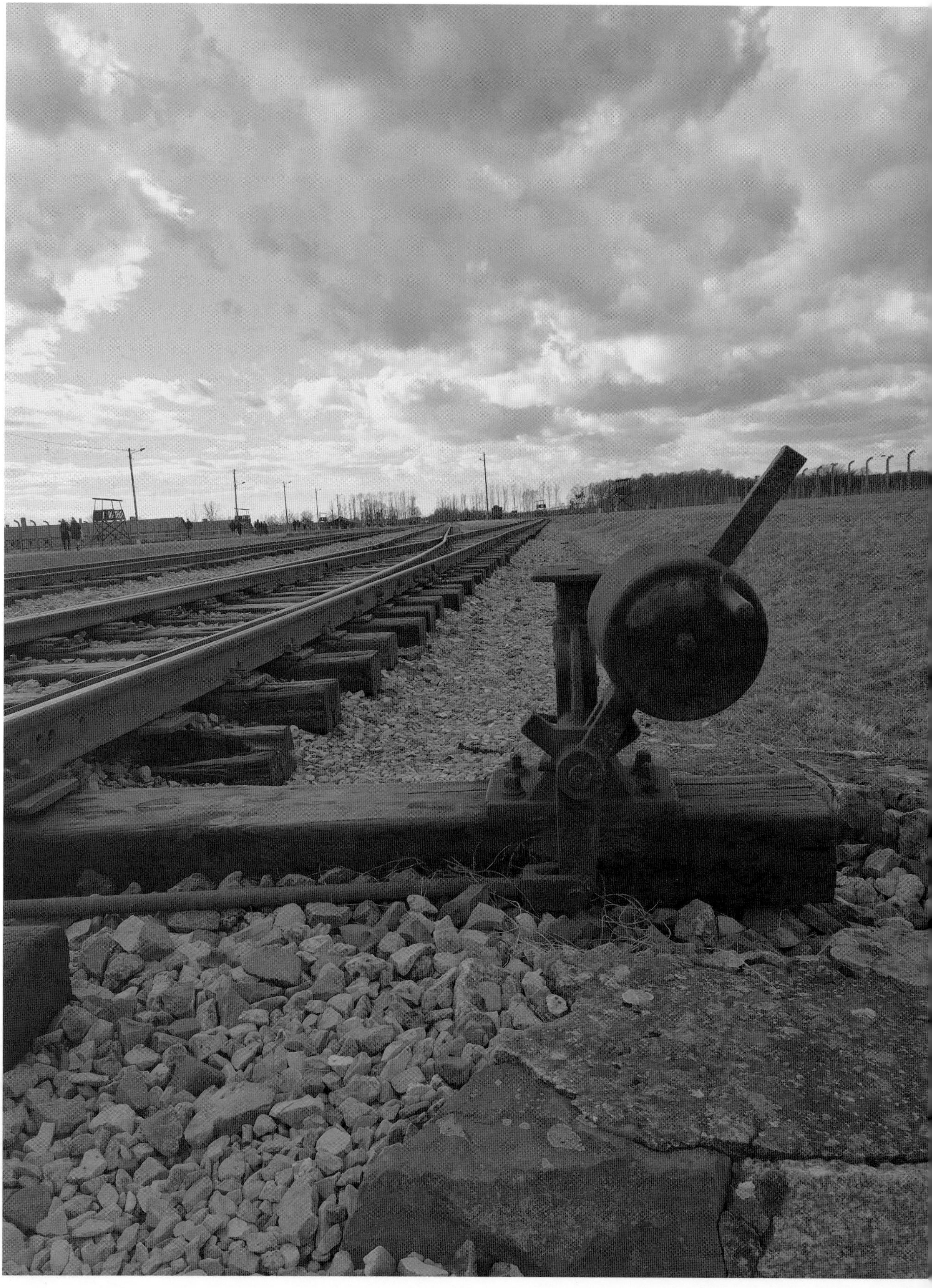

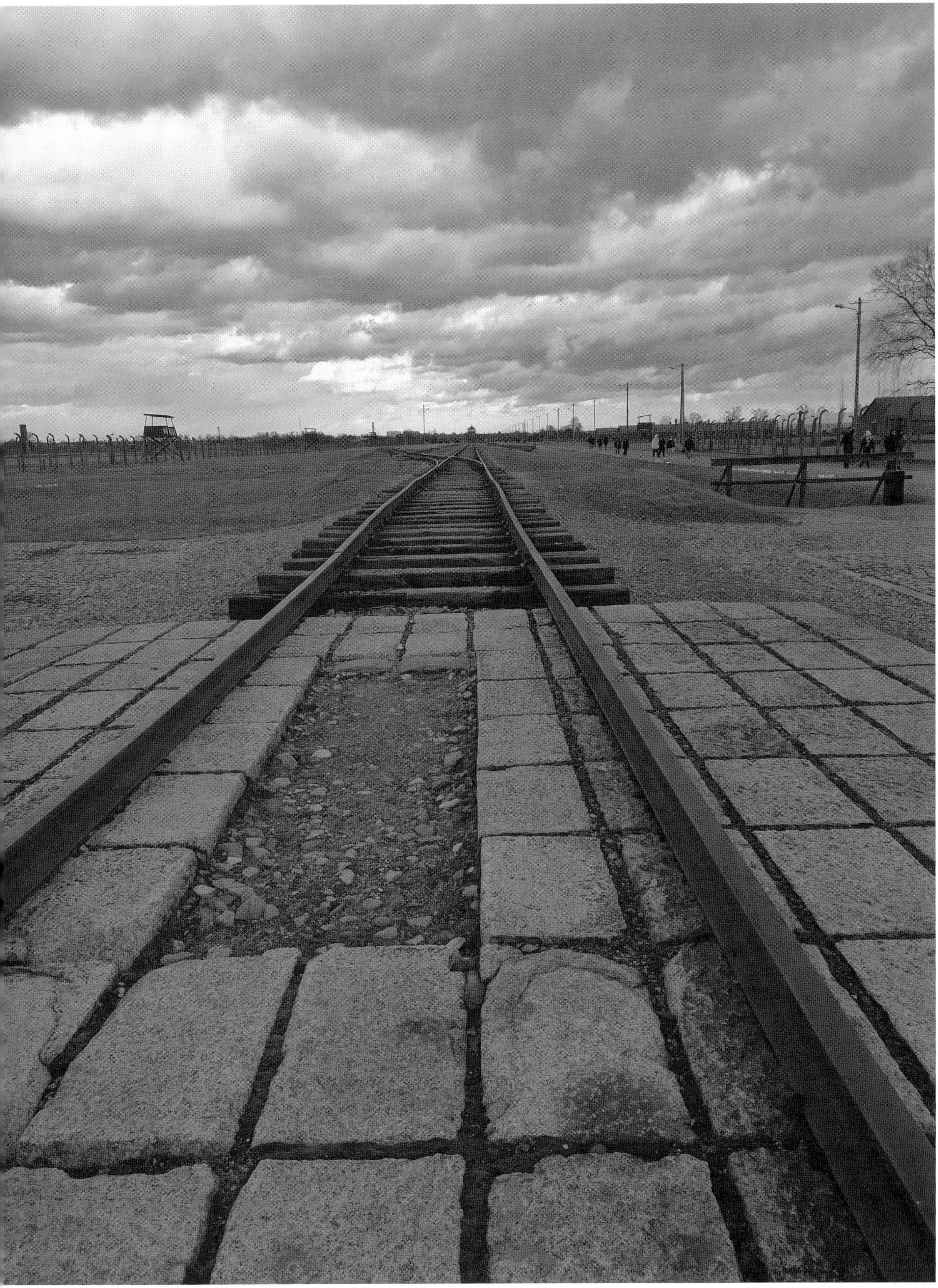

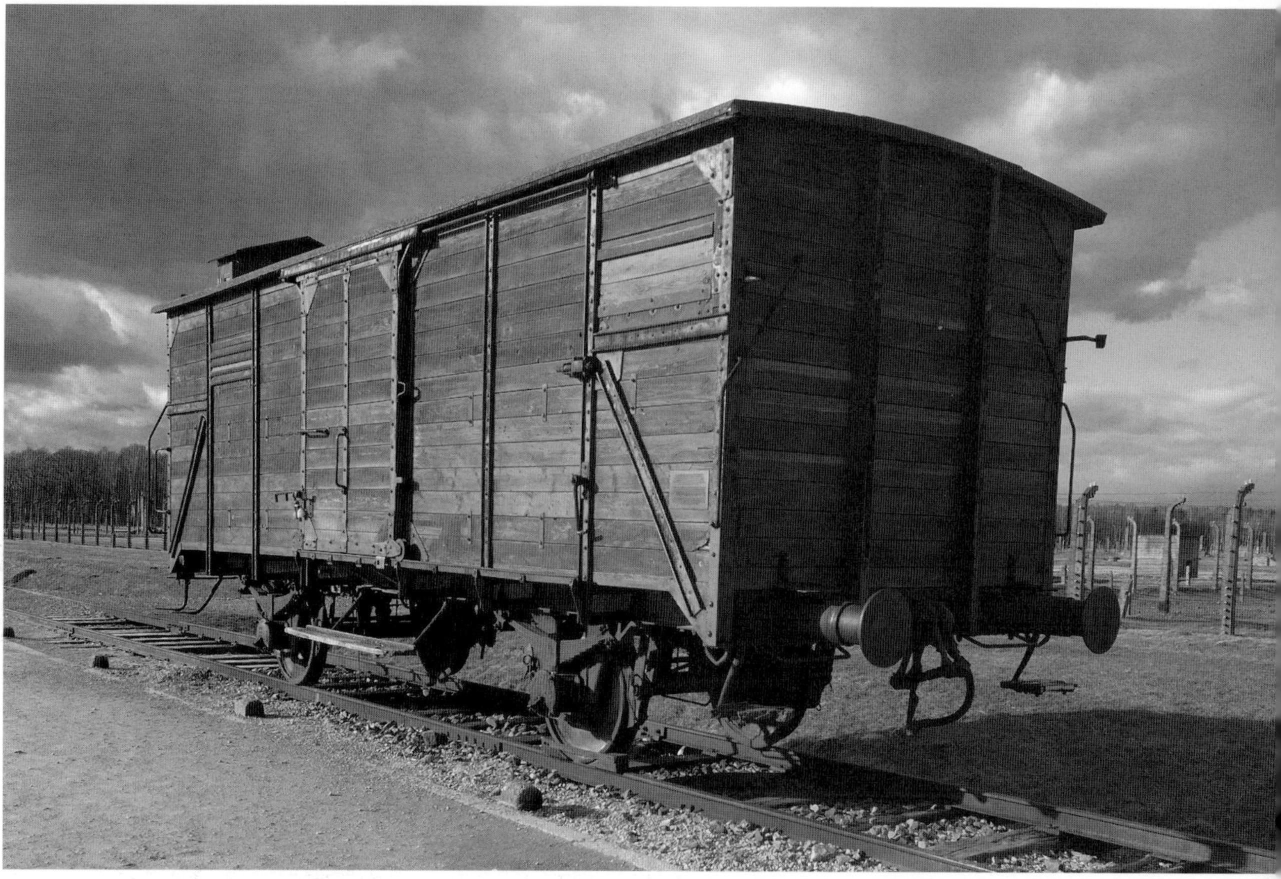

Three photographs taken by the author's niece during a visit to Auschwitz in February 2022, including one of the boxcars used to transport Jews to Auschwitz. This 15-ton boxcar is one of a number of types that were used. Its cramped interior would have held 80 to 100 people. Deportation trains usually carried between 1,000 and 2,000 people. *(Lilly Corner)*

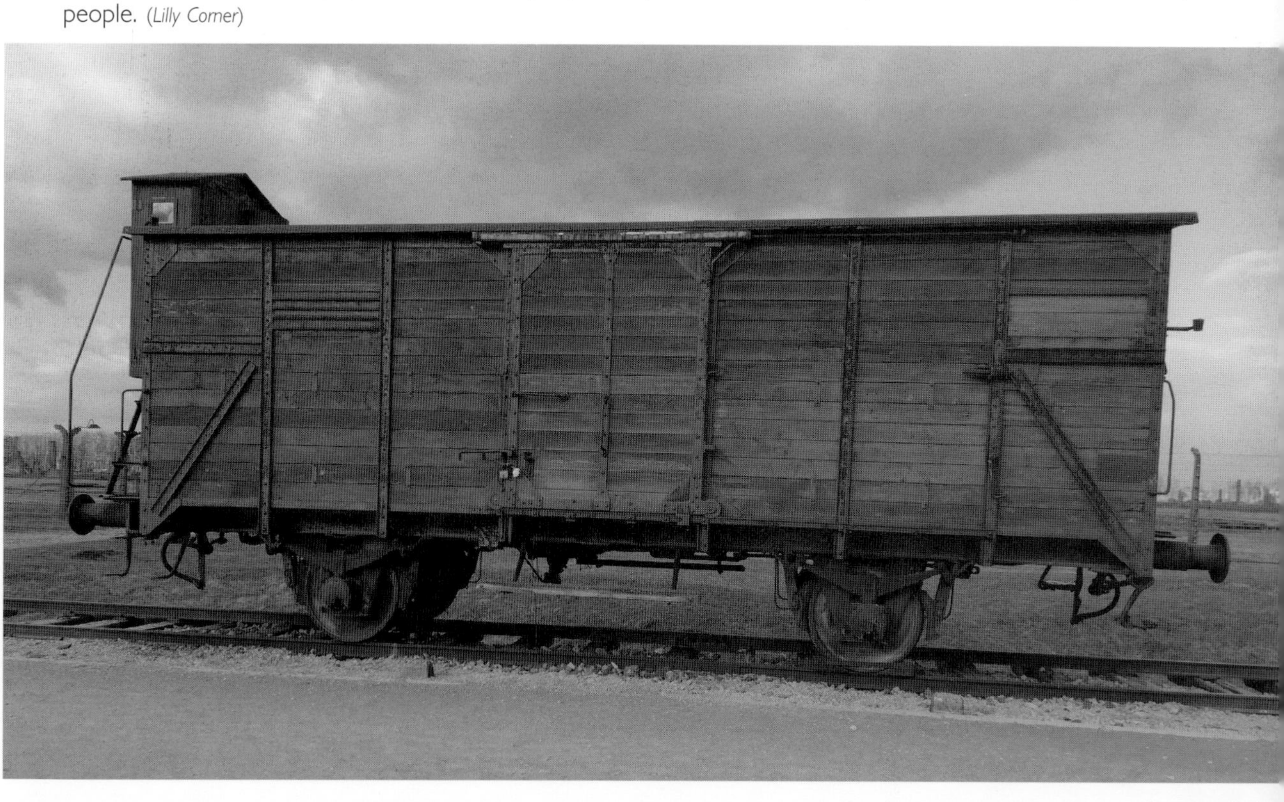

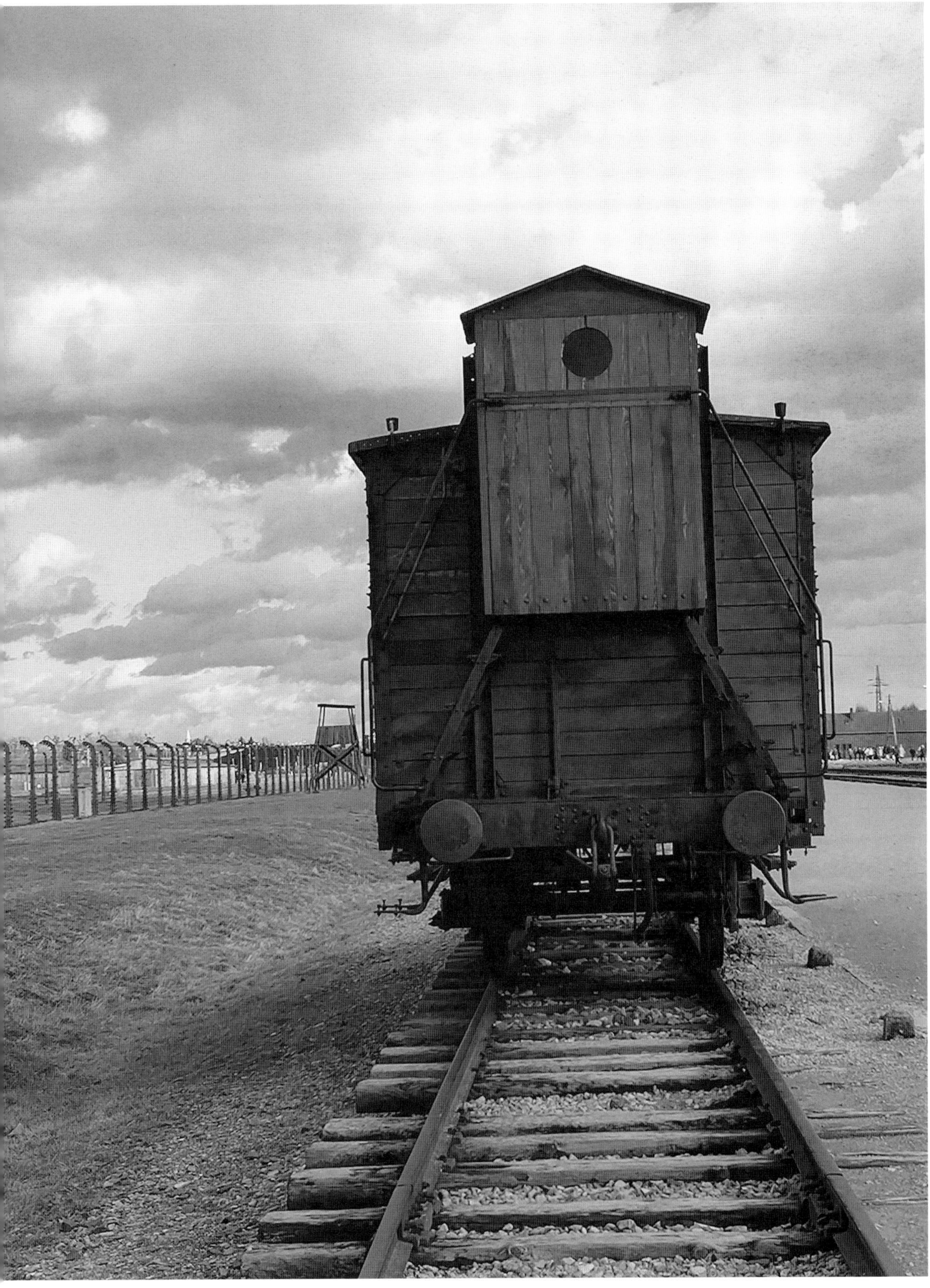

Notes

Notes

Notes

Notes

Notes

Notes

Notes